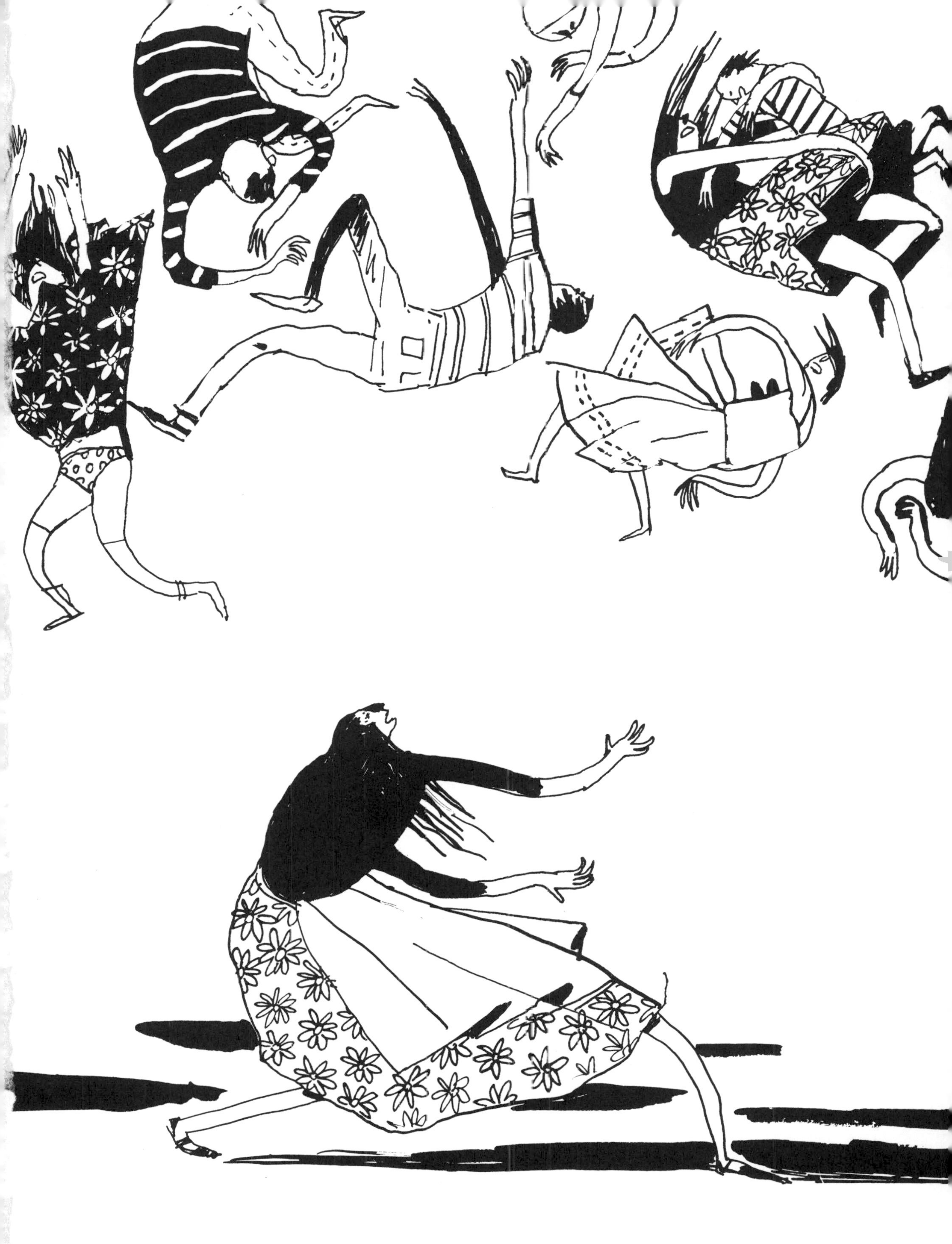

HOW TO BE **HAPPY**

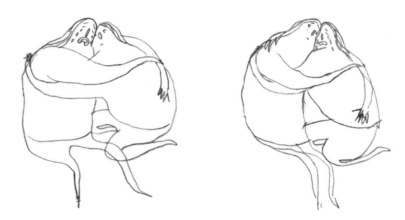

ELEANOR DAVIS
FANTAGRAPHICS BOOKS
SEATTLE 2014

AUTHOR'S NOTE

THIS IS NOT ACTUALLY A BOOK ABOUT HOW TO BE HAPPY. I'VE READ
A LOT OF BOOKS ABOUT HOW TO BE HAPPY, HOWEVER, AND IF
YOU'RE STRUGGLING, THE FOLLOWING HAVE BEEN HELPFUL TO ME.

DEPRESSED AND ANXIOUS: THE DIALECTICAL BEHAVIOR THERAPY
WORKBOOK FOR OVERCOMING DEPRESSION & ANXIETY
BY THOMAS MARRA

NONVIOLENT COMMUNICATION: A LANGUAGE OF LIFE
BY MARSHALL B. ROSENBERG

TO DREW, WHO SWIMS WITH IT,

AND

TO KATE, WHO SWIMS AGAINST.

EDITOR: GARY GROTH

DESIGN: ELEANOR DAVIS

PRODUCTION: PAUL BARESH AND KEELI MCCARTHY

ASSOCIATE PUBLISHER: ERIC REYNOLDS

PUBLISHER: GARY GROTH

PUBLISHED BY

FANTAGRAPHICS BOOKS

7563 LAKE CITY WAY

SEATTLE, WA 98115

"IN OUR EDEN" ORIGINALLY PRINTED IN *NOBROW*

"NITA GOES HOME," "STICK AND STRING," "SEVEN SACKS,"

AND "THOMAS THE LEADER" ORIGINALLY PRINTED IN *MOME*

"BUS TRIP" ORIGINALLY PRINTED IN *LUCKY PEACH MAGAZINE*

SECOND PRINTING: DECEMBER 2014

ISBN 978-1-60699-740-6

PRINTED IN SINGAPORE

SPECIAL THANKS TO: RANDALL BETHUNE, BIG PLANET COMICS, BLACK HOOK PRESS
OF JAPAN, NICK CAPETILLO, KEVIN CZAPIEWSKI, JOHN DIBELLO, JUAN MANUEL
DOMÍNGUEZ, MATHIEU D'OUBLET, DAN EVANS III, THOMAS EYKEMANS, SCOTT FRITSCH-
HAMMES, COCO AND EDDIE GORODETSKY, KAREN GREEN, TED HAYCRAFT, EDUARDO
TAKEO "LIZARKEO" IGARASHI, NEVDON JAMGOCHIAN, ANDY KOOPMANS, PHILIP NEL,
VANESSA PALACIOS, KURT SAYENGA, ANNE LISE ROSTGAARD SCHMIDT, CHRISTIAN
SCHREMSER, SECRET HEADQUARTERS, PAUL VAN DIJKEN, MUNGO VAN KRIMPEN-HALL,
JASON AARON WONG, AND THOMAS ZIMMERMANN

THANK YOU TO EVERYONE, FOR EVERYTHING.

WRITE A
STORY

A STORY
ABOUT
YOURSELF

A STORY
ABOUT
YOUR LIFE

NOW,
BELIEVE
IT

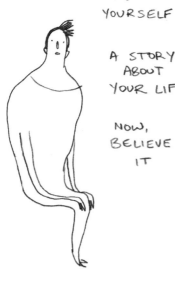

NOW WRITE
ANOTHER
STORY, SAME
SUBJECT

A BETTER
STORY

MORE
INTERESTING

STRONGER
CHARACTERS.

NOW,
BELIEVE
THAT.

JUST KEEP
WRITING.

YOU HAVE
PLENTY
OF
TIME

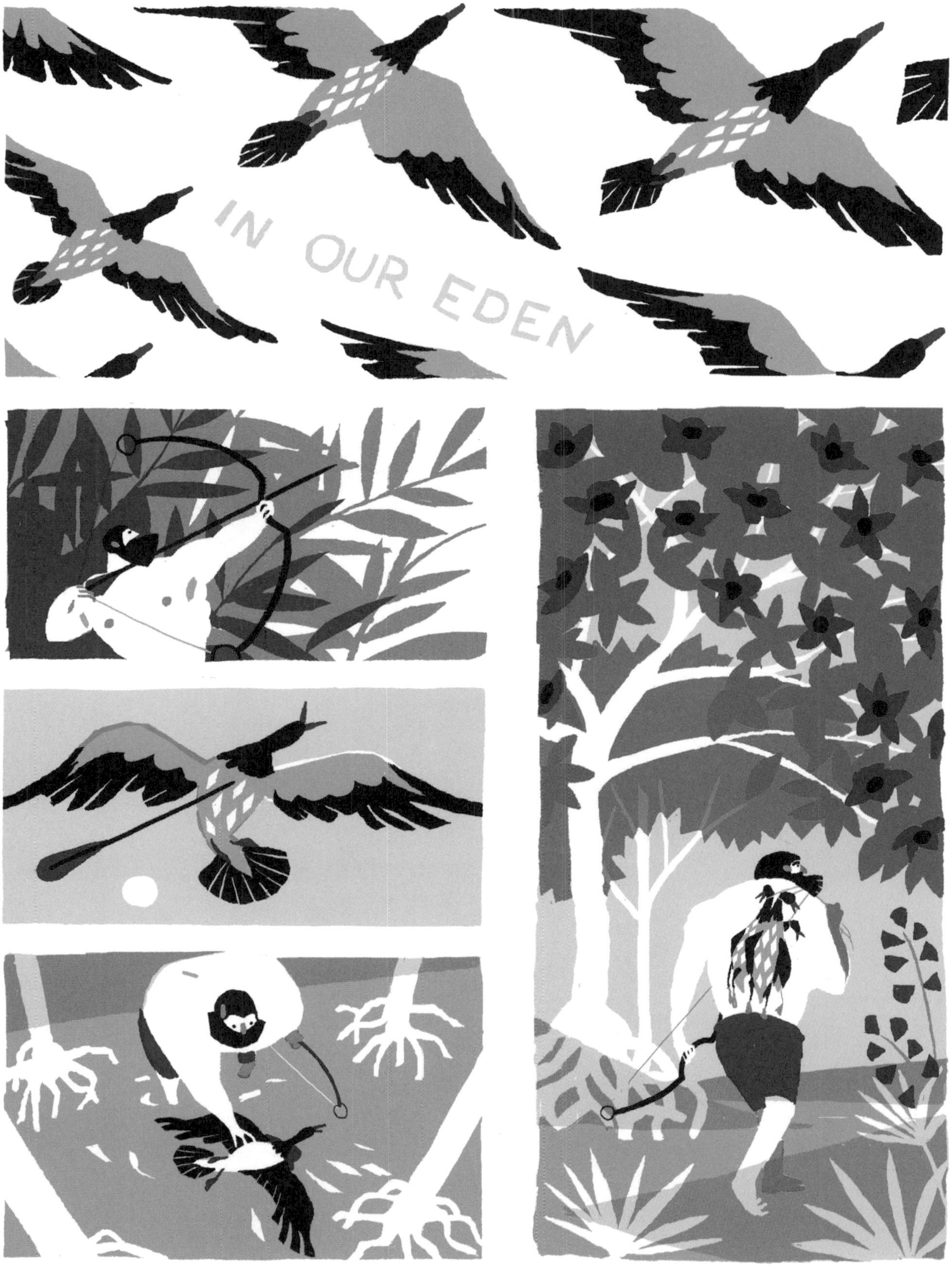
IN OUR EDEN

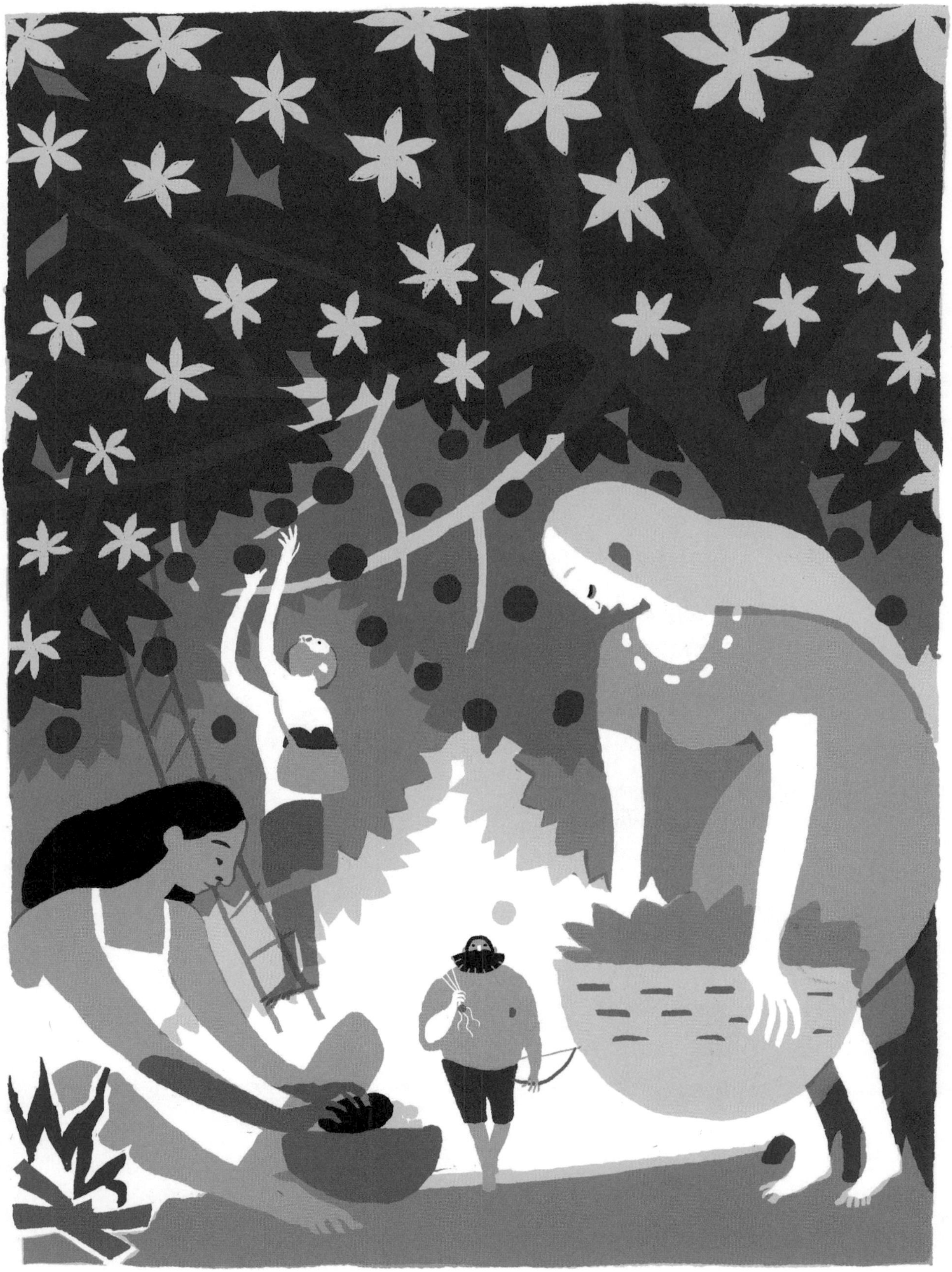

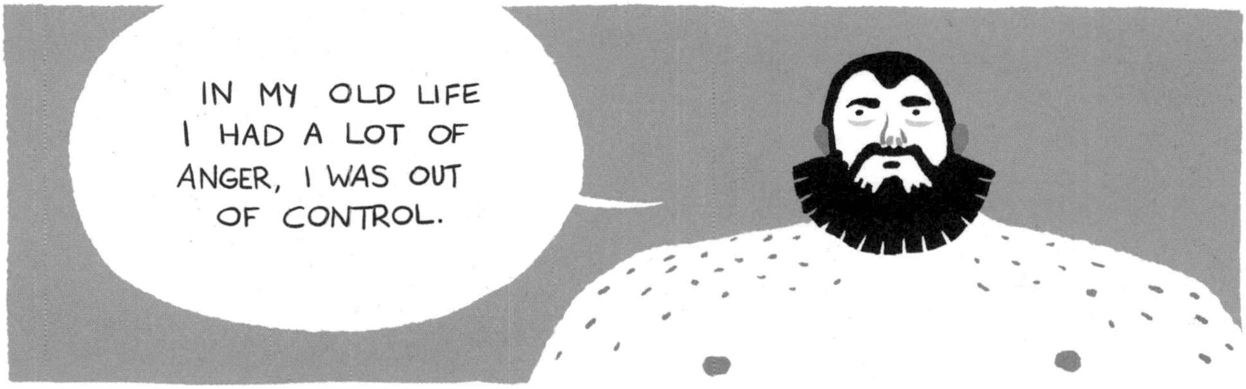
IN MY OLD LIFE I HAD A LOT OF ANGER, I WAS OUT OF CONTROL.

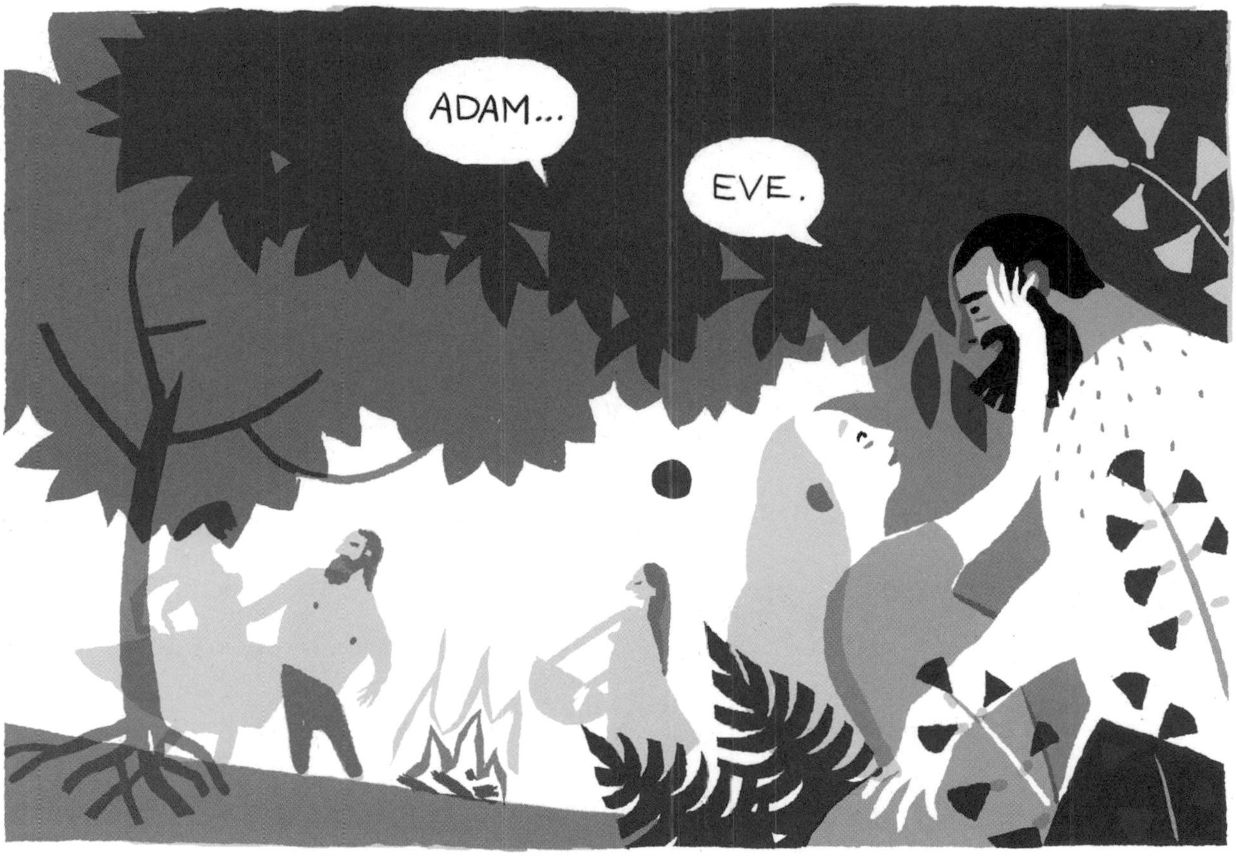
ADAM...
EVE.

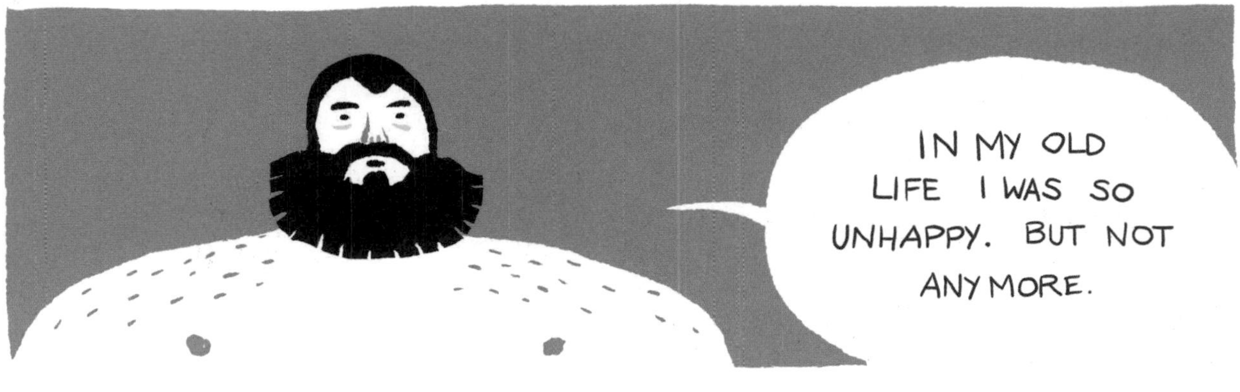
IN MY OLD LIFE I WAS SO UNHAPPY. BUT NOT ANYMORE.

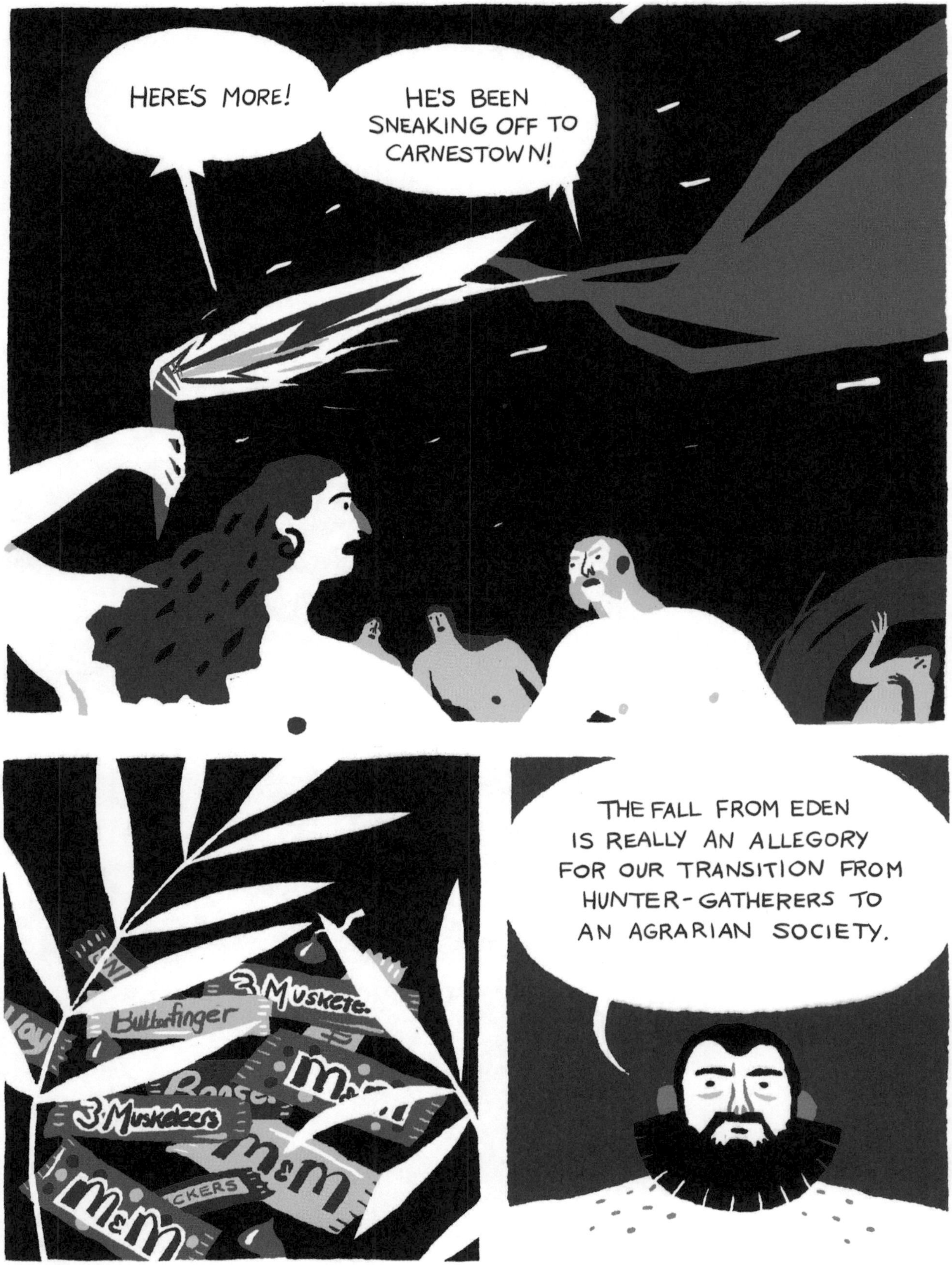

HERE'S MORE!
HE'S BEEN SNEAKING OFF TO CARNESTOWN!
Butterfinger
3 Musketeers
THE FALL FROM EDEN IS REALLY AN ALLEGORY FOR OUR TRANSITION FROM HUNTER-GATHERERS TO AN AGRARIAN SOCIETY.

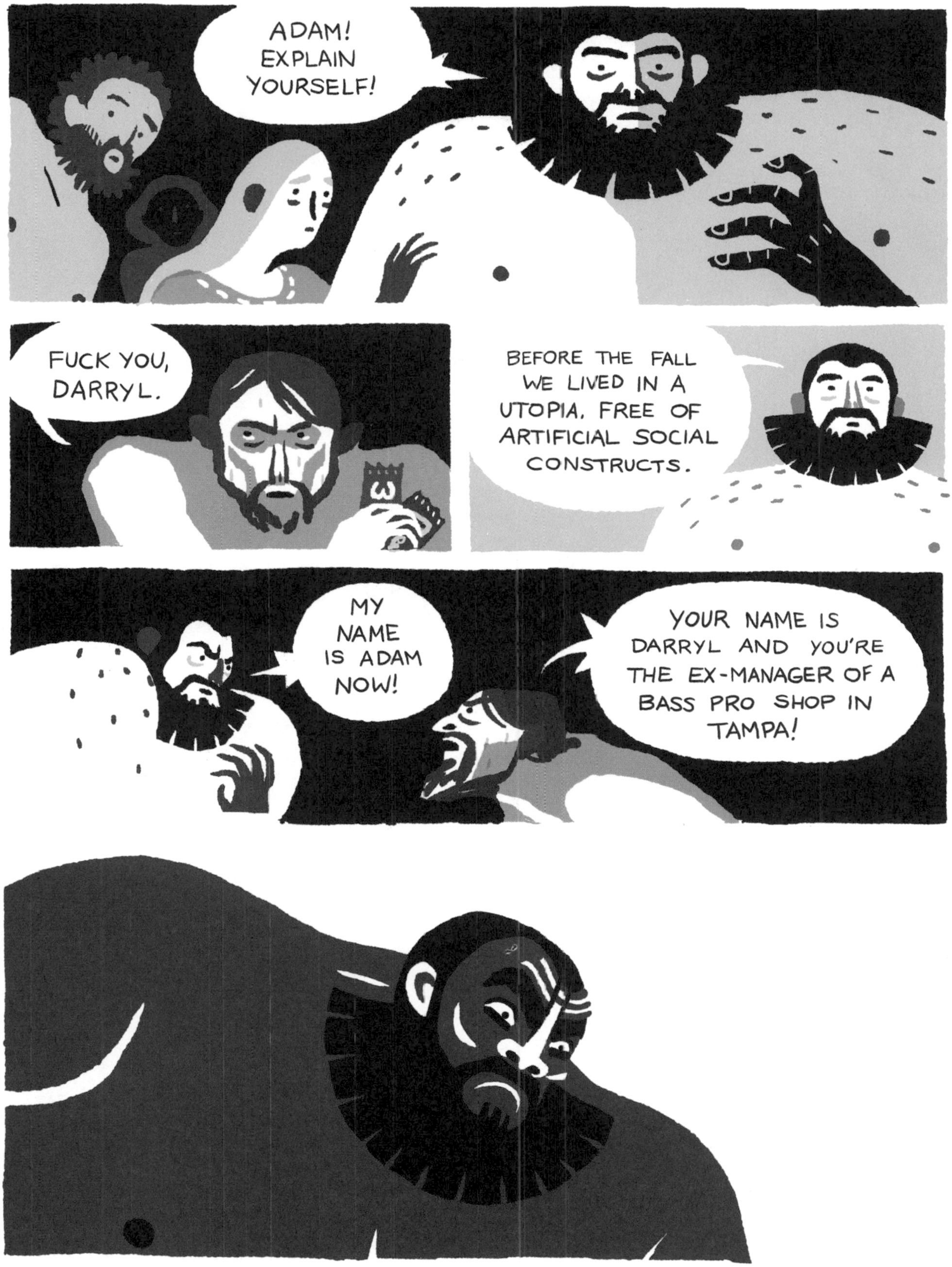
ADAM! EXPLAIN YOURSELF!
FUCK YOU, DARRYL.
BEFORE THE FALL WE LIVED IN A UTOPIA, FREE OF ARTIFICIAL SOCIAL CONSTRUCTS.
MY NAME IS ADAM NOW!
YOUR NAME IS DARRYL AND YOU'RE THE EX-MANAGER OF A BASS PRO SHOP IN TAMPA!

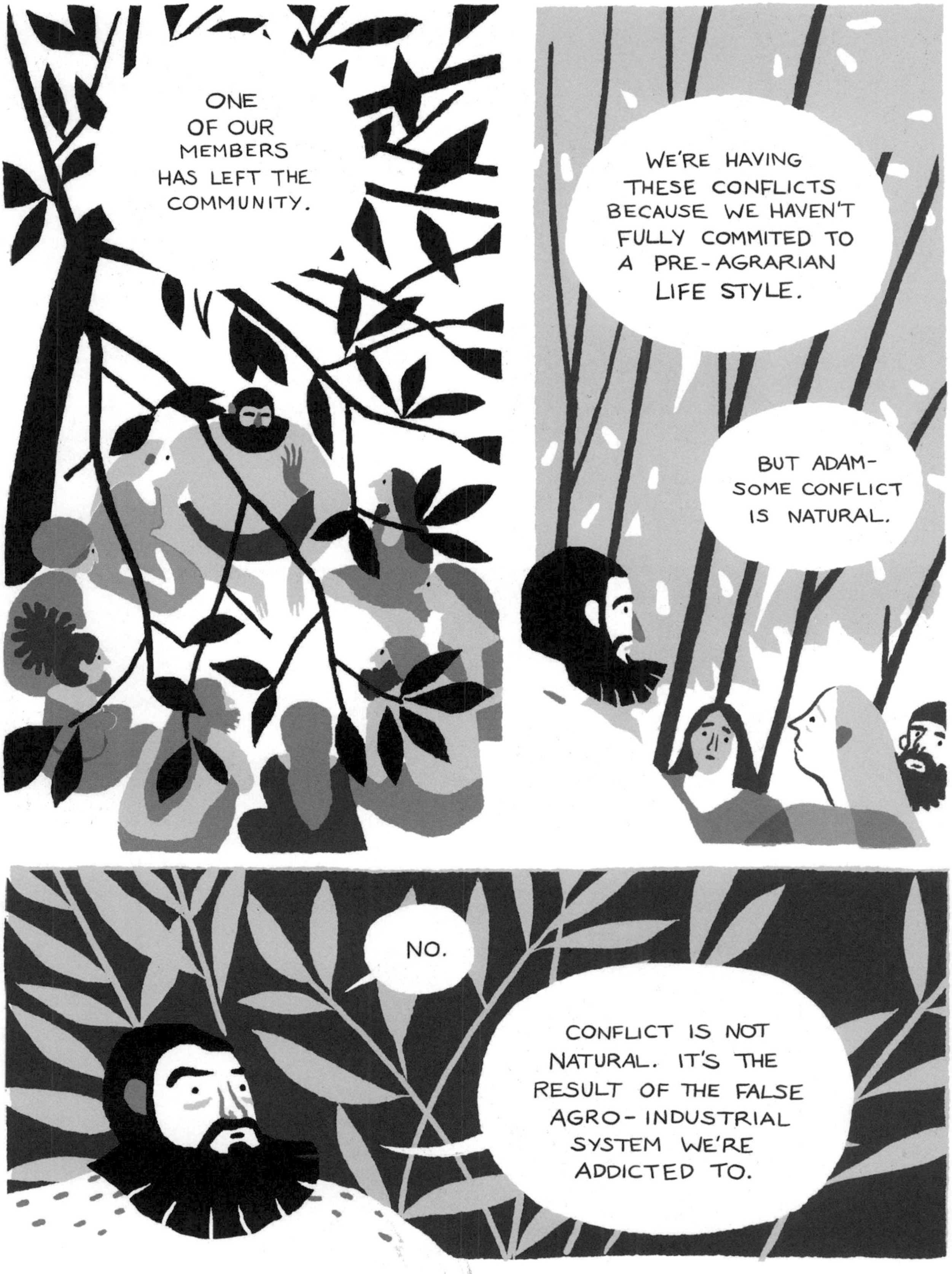
ONE OF OUR MEMBERS HAS LEFT THE COMMUNITY.
WE'RE HAVING THESE CONFLICTS BECAUSE WE HAVEN'T FULLY COMMITED TO A PRE-AGRARIAN LIFE STYLE.
BUT ADAM- SOME CONFLICT IS NATURAL.
NO.
CONFLICT IS NOT NATURAL. IT'S THE RESULT OF THE FALSE AGRO-INDUSTRIAL SYSTEM WE'RE ADDICTED TO.

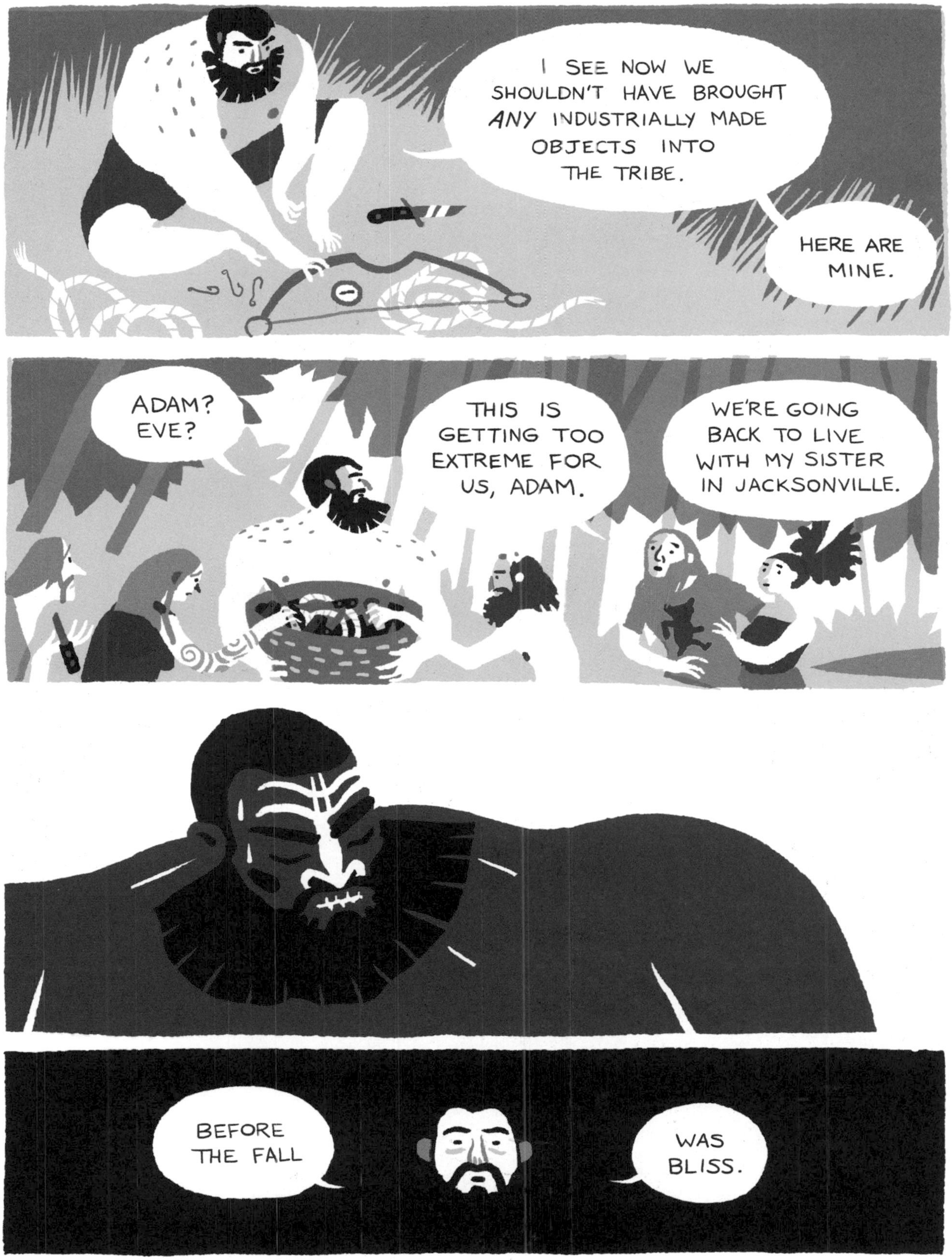
I SEE NOW WE SHOULDN'T HAVE BROUGHT *ANY* INDUSTRIALLY MADE OBJECTS INTO THE TRIBE.
HERE ARE MINE.
ADAM? EVE?
THIS IS GETTING TOO EXTREME FOR US, ADAM.
WE'RE GOING BACK TO LIVE WITH MY SISTER IN JACKSONVILLE.
BEFORE THE FALL
WAS BLISS.

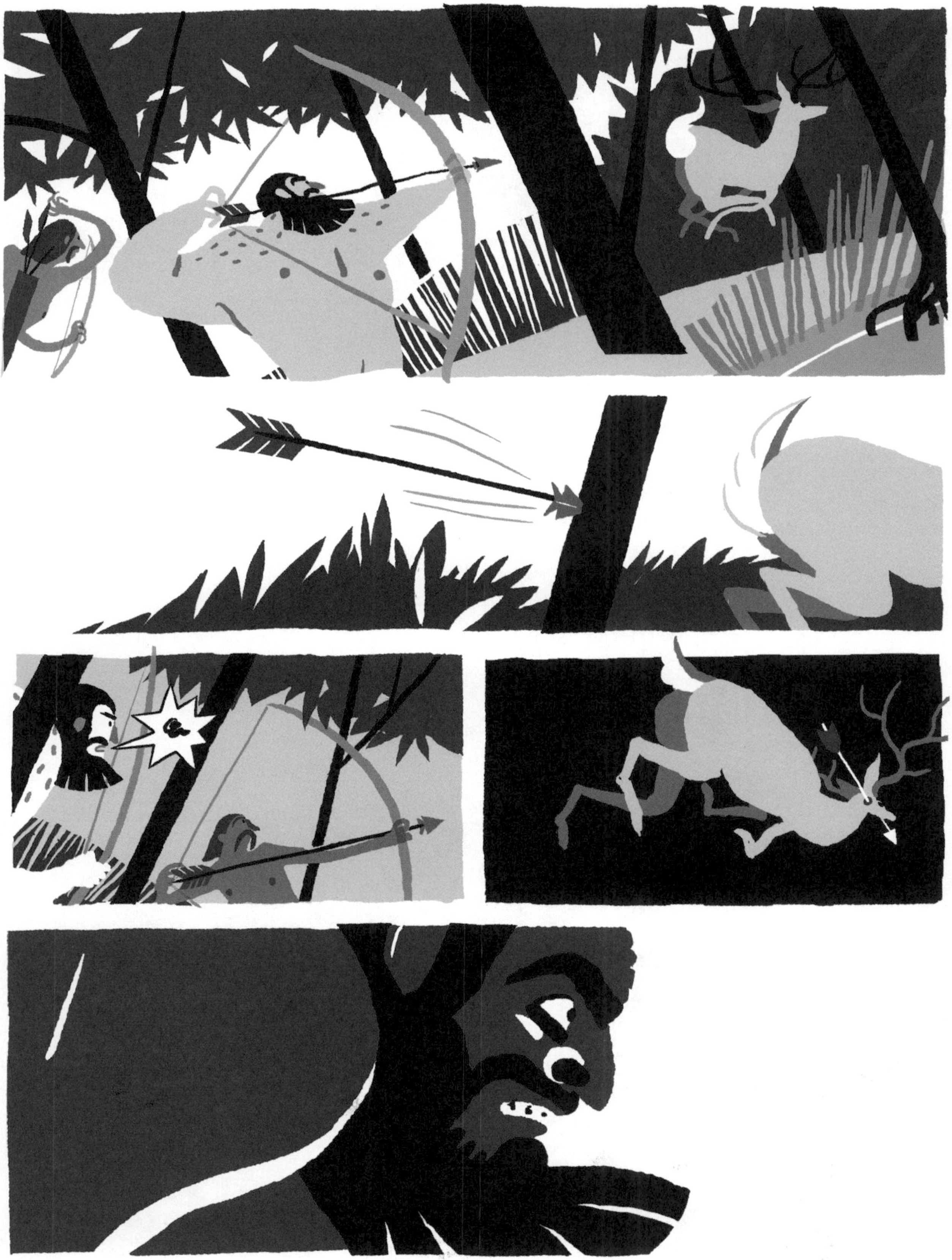

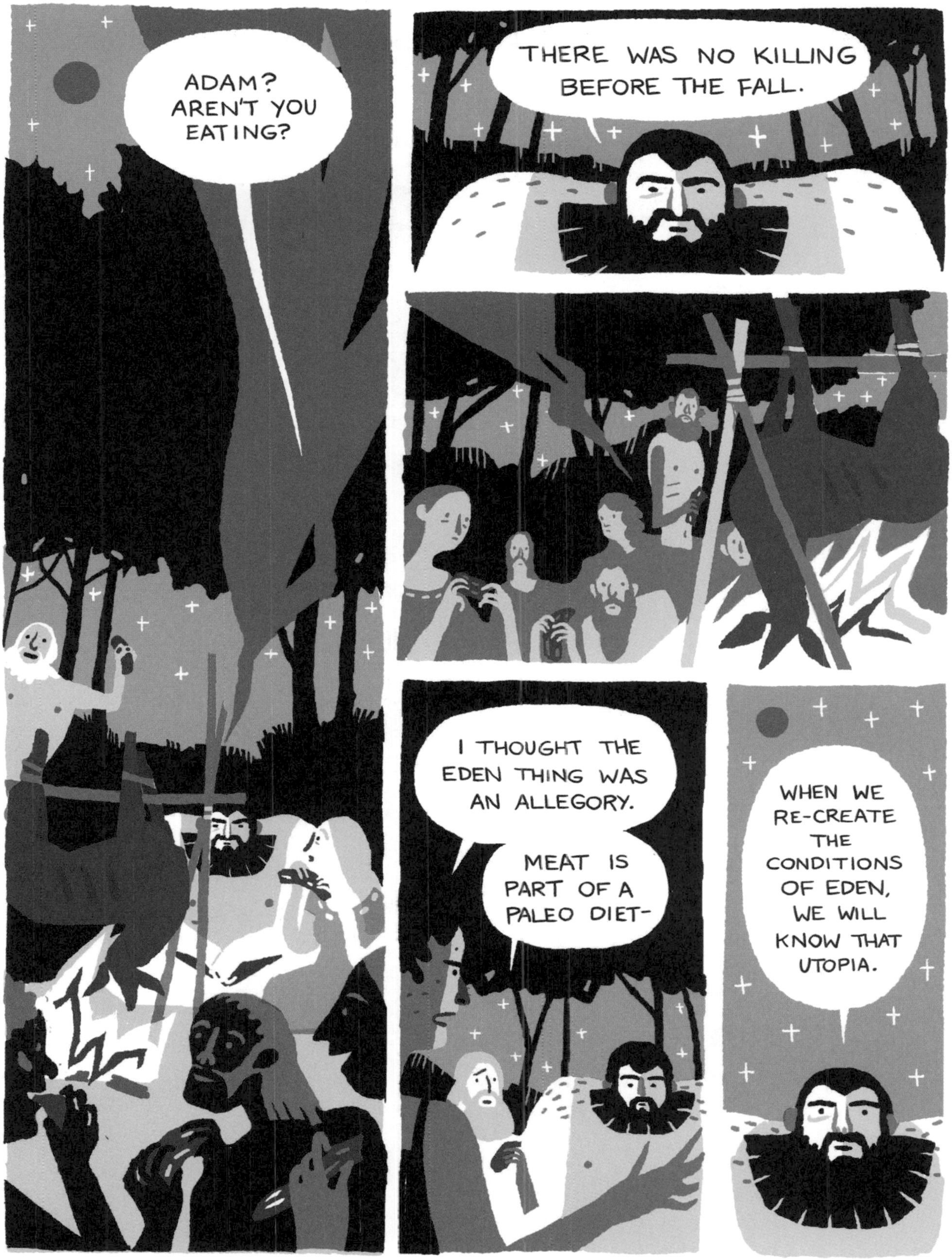
ADAM? AREN'T YOU EATING?
THERE WAS NO KILLING BEFORE THE FALL.
I THOUGHT THE EDEN THING WAS AN ALLEGORY.
MEAT IS PART OF A PALEO DIET-
WHEN WE RE-CREATE THE CONDITIONS OF EDEN, WE WILL KNOW THAT UTOPIA.

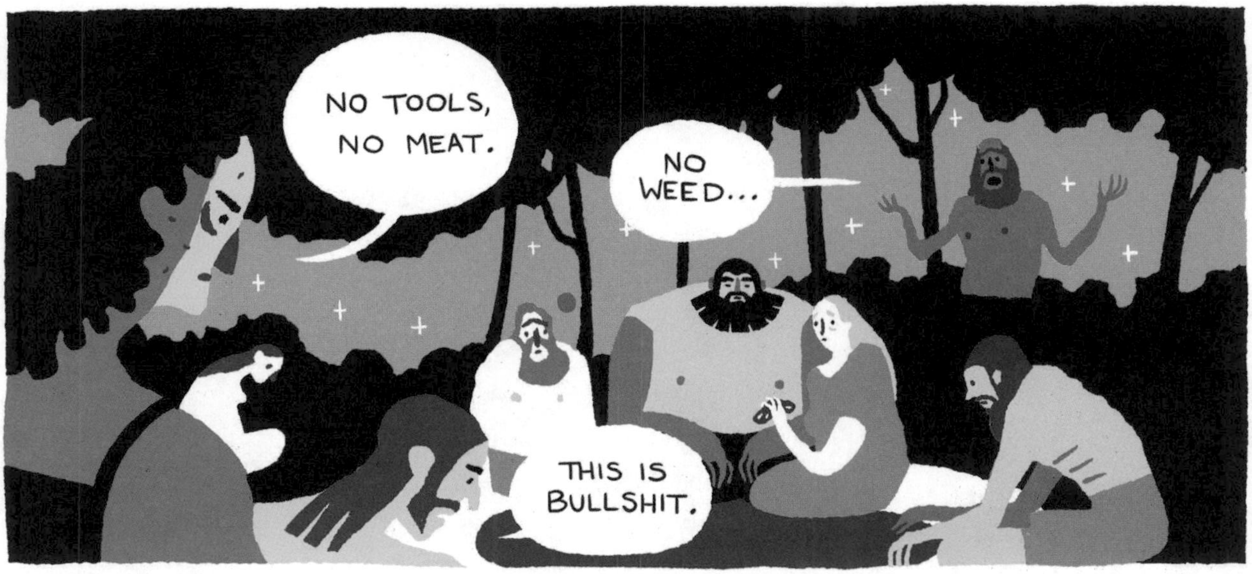
NO TOOLS, NO MEAT.
NO WEED...
THIS IS BULLSHIT.

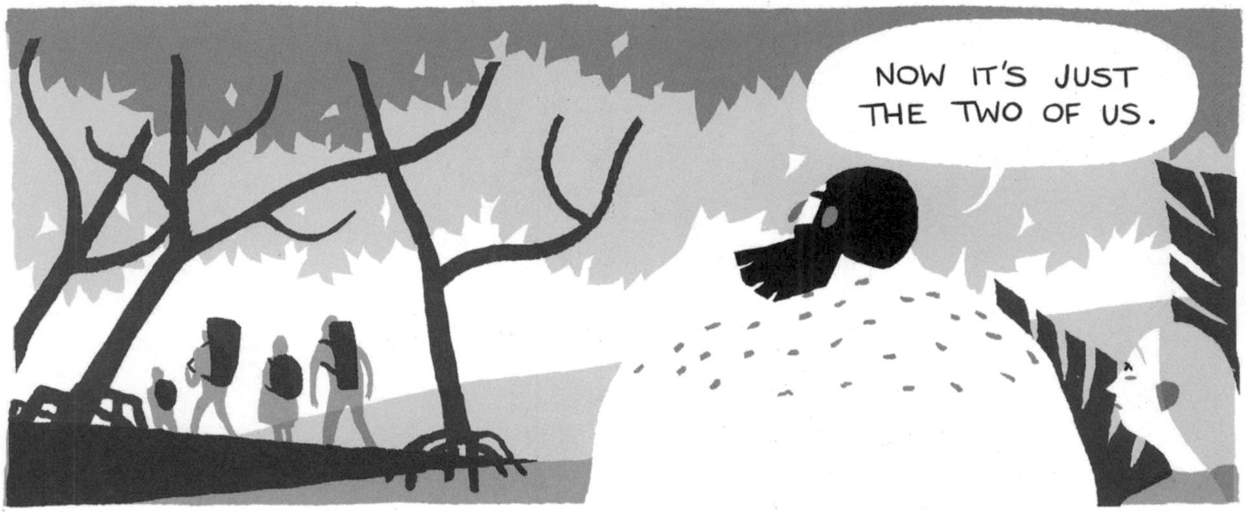
NOW IT'S JUST THE TWO OF US.

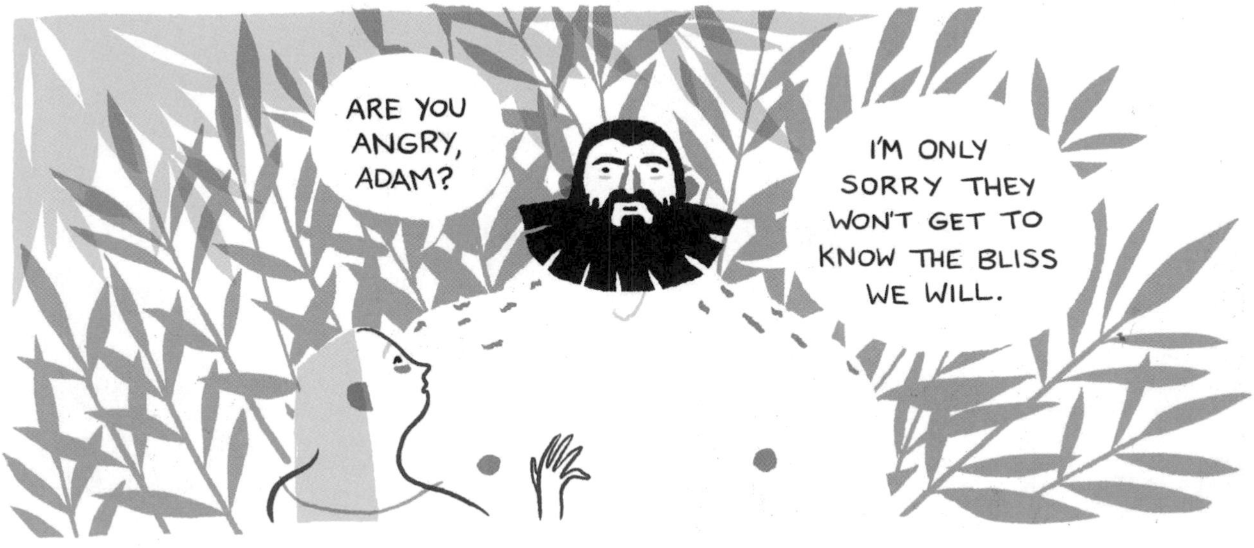
ARE YOU ANGRY, ADAM?
I'M ONLY SORRY THEY WON'T GET TO KNOW THE BLISS WE WILL.

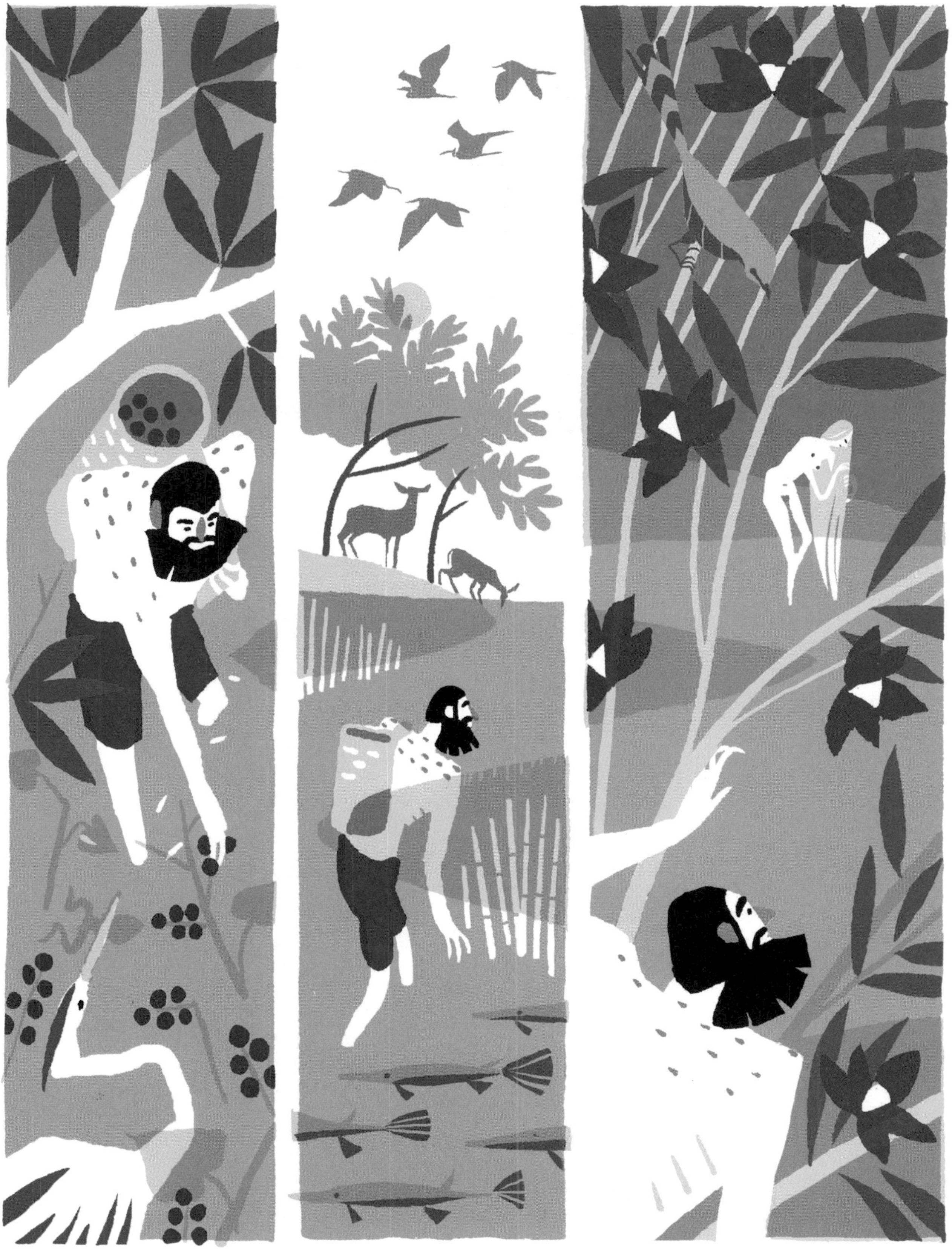

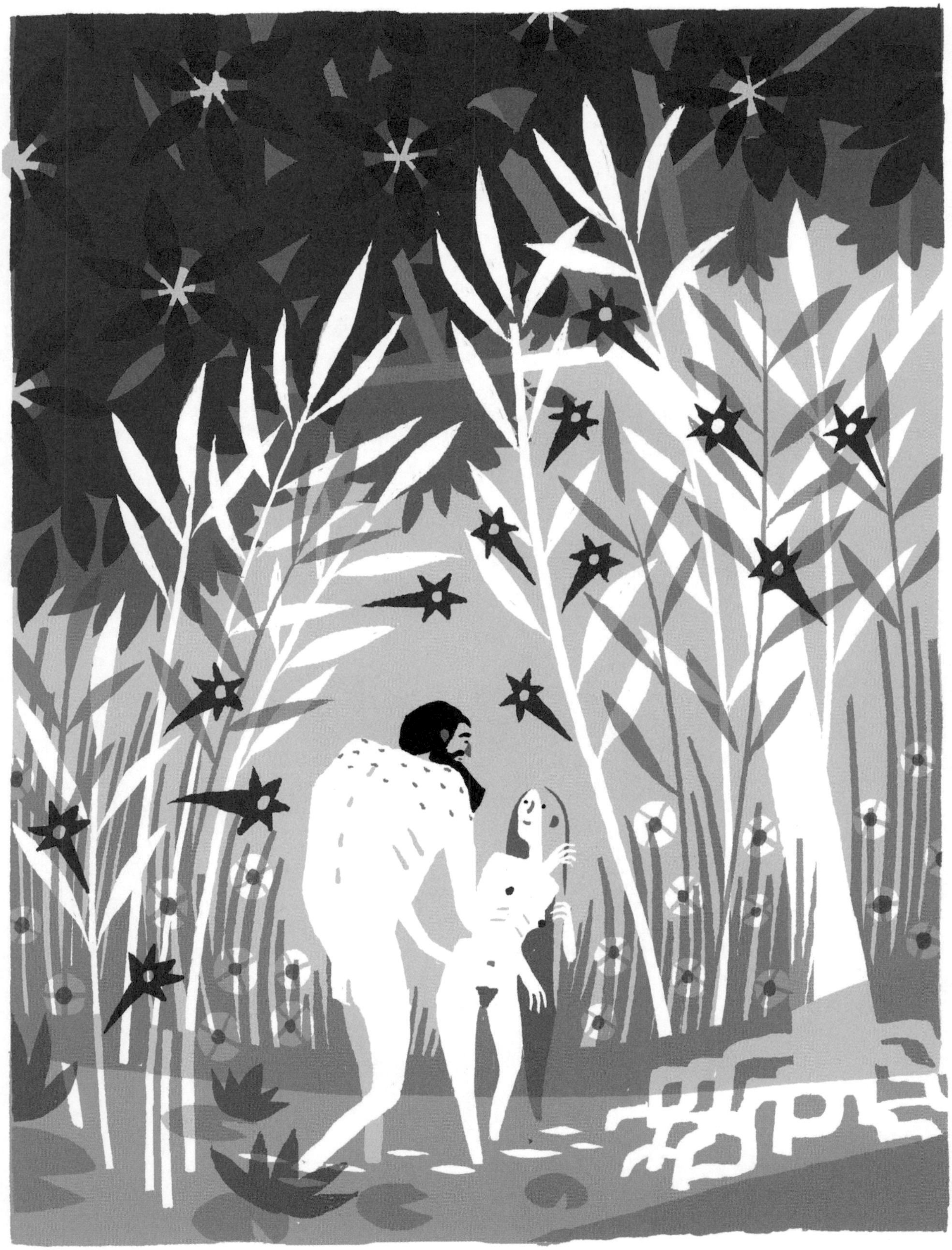

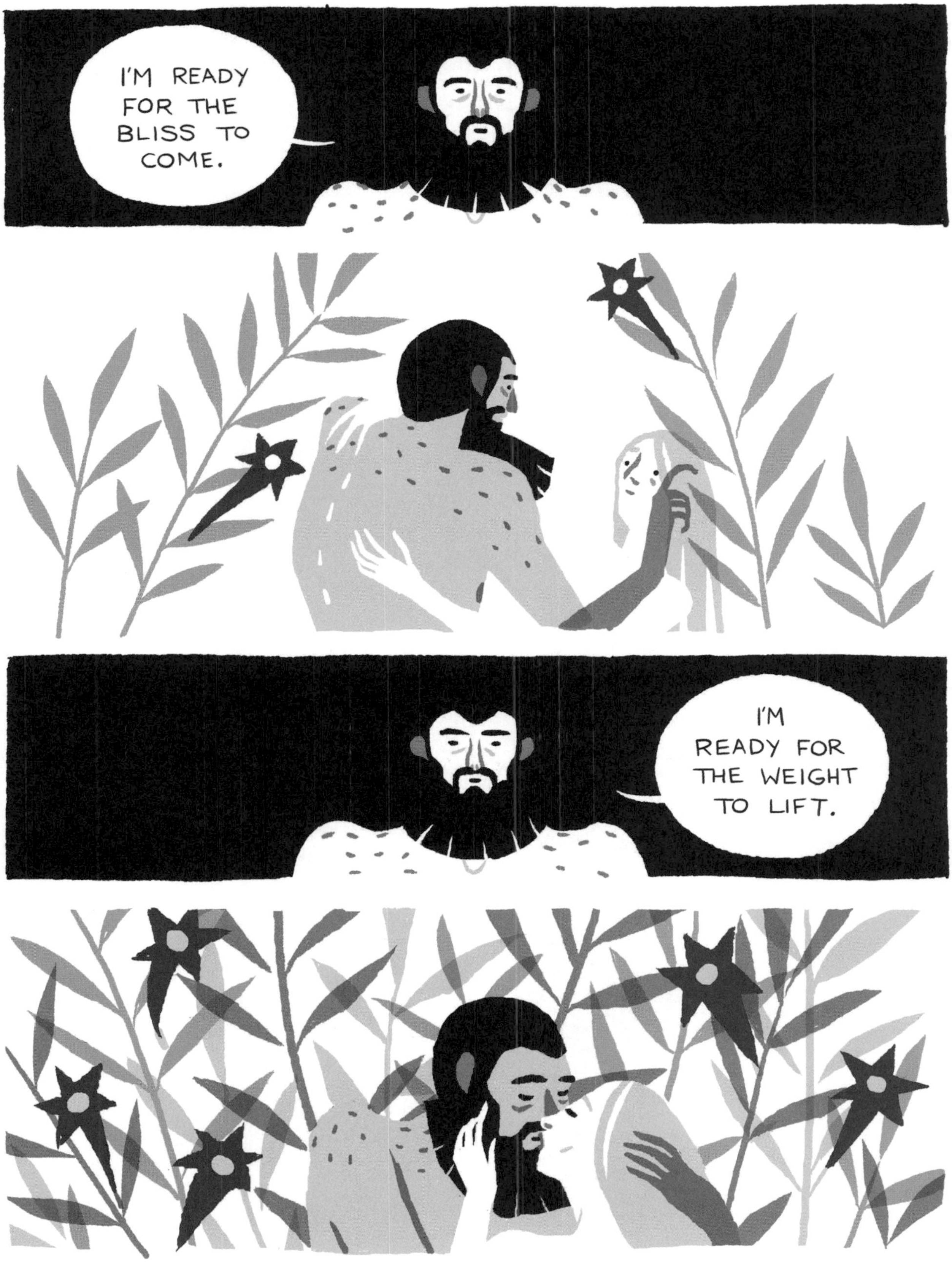
I'M READY FOR THE BLISS TO COME.
I'M READY FOR THE WEIGHT TO LIFT.

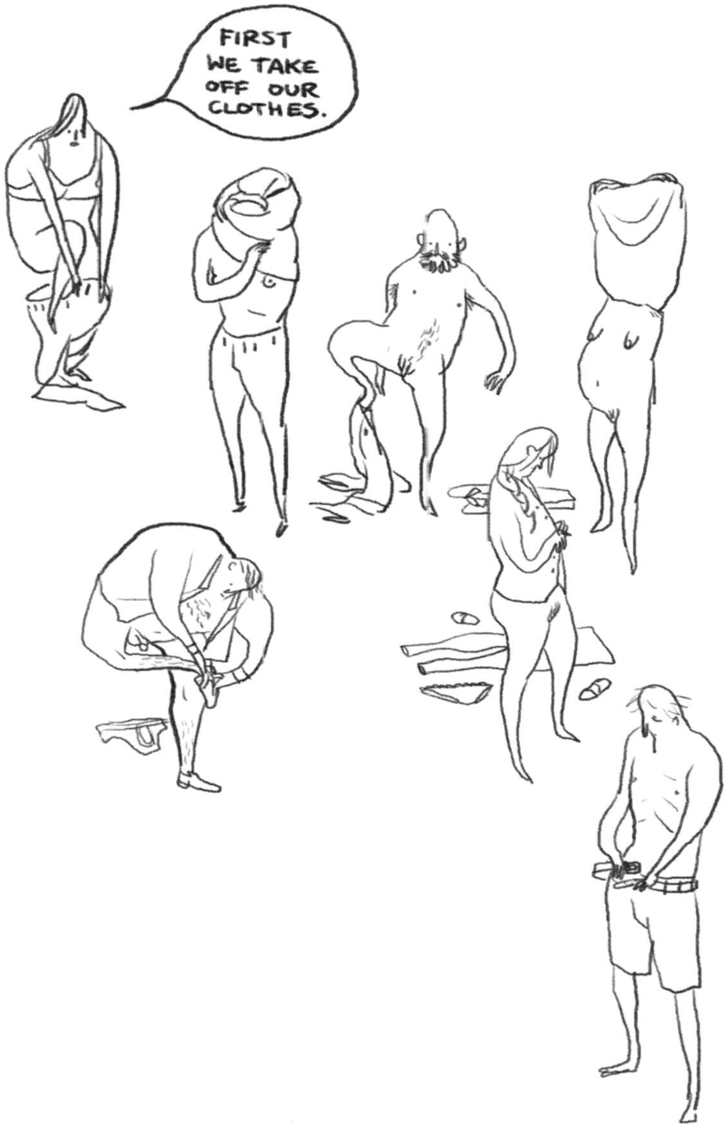
FIRST WE TAKE OFF OUR CLOTHES.

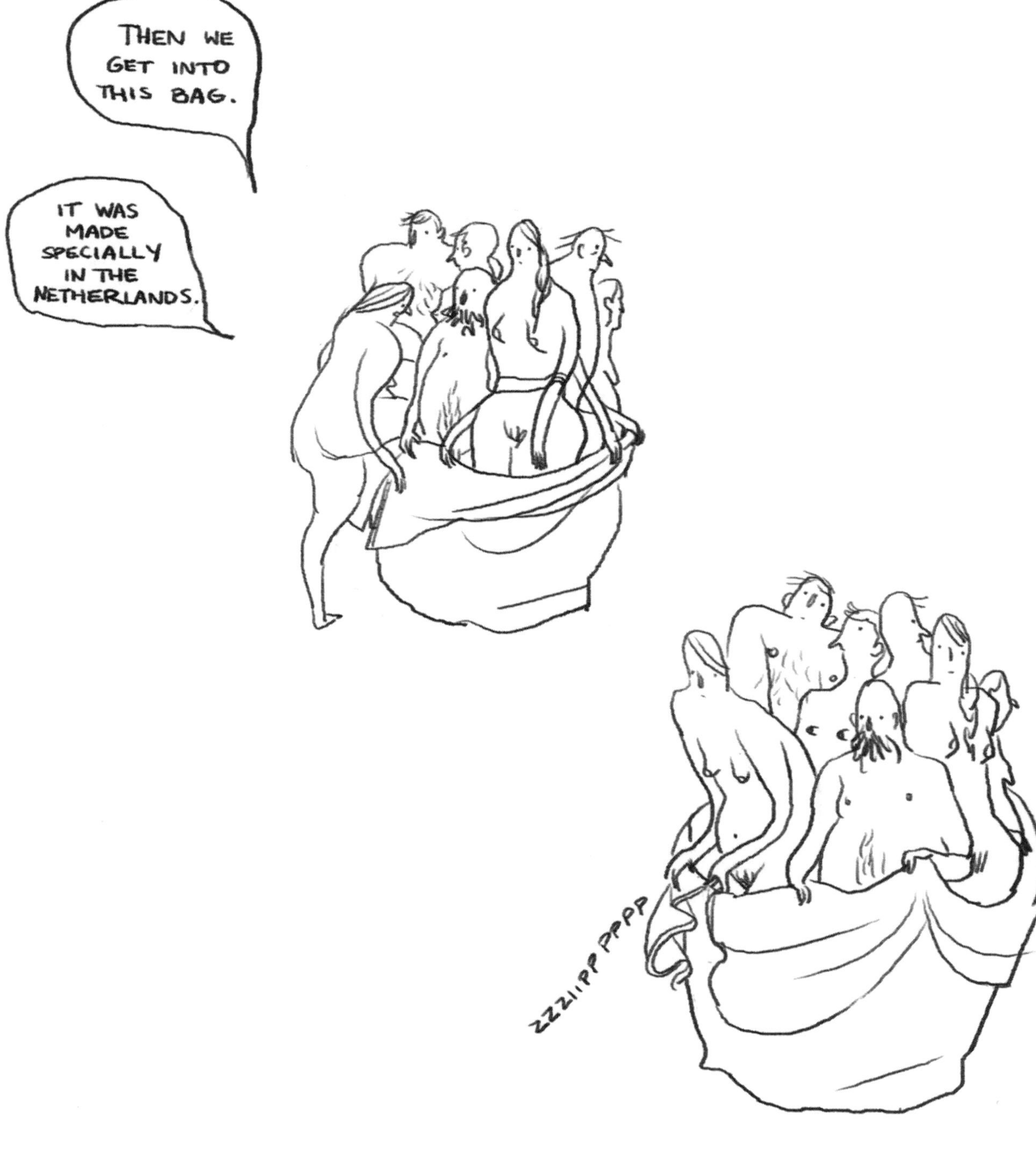
THEN WE GET INTO THIS BAG.
IT WAS MADE SPECIALLY IN THE NETHERLANDS.
ZZZIIPPPPPP

ZZZIPPPP

ZZZIPP

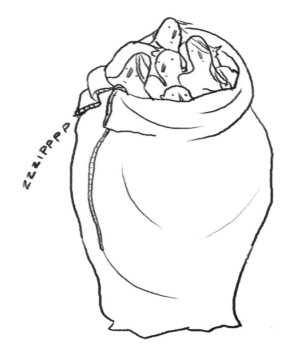

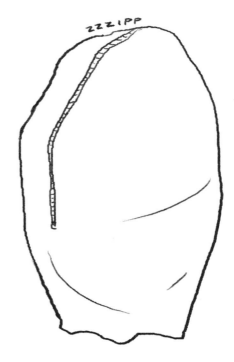

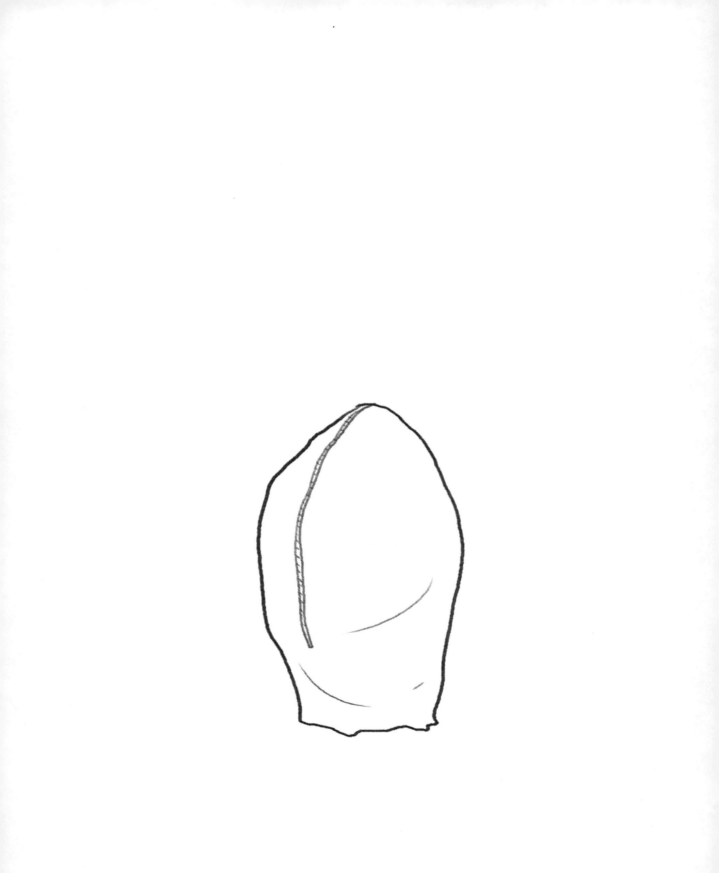

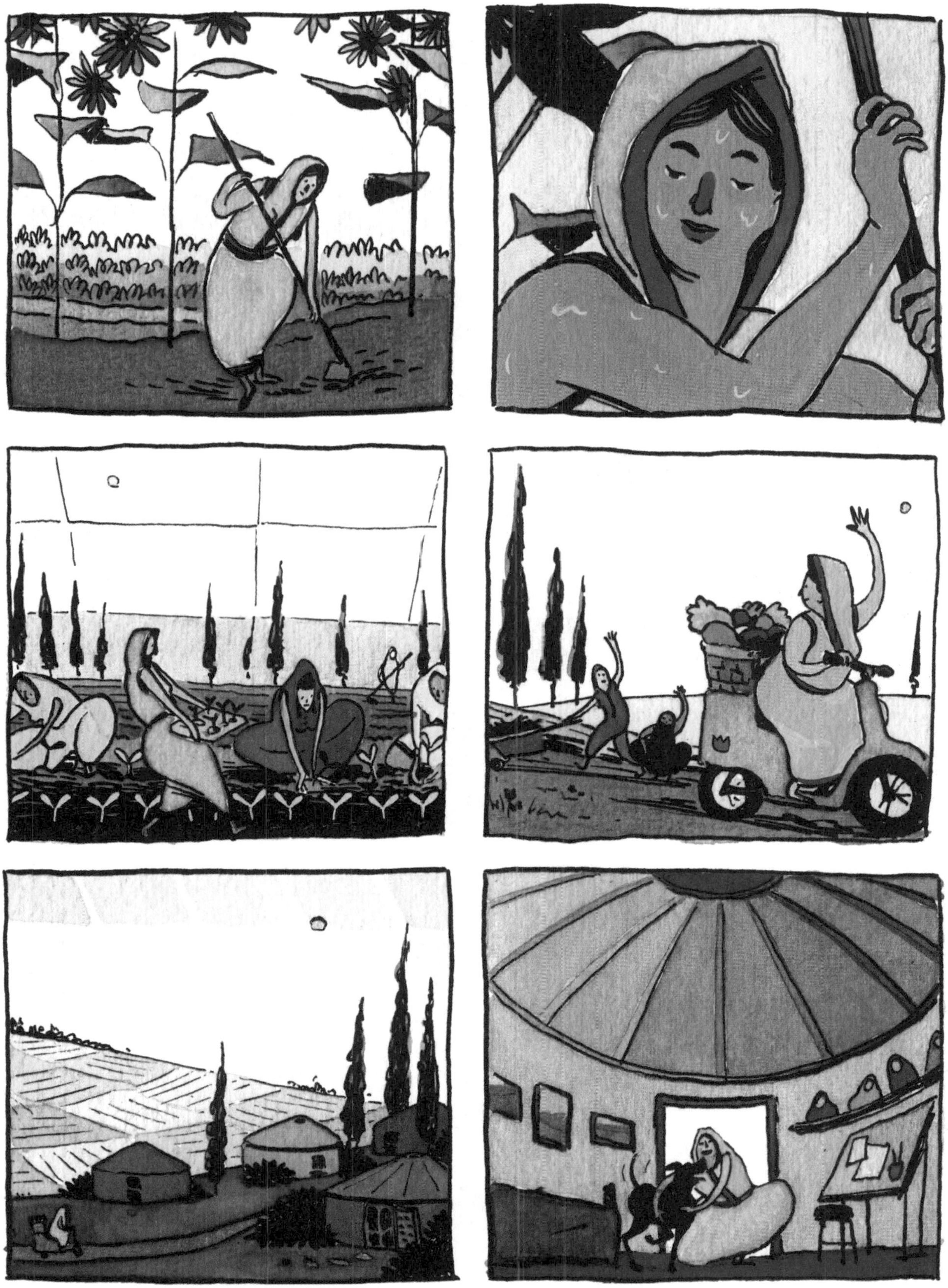

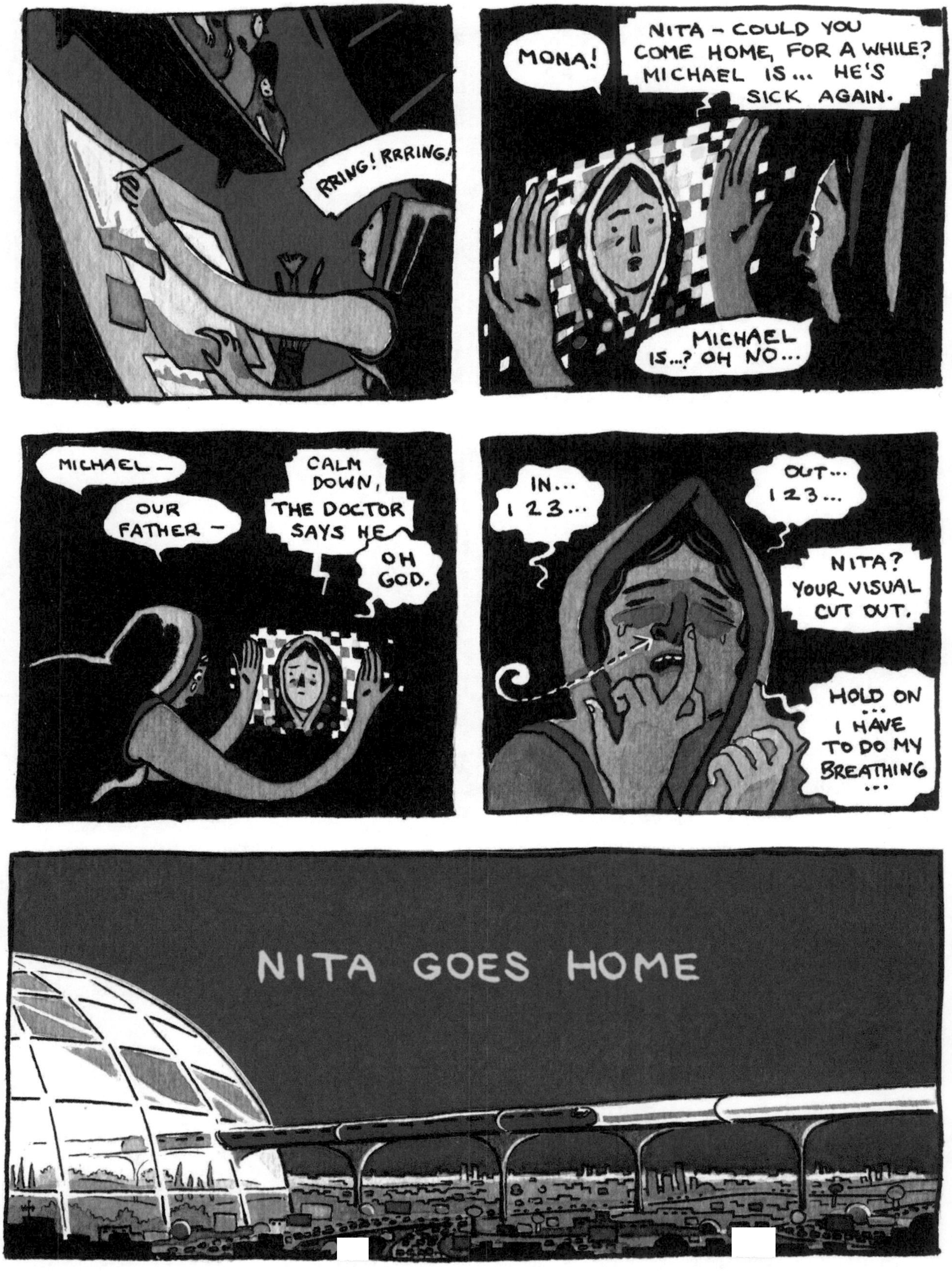
RRING! RRRING!
MONA!
NITA - COULD YOU COME HOME, FOR A WHILE? MICHAEL IS... HE'S SICK AGAIN.
MICHAEL IS...? OH NO...
MICHAEL —
OUR FATHER —
CALM DOWN, THE DOCTOR SAYS HE
OH GOD.
IN... 1 2 3...
OUT... 1 2 3...
NITA? YOUR VISUAL CUT OUT.
HOLD ON ... I HAVE TO DO MY BREATHING ...
NITA GOES HOME

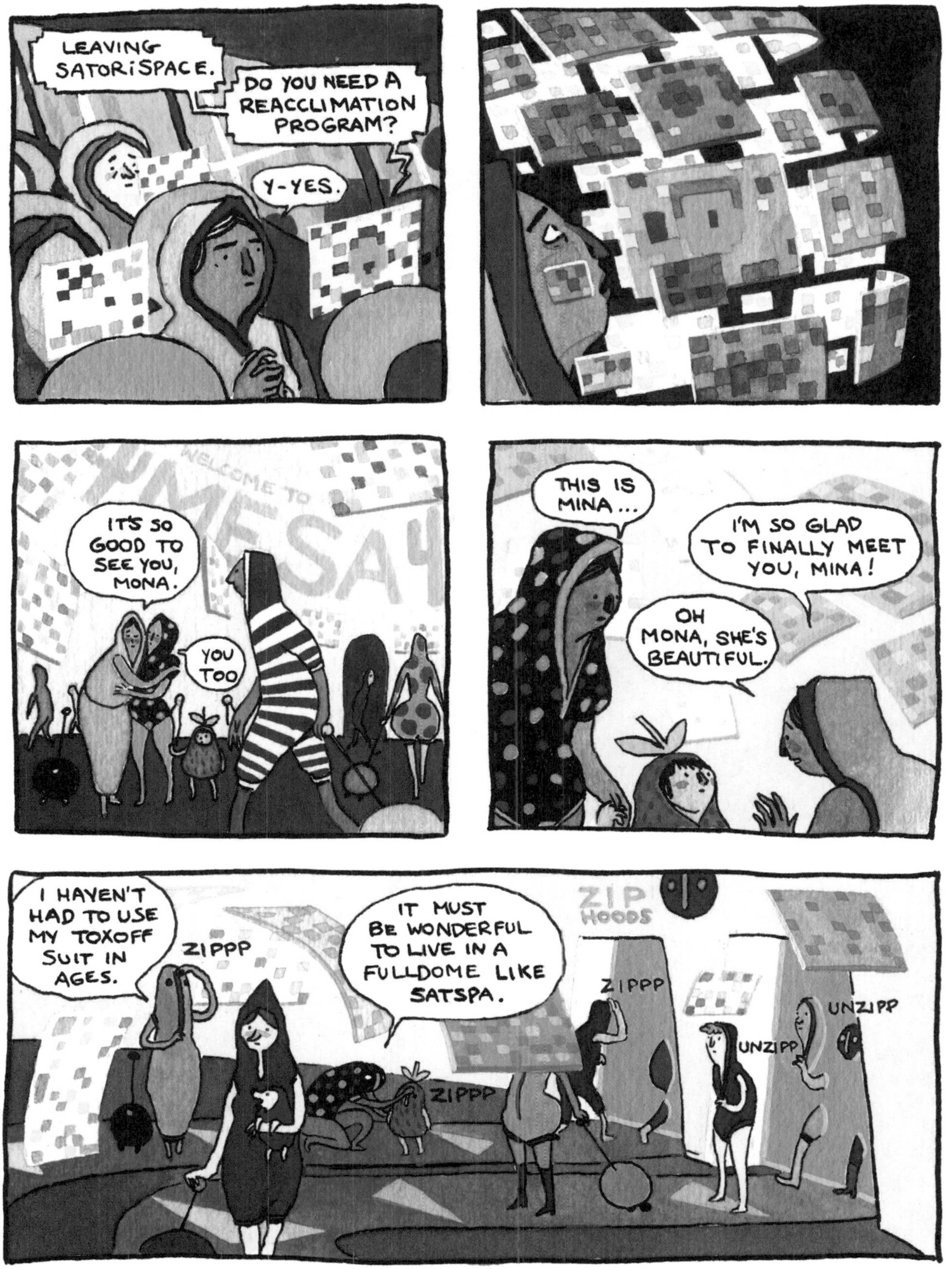
LEAVING SATORiSPACE.
DO YOU NEED A REACCLIMATION PROGRAM?
Y-YES.
WELCOME TO MESA4
IT'S SO GOOD TO SEE YOU, MONA.
YOU TOO
THIS IS MINA...
I'M SO GLAD TO FINALLY MEET YOU, MINA!
OH MONA, SHE'S BEAUTIFUL.
I HAVEN'T HAD TO USE MY TOXOFF SUIT IN AGES.
ZIPPP
IT MUST BE WONDERFUL TO LIVE IN A FULLDOME LIKE SATSPA.
ZIP HOODS
ZIPPP
ZIPPP
UNZIPP
UNZIPP

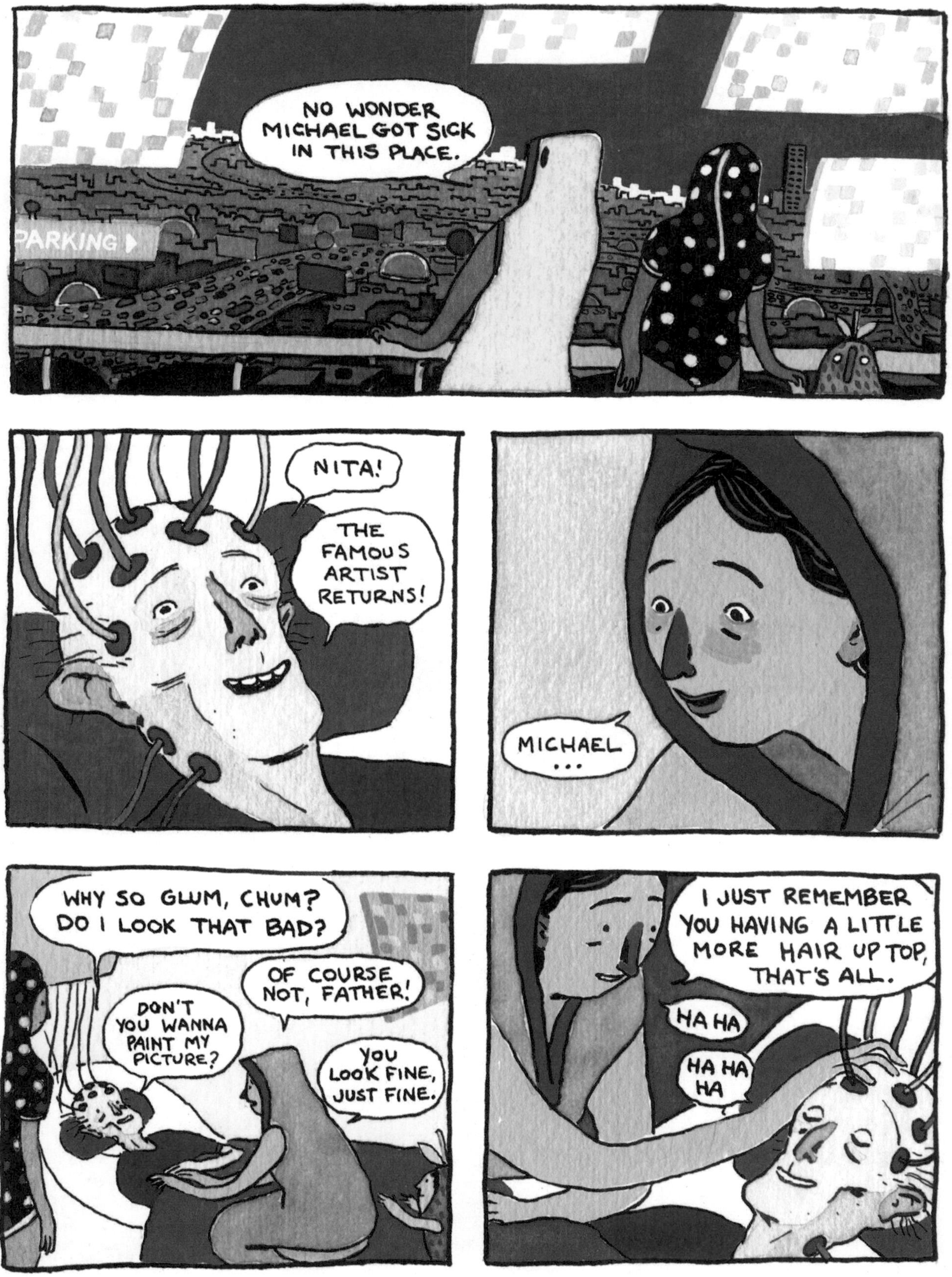
NO WONDER MICHAEL GOT SICK IN THIS PLACE.
PARKING
NITA!
THE FAMOUS ARTIST RETURNS!
MICHAEL ...
WHY SO GLUM, CHUM? DO I LOOK THAT BAD?
OF COURSE NOT, FATHER!
DON'T YOU WANNA PAINT MY PICTURE?
YOU LOOK FINE, JUST FINE.
I JUST REMEMBER YOU HAVING A LITTLE MORE HAIR UP TOP, THAT'S ALL.
HA HA
HA HA HA

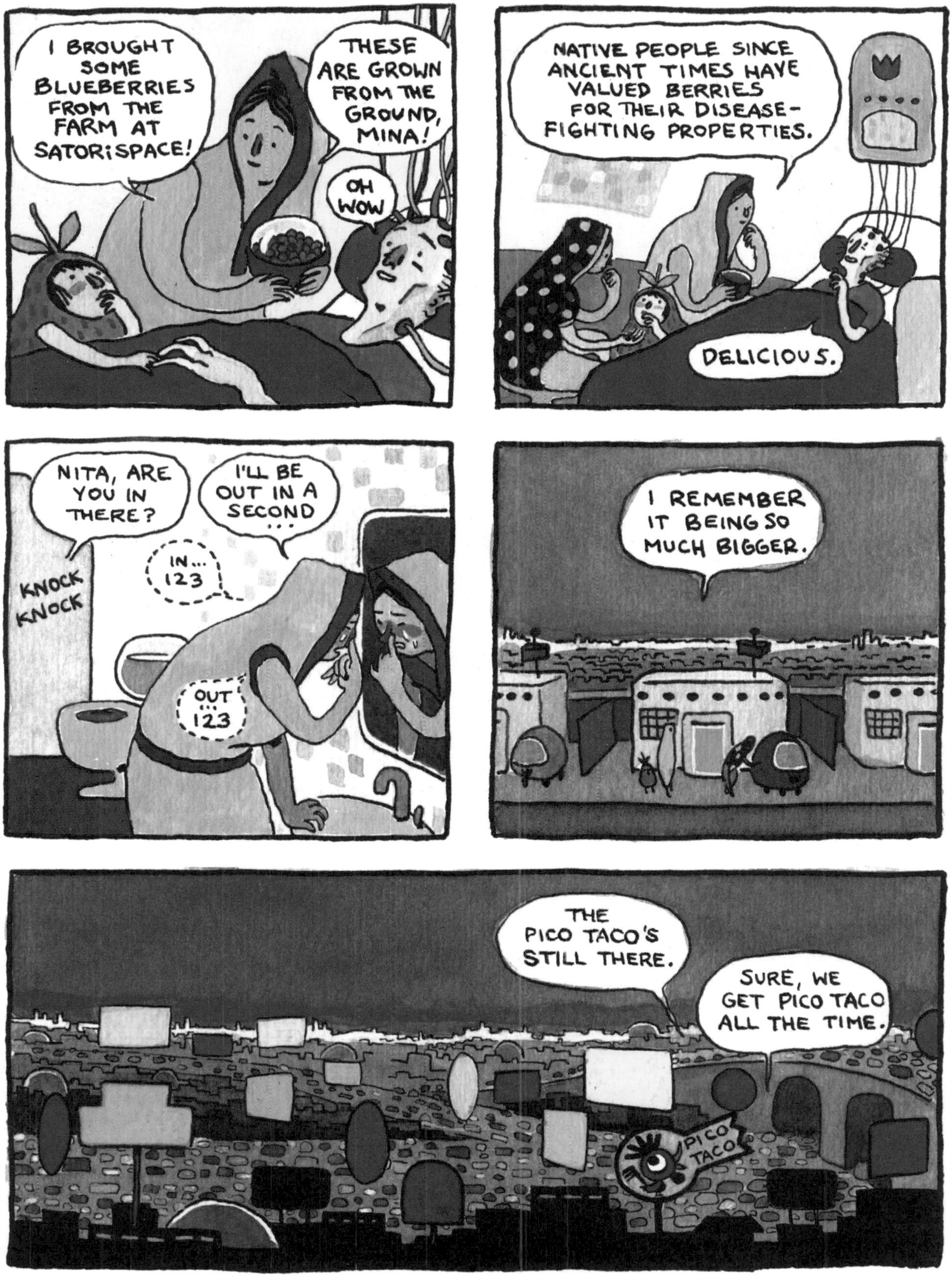
I BROUGHT SOME BLUEBERRIES FROM THE FARM AT SATORI SPACE!
THESE ARE GROWN FROM THE GROUND, MINA!
OH WOW
NATIVE PEOPLE SINCE ANCIENT TIMES HAVE VALUED BERRIES FOR THEIR DISEASE-FIGHTING PROPERTIES.
DELICIOUS.
NITA, ARE YOU IN THERE?
KNOCK KNOCK
I'LL BE OUT IN A SECOND...
IN... 123
OUT... 123
I REMEMBER IT BEING SO MUCH BIGGER.
THE PICO TACO'S STILL THERE.
SURE, WE GET PICO TACO ALL THE TIME.
PICO TACO

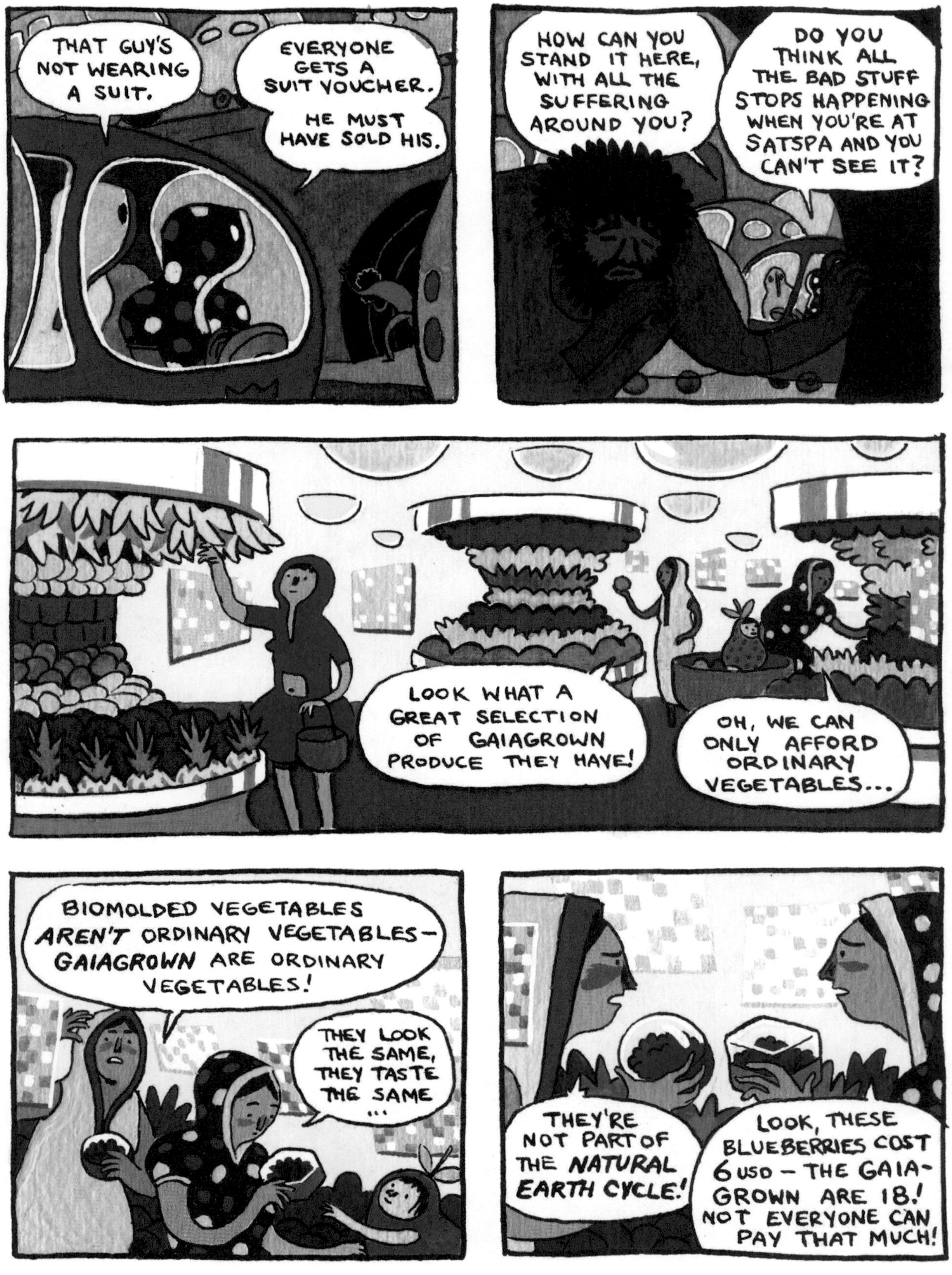
THAT GUY'S NOT WEARING A SUIT.
EVERYONE GETS A SUIT VOUCHER.
HE MUST HAVE SOLD HIS.
HOW CAN YOU STAND IT HERE, WITH ALL THE SUFFERING AROUND YOU?
DO YOU THINK ALL THE BAD STUFF STOPS HAPPENING WHEN YOU'RE AT SATSPA AND YOU CAN'T SEE IT?
LOOK WHAT A GREAT SELECTION OF GAIAGROWN PRODUCE THEY HAVE!
OH, WE CAN ONLY AFFORD ORDINARY VEGETABLES...
BIOMOLDED VEGETABLES AREN'T ORDINARY VEGETABLES— GAIAGROWN ARE ORDINARY VEGETABLES!
THEY LOOK THE SAME, THEY TASTE THE SAME ...
THEY'RE NOT PART OF THE NATURAL EARTH CYCLE!
LOOK, THESE BLUEBERRIES COST 6 USD — THE GAIA-GROWN ARE 18! NOT EVERYONE CAN PAY THAT MUCH!

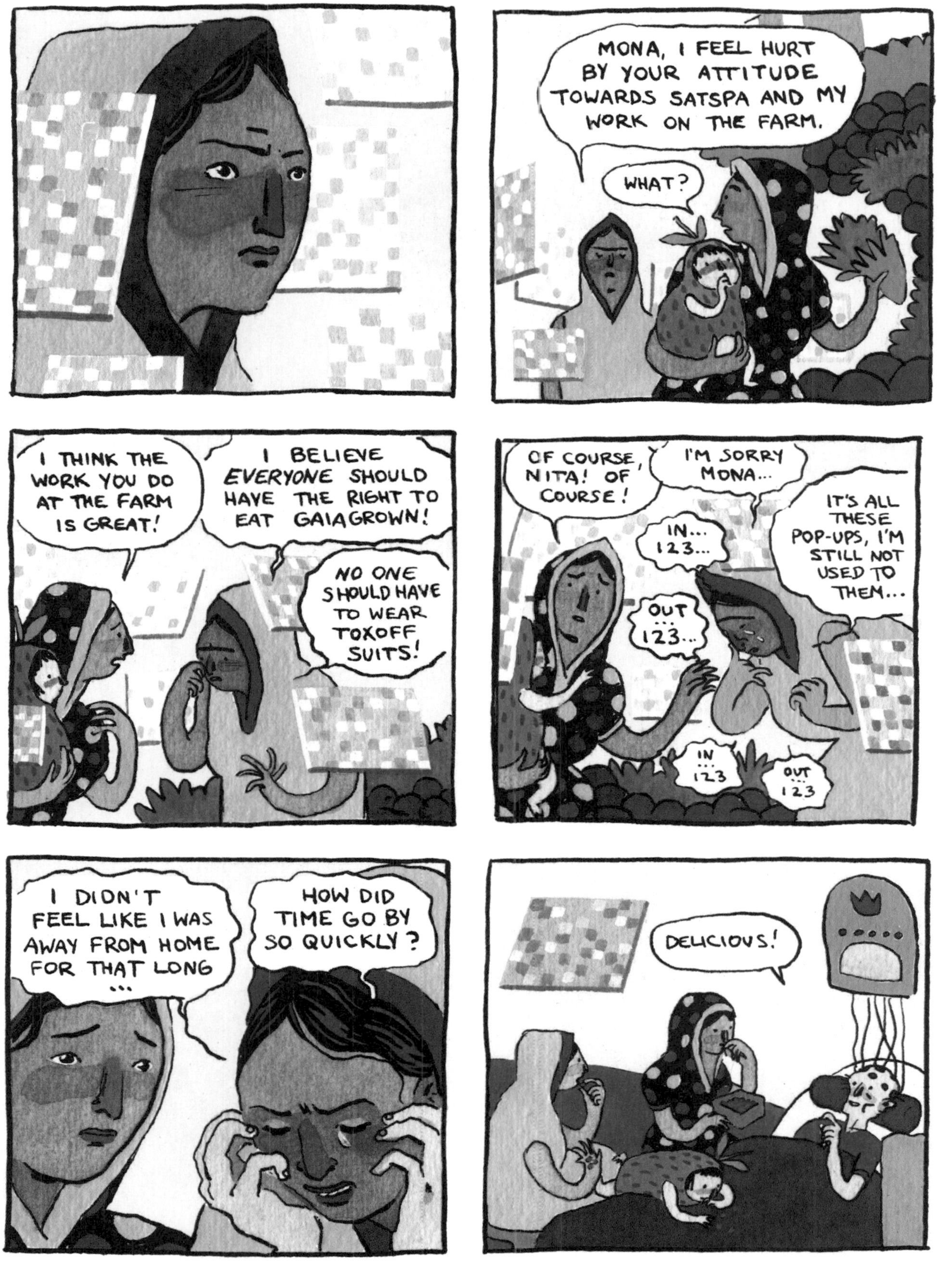
MONA, I FEEL HURT BY YOUR ATTITUDE TOWARDS SATSPA AND MY WORK ON THE FARM.
WHAT?
I THINK THE WORK YOU DO AT THE FARM IS GREAT!
I BELIEVE EVERYONE SHOULD HAVE THE RIGHT TO EAT GAIAGROWN!
NO ONE SHOULD HAVE TO WEAR TOXOFF SUITS!
OF COURSE, NITA! OF COURSE!
I'M SORRY MONA...
IT'S ALL THESE POP-UPS, I'M STILL NOT USED TO THEM...
IN... 123...
OUT... 123...
IN... 123
OUT... 123
I DIDN'T FEEL LIKE I WAS AWAY FROM HOME FOR THAT LONG...
HOW DID TIME GO BY SO QUICKLY?
DELICIOUS!

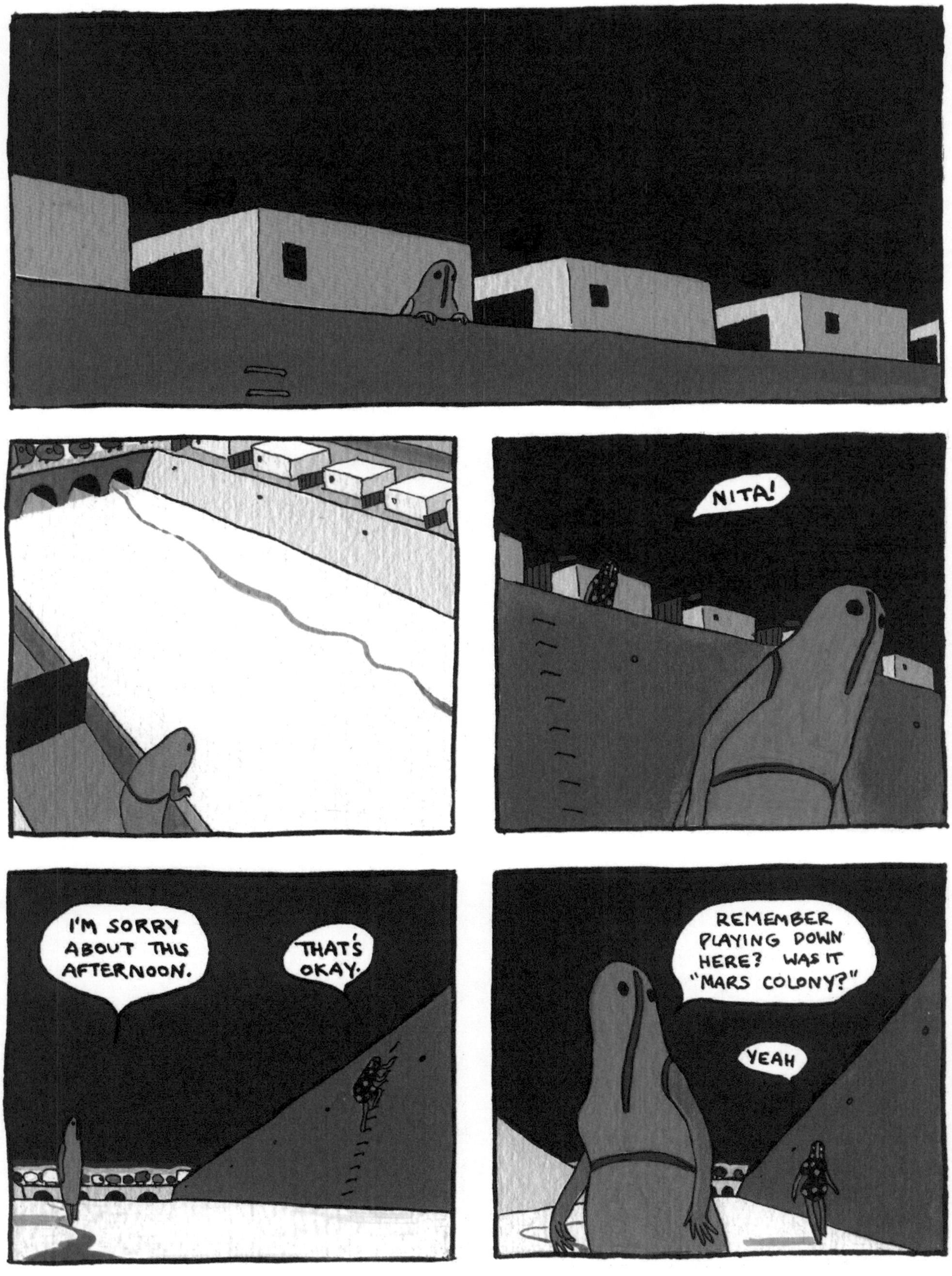
NITA!
I'M SORRY ABOUT THIS AFTERNOON.
THAT'S OKAY.
REMEMBER PLAYING DOWN HERE? WAS IT "MARS COLONY?"
YEAH

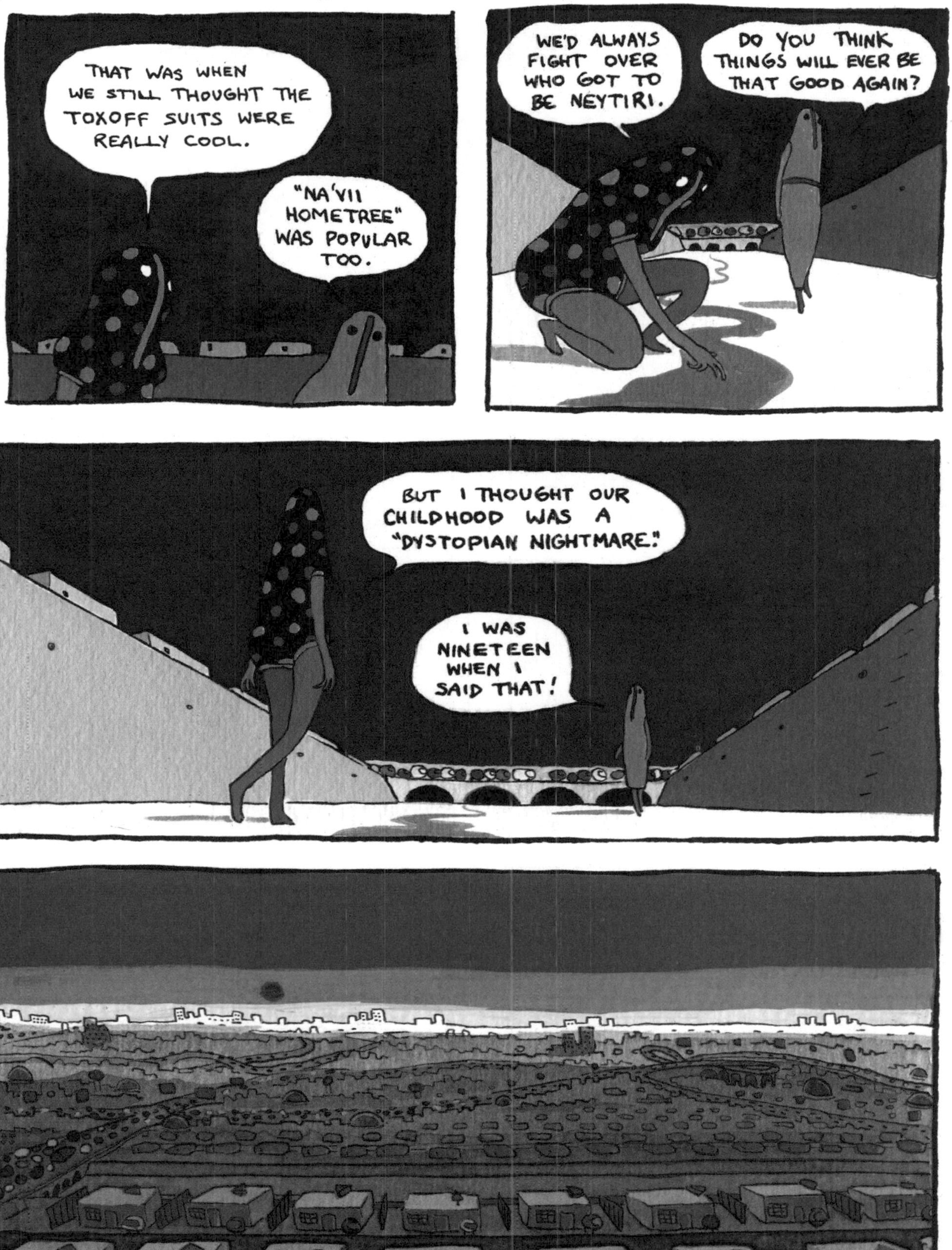
THAT WAS WHEN WE STILL THOUGHT THE TOXOFF SUITS WERE REALLY COOL.
"NA'VII HOMETREE" WAS POPULAR TOO.
WE'D ALWAYS FIGHT OVER WHO GOT TO BE NEYTIRI.
DO YOU THINK THINGS WILL EVER BE THAT GOOD AGAIN?
BUT I THOUGHT OUR CHILDHOOD WAS A "DYSTOPIAN NIGHTMARE."
I WAS NINETEEN WHEN I SAID THAT!

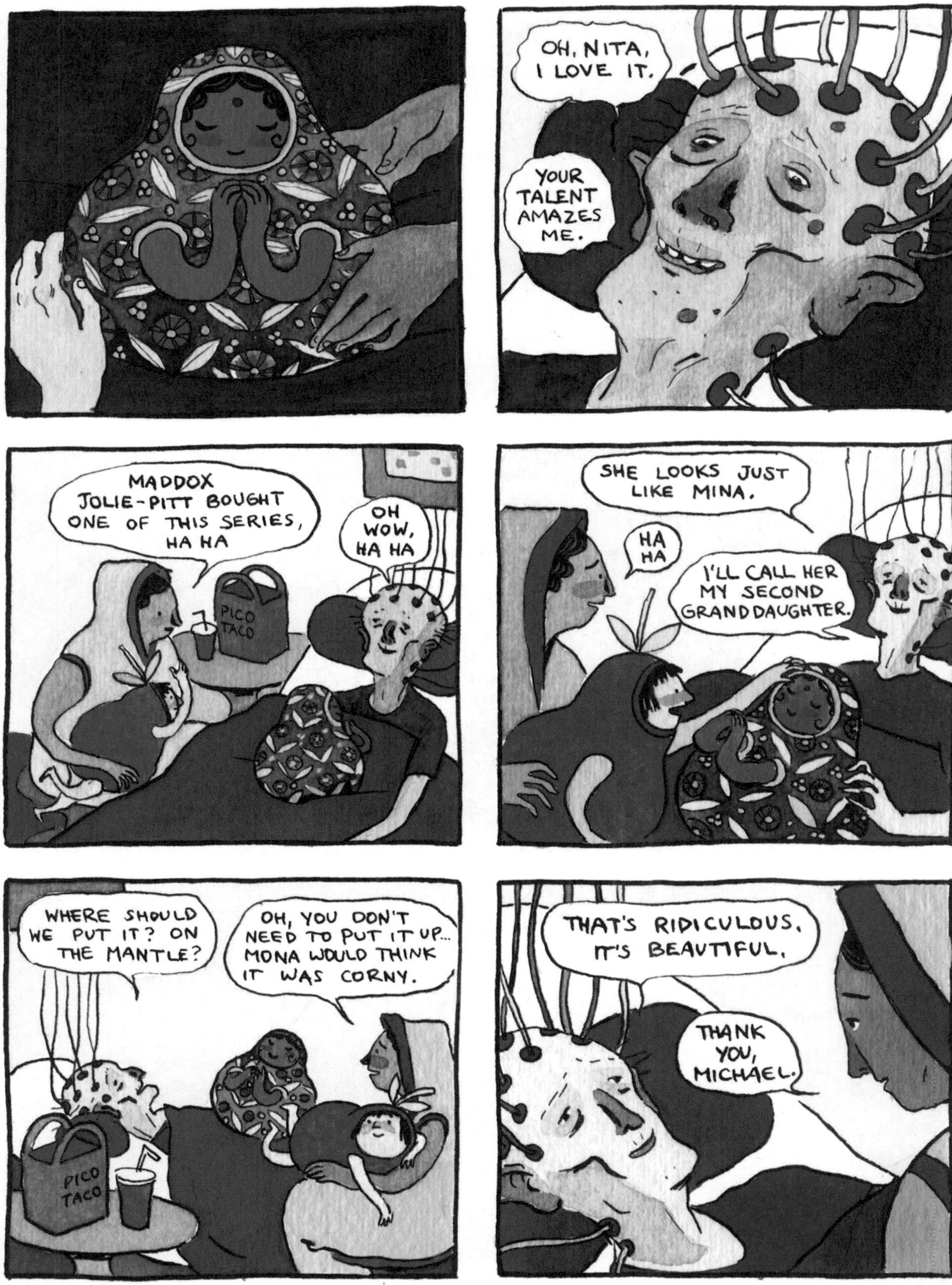
OH, NITA, I LOVE IT.
YOUR TALENT AMAZES ME.
MADDOX JOLIE-PITT BOUGHT ONE OF THIS SERIES, HA HA
OH WOW, HA HA
PICO TACO
SHE LOOKS JUST LIKE MINA.
HA HA
I'LL CALL HER MY SECOND GRANDDAUGHTER.
WHERE SHOULD WE PUT IT? ON THE MANTLE?
OH, YOU DON'T NEED TO PUT IT UP... MONA WOULD THINK IT WAS CORNY.
PICO TACO
THAT'S RIDICULOUS. IT'S BEAUTIFUL.
THANK YOU, MICHAEL.

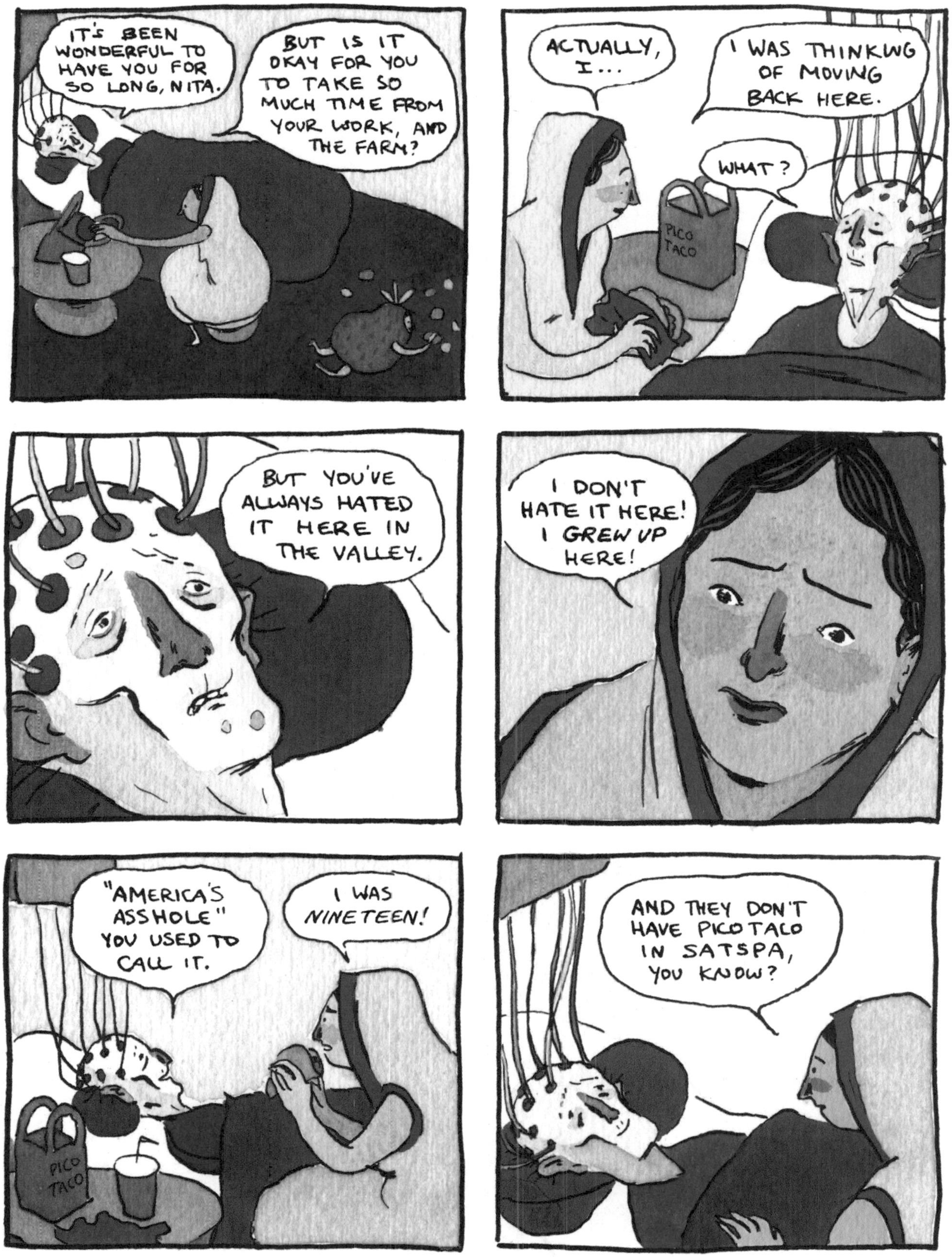
IT'S BEEN WONDERFUL TO HAVE YOU FOR SO LONG, NITA.
BUT IS IT OKAY FOR YOU TO TAKE SO MUCH TIME FROM YOUR WORK, AND THE FARM?
ACTUALLY, I...
I WAS THINKING OF MOVING BACK HERE.
WHAT?
PICO TACO
BUT YOU'VE ALWAYS HATED IT HERE IN THE VALLEY.
I DON'T HATE IT HERE! I GREW UP HERE!
"AMERICA'S ASSHOLE" YOU USED TO CALL IT.
I WAS NINETEEN!
PICO TACO
AND THEY DON'T HAVE PICO TACO IN SATSPA, YOU KNOW?

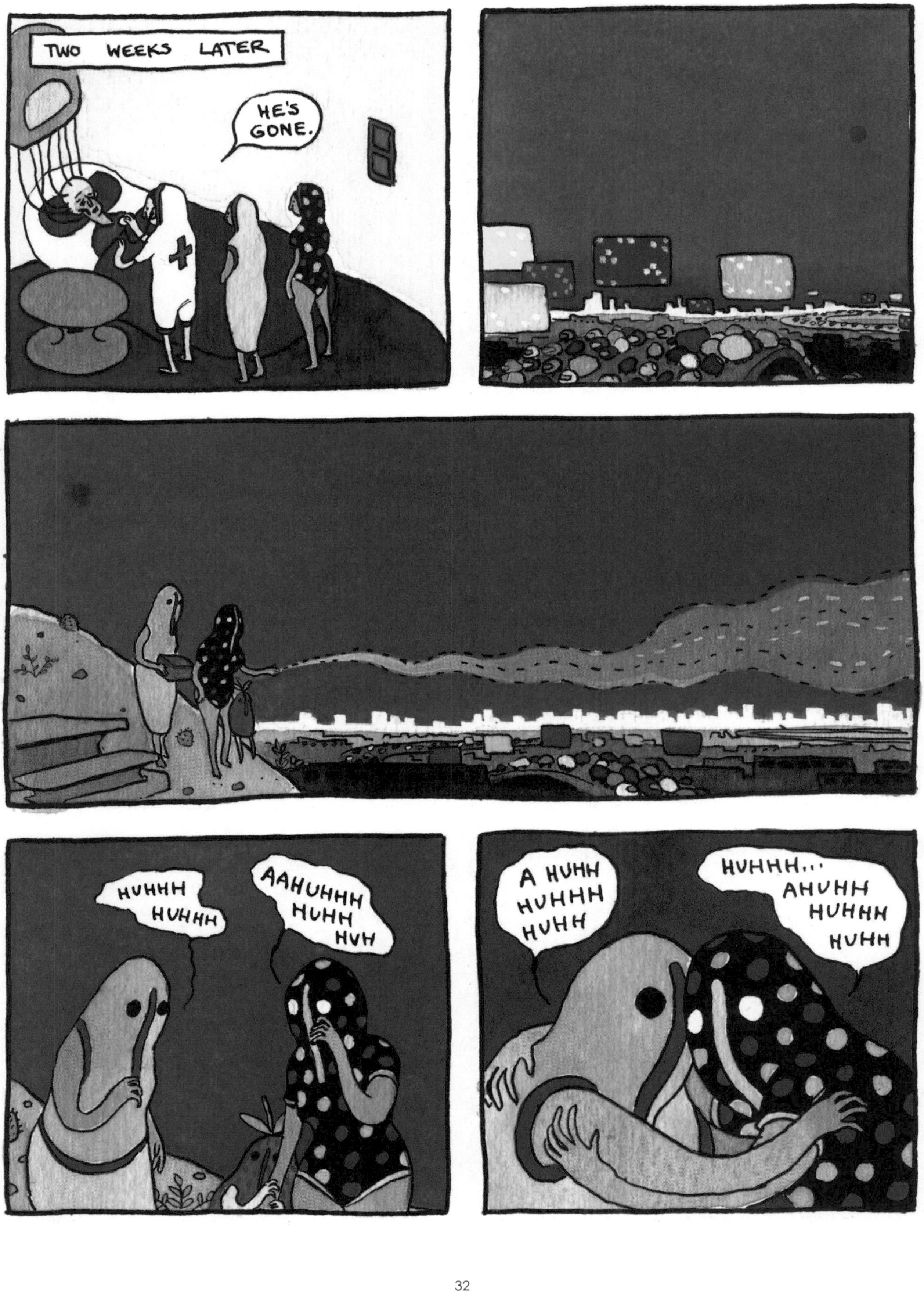
TWO WEEKS LATER
HE'S GONE.
HUHHH HUHHH
AAHUHHH HUHH HUH
A HUHH HUHHH HUHH
HUHHH... AHUHH HUHHH HUHH

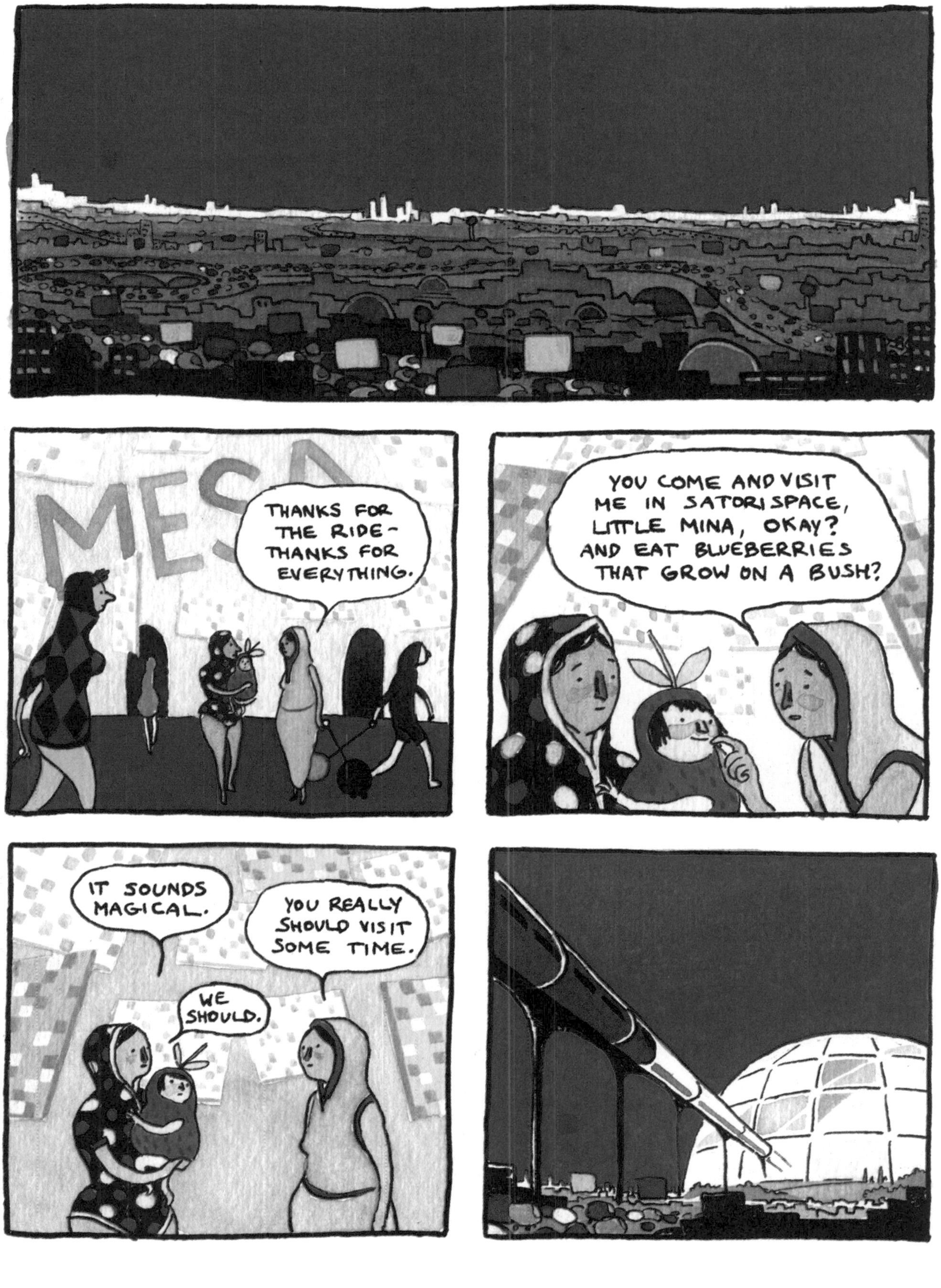
MESA
THANKS FOR THE RIDE- THANKS FOR EVERYTHING.
YOU COME AND VISIT ME IN SATORISPACE, LITTLE MINA, OKAY? AND EAT BLUEBERRIES THAT GROW ON A BUSH?
IT SOUNDS MAGICAL.
YOU REALLY SHOULD VISIT SOME TIME.
WE SHOULD.

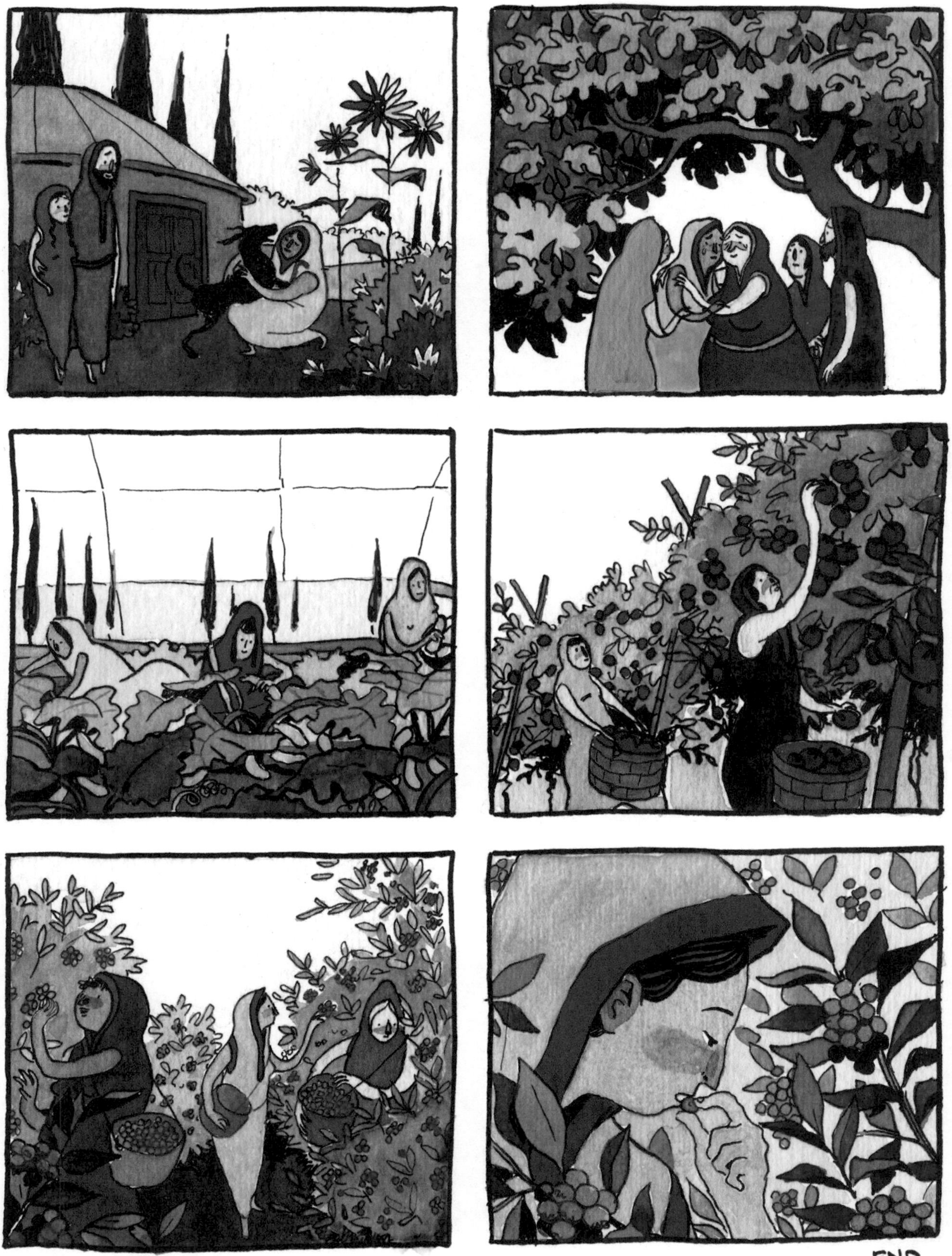
END

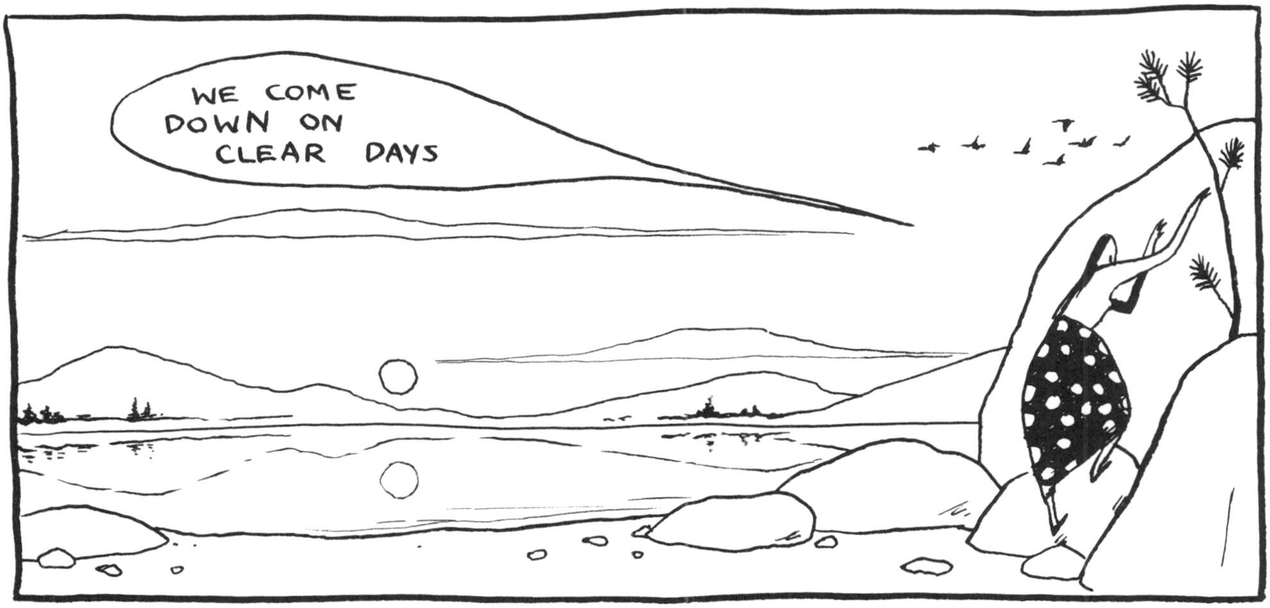
WE COME DOWN ON CLEAR DAYS

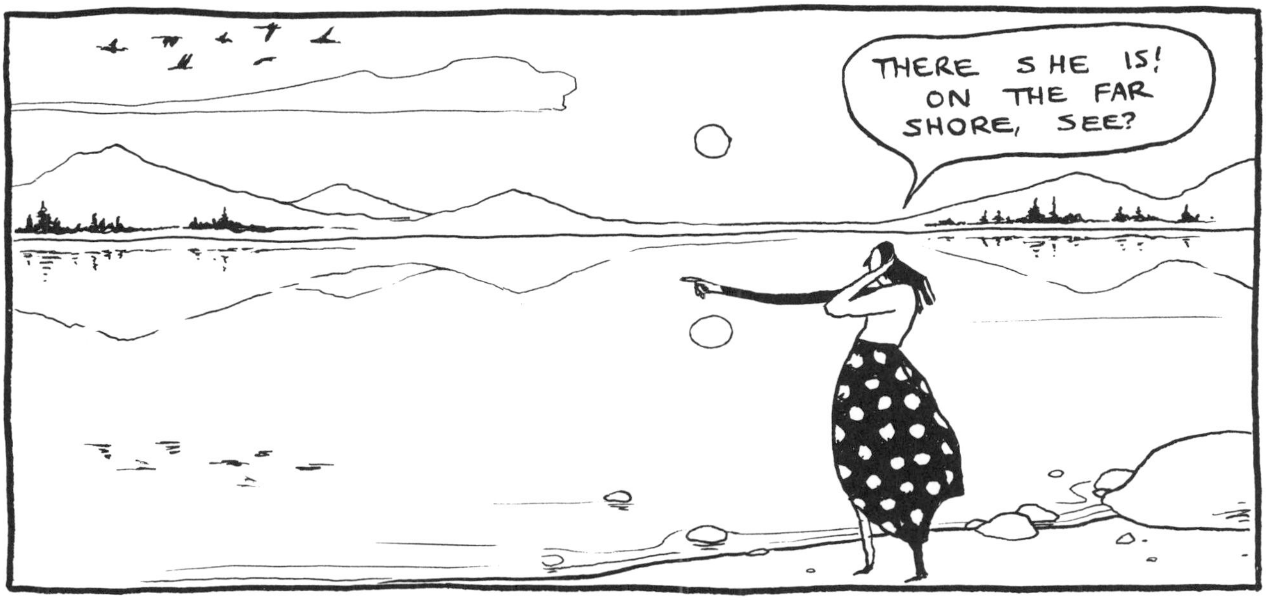
THERE SHE IS! ON THE FAR SHORE, SEE?

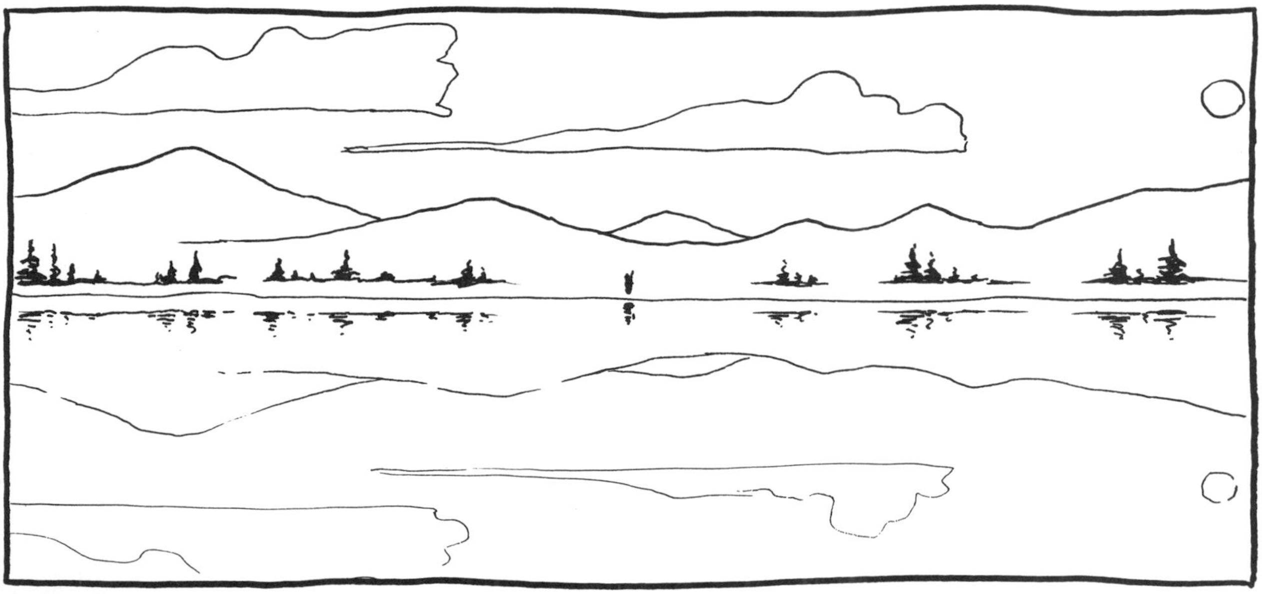

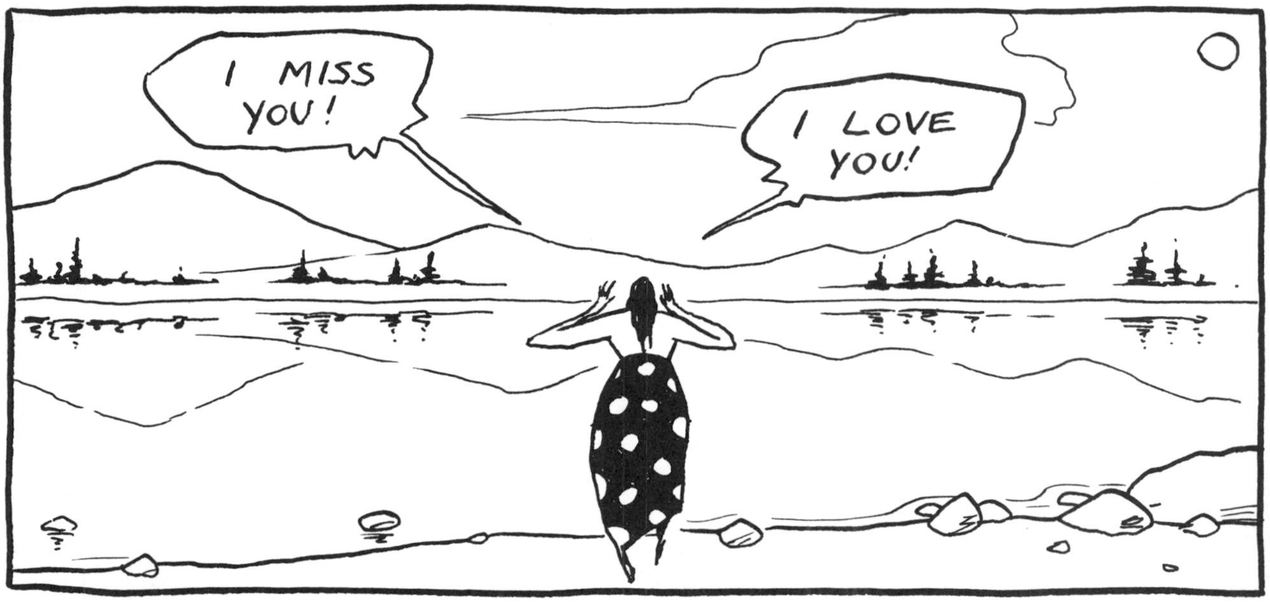
I MISS YOU!
I LOVE YOU!

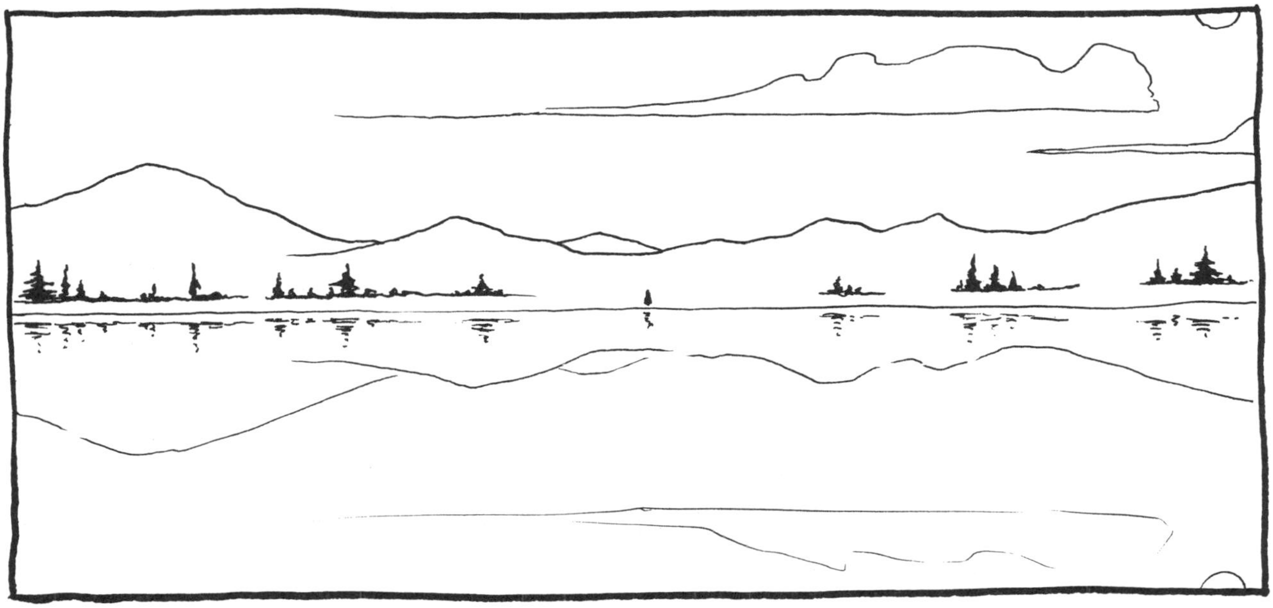

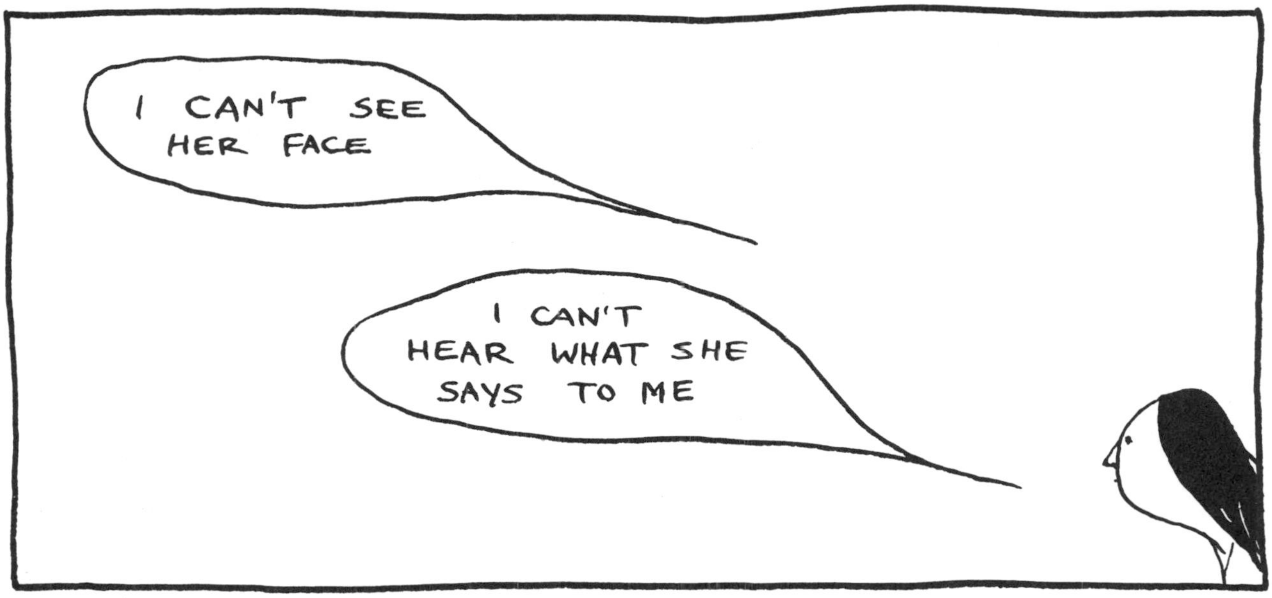
I CAN'T SEE HER FACE
I CAN'T HEAR WHAT SHE SAYS TO ME

END

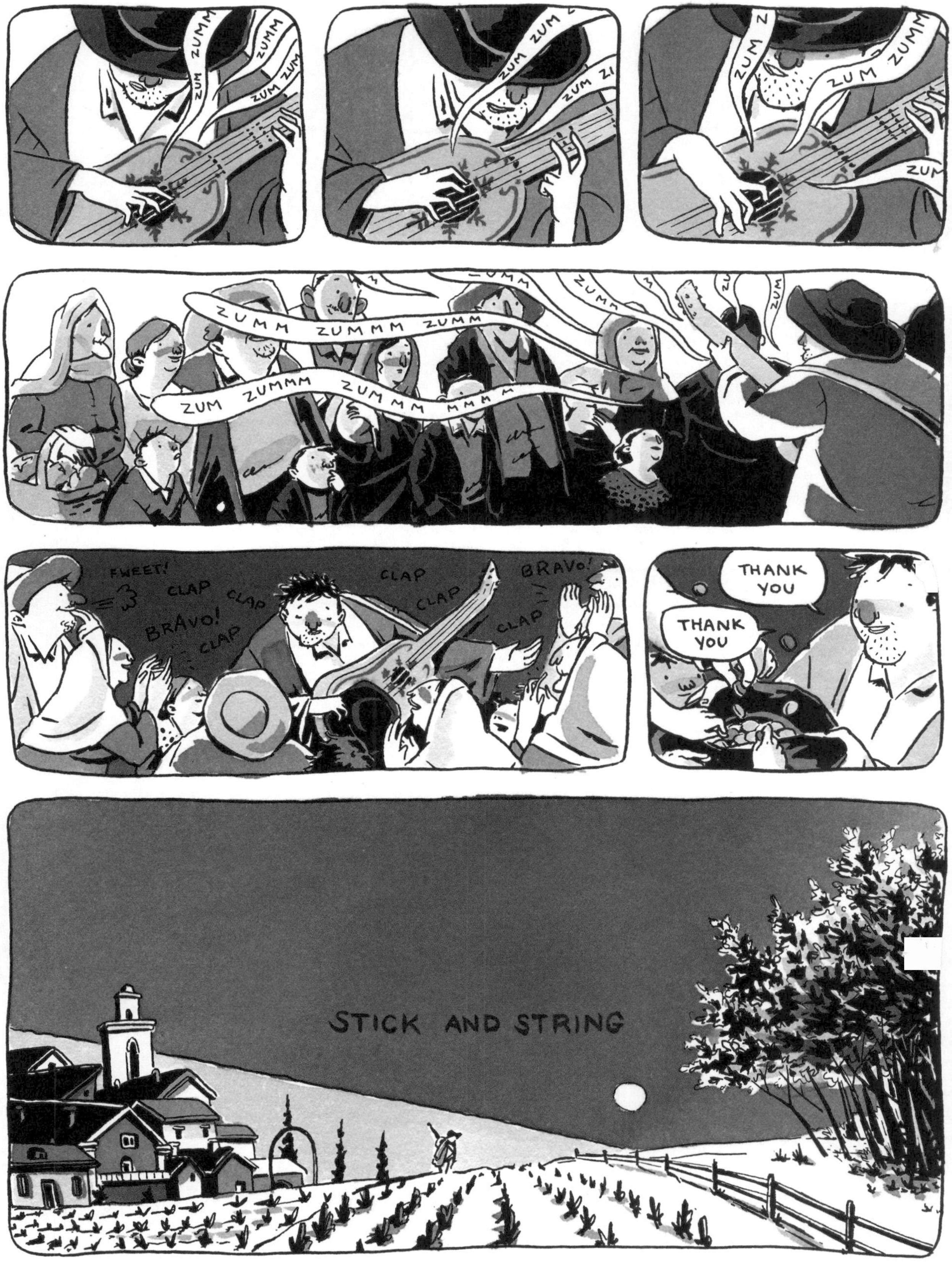
ZUMM ZUMM
ZUM ZUM
ZUMM
ZUM ZUMM
ZUM ZI
ZUMM
ZUMM
ZUM
ZUMM ZUMMM ZUMM
ZUM ZUMMM ZUMMM MMMM
ZUM
FWEET!
CLAP
CLAP
BRAVO!
CLAP
CLAP
CLAP
BRAVO!
CLAP
THANK YOU
THANK YOU
STICK AND STRING

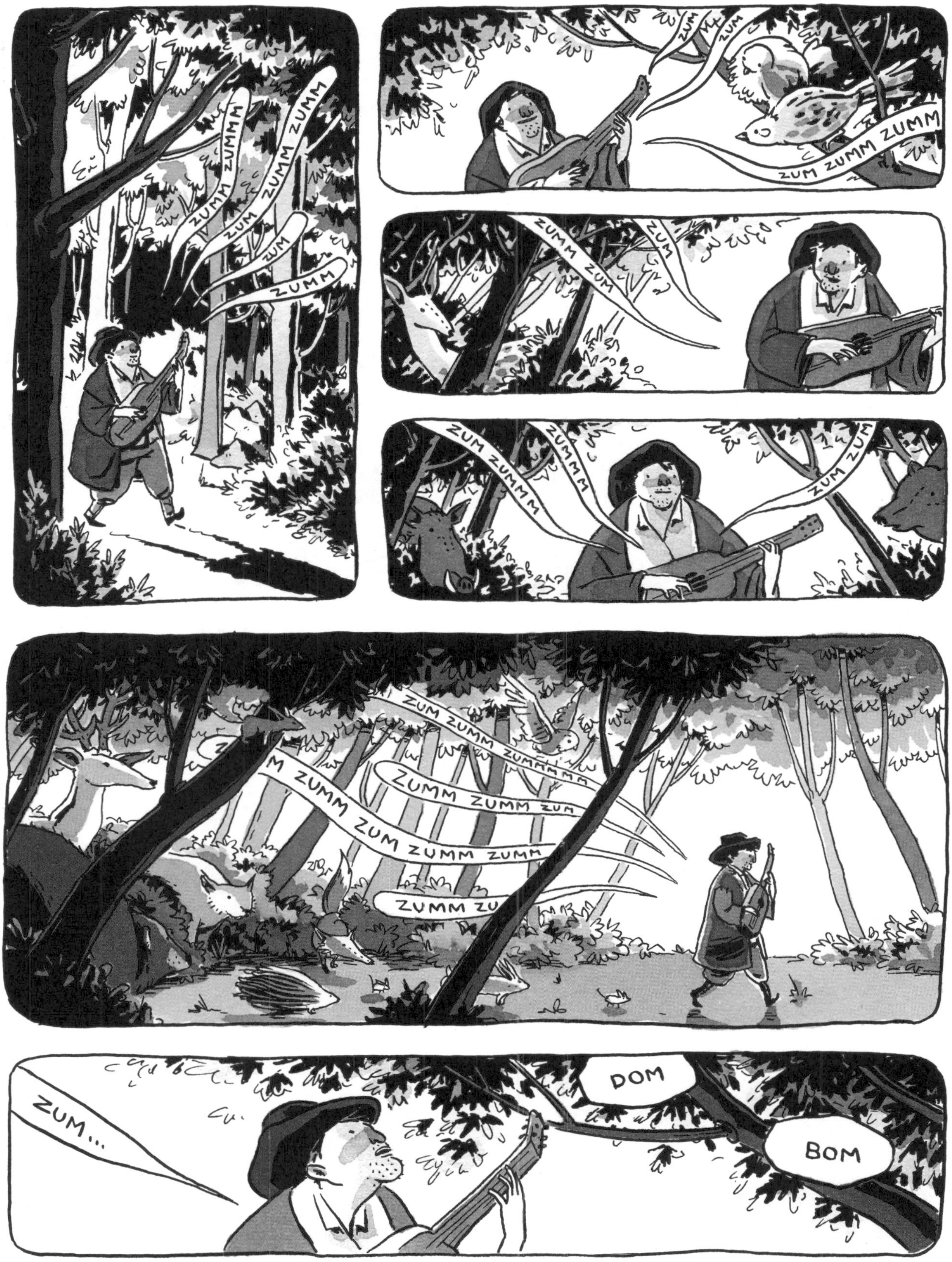

ZUMM ZUMM ZUMM
ZUMM ZUM ZUMM
ZUM ZUMM
ZUMM
ZUM
ZUM
ZUM ZUMM ZUMM
ZUMM ZUM
ZUM
ZUM ZUMMM
ZUMMM
ZUM ZUM
ZUM ZUMM ZUMMMM
M ZUMM
ZUMM ZUMM ZUM
ZUM ZUMM ZUMM
ZUMM ZU
ZUM...
DOM
BOM

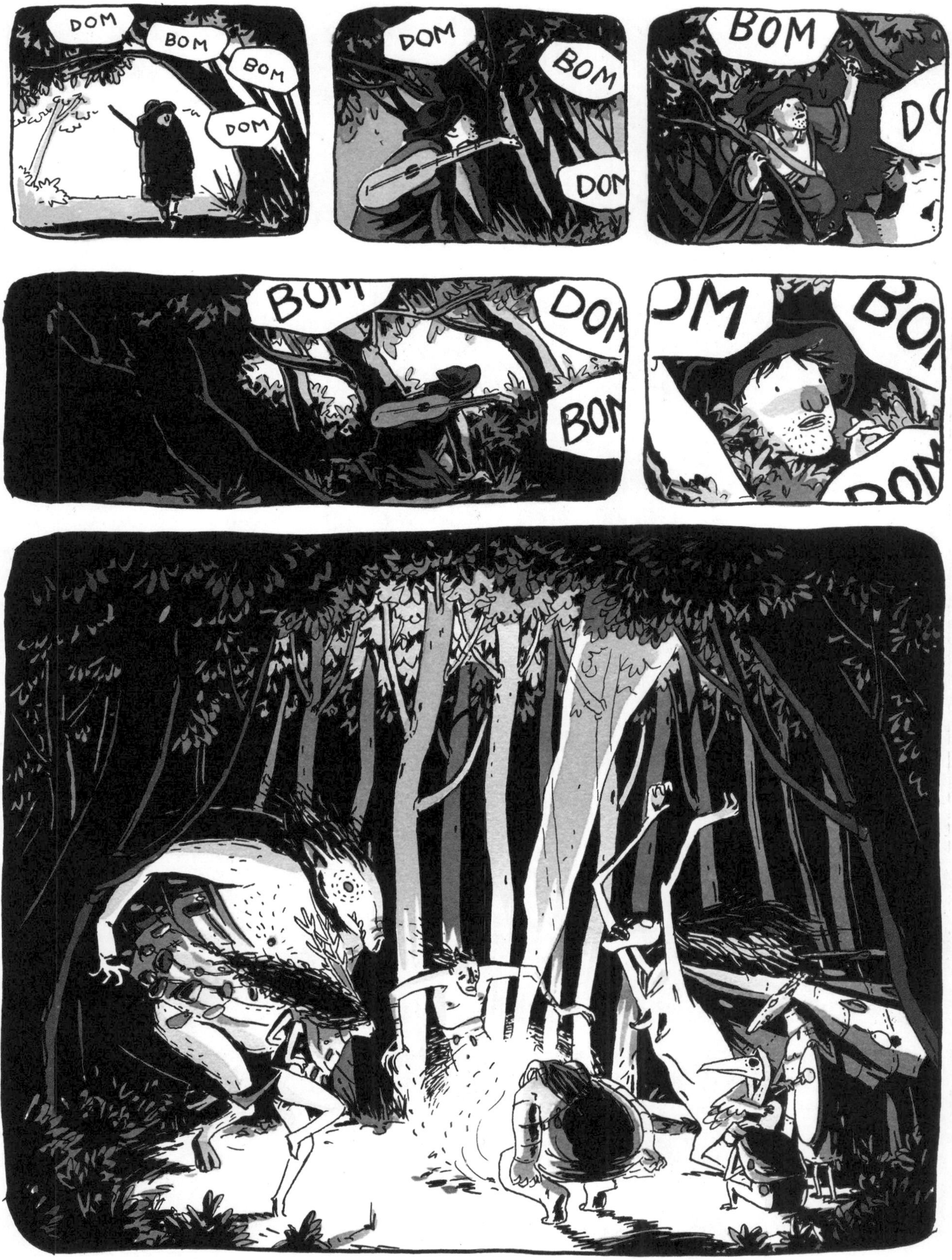
DOM
BOM
BOM
DOM
DOM
BOM
BOM

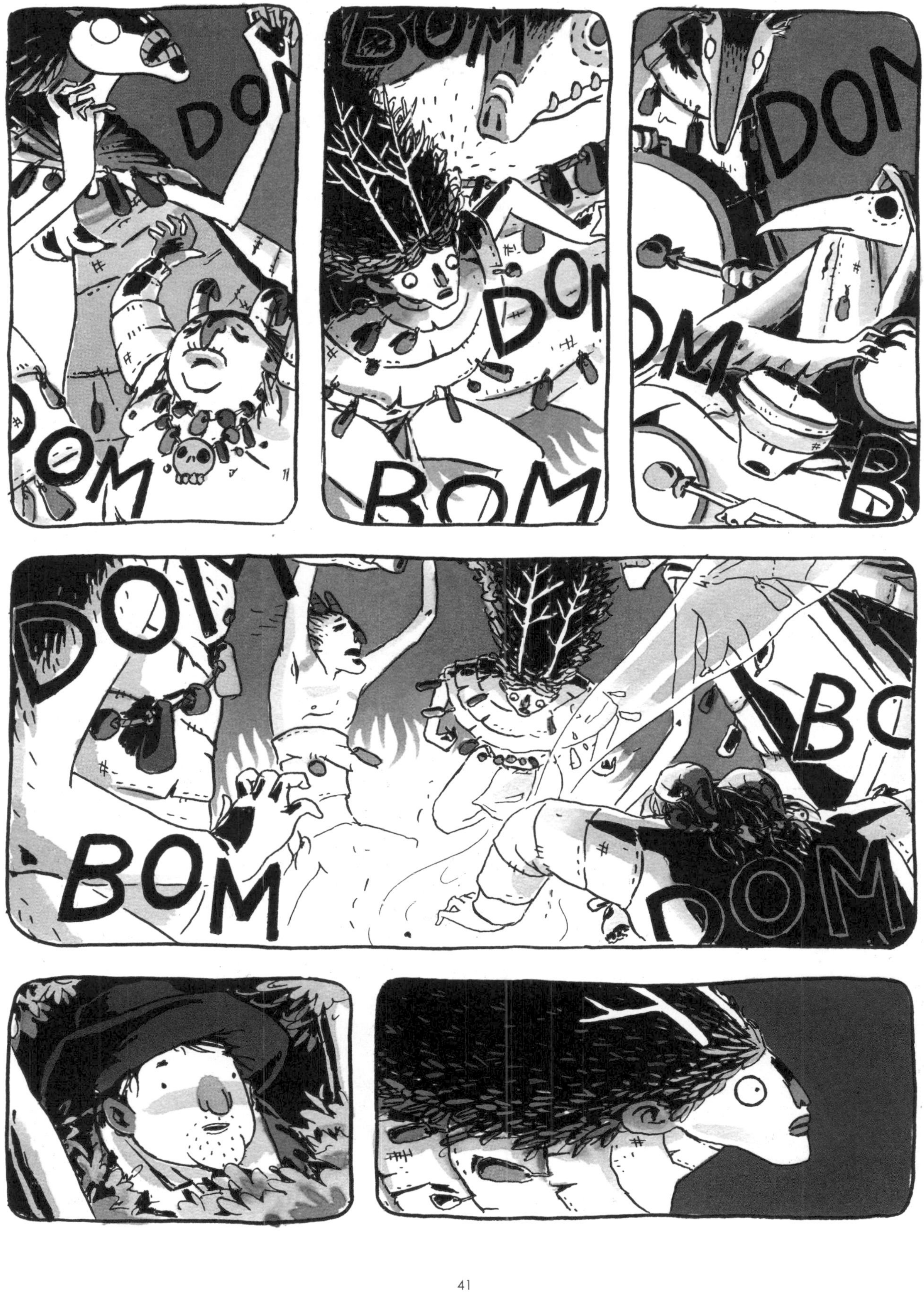
DOM
DOM
BOM
DOM
BOM
DOM
OM
B
DOM
BOM
BO
DOM

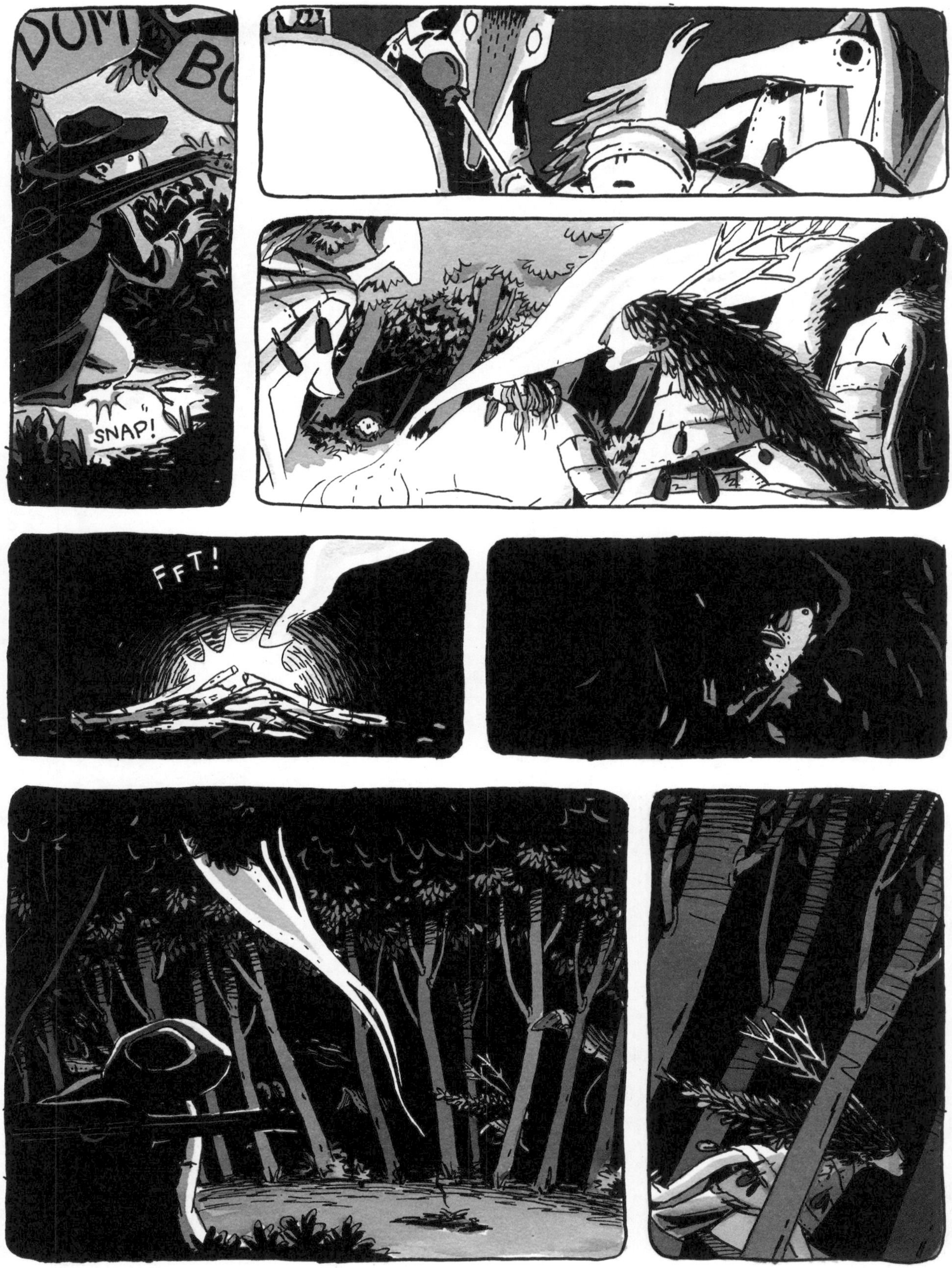
DUM
BO
SNAP!
FFT!

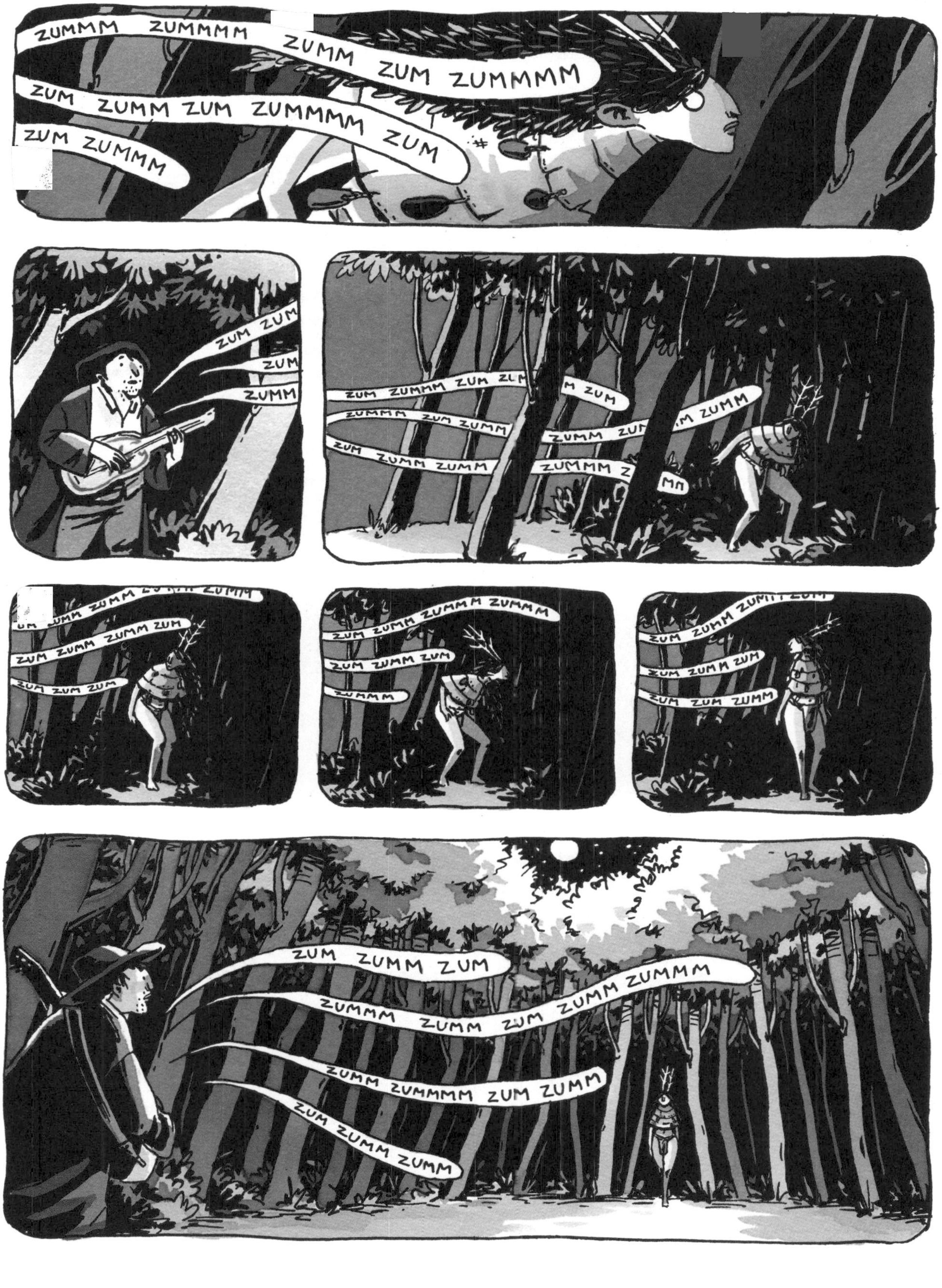
ZUMMM ZUMMMM ZUMM ZUM ZUMMMM
ZUM ZUMM ZUM ZUMMMM ZUM
ZUM ZUMMM
ZUM ZUM
ZUM
ZUMM
ZUM ZUMMM ZUM
ZUMMM ZUM ZUMM
ZUM ZUMM ZUMM
ZUM ZUM
ZUMM ZUMM
ZUMMM
ZUM ZUMM ZUMM ZUM
ZUM ZUM ZUM
ZUM ZUMM ZUMMM ZUMMM
ZUM ZUMM ZUM
ZUMMM
ZUM ZUMM
ZUM ZUMM ZUM
ZUM ZUM ZUMM
ZUM ZUMM ZUM
ZUMMM ZUMM ZUM ZUMM ZUMMM
ZUMM ZUMMMM ZUM ZUMM
ZUM ZUMM ZUMM

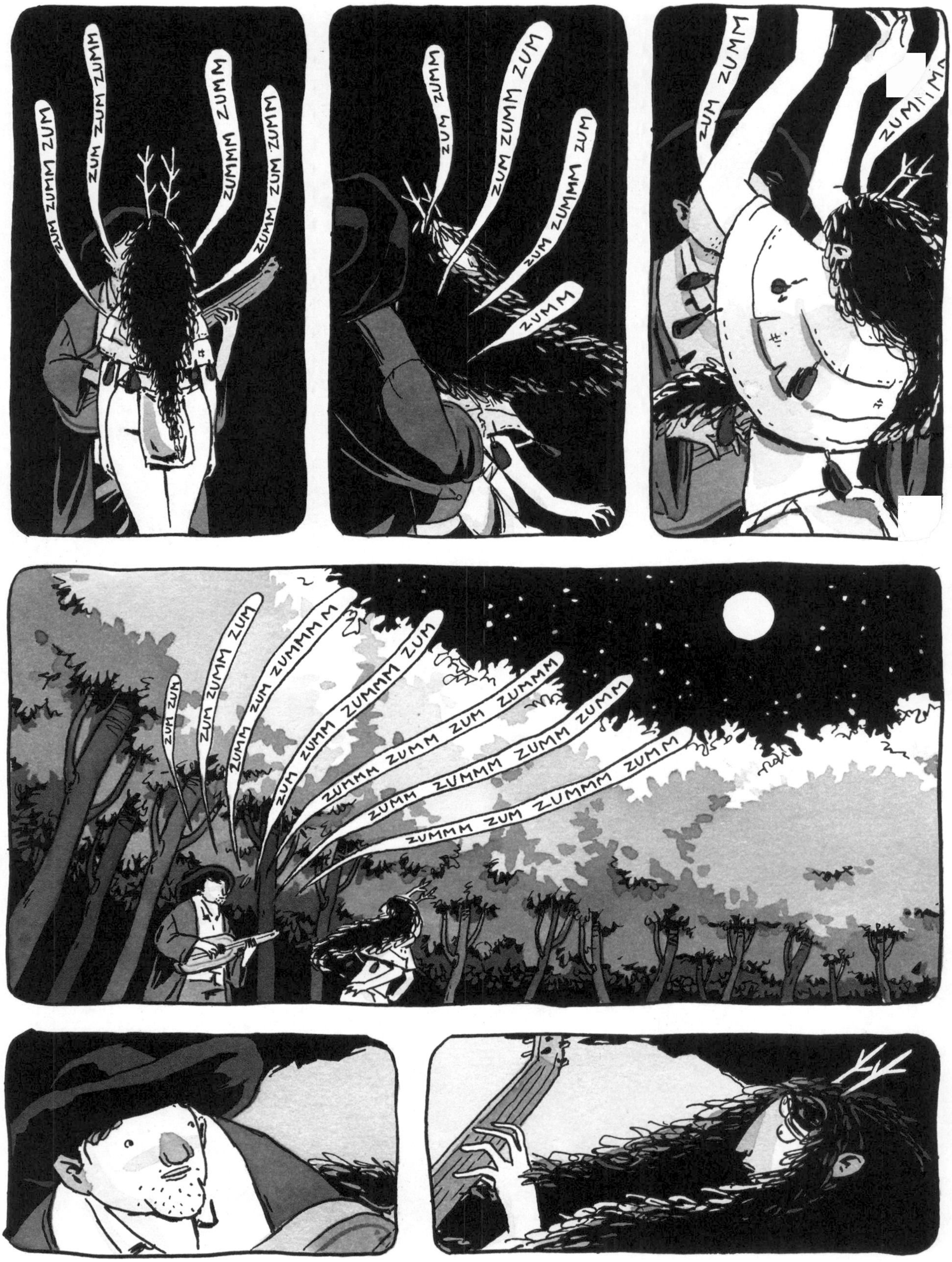

ZUM ZUMM ZUM
ZUM ZUM ZUMM
ZUMMM ZUMM
ZUMM ZUM ZUMM
ZUM ZUMM
ZUM ZUMM ZUM
ZUM ZUMMM ZUM
ZUMM
ZUM ZUMM
ZUM ZUM
ZUM ZUMM ZUM
ZUMM ZUM ZUMMMM
ZUM ZUMM ZUMMM ZUM
ZUMMM ZUMM ZUM ZUMMM
ZUMM ZUMMM ZUMM ZUMM
ZUMMM ZUM ZUMMM ZUMM

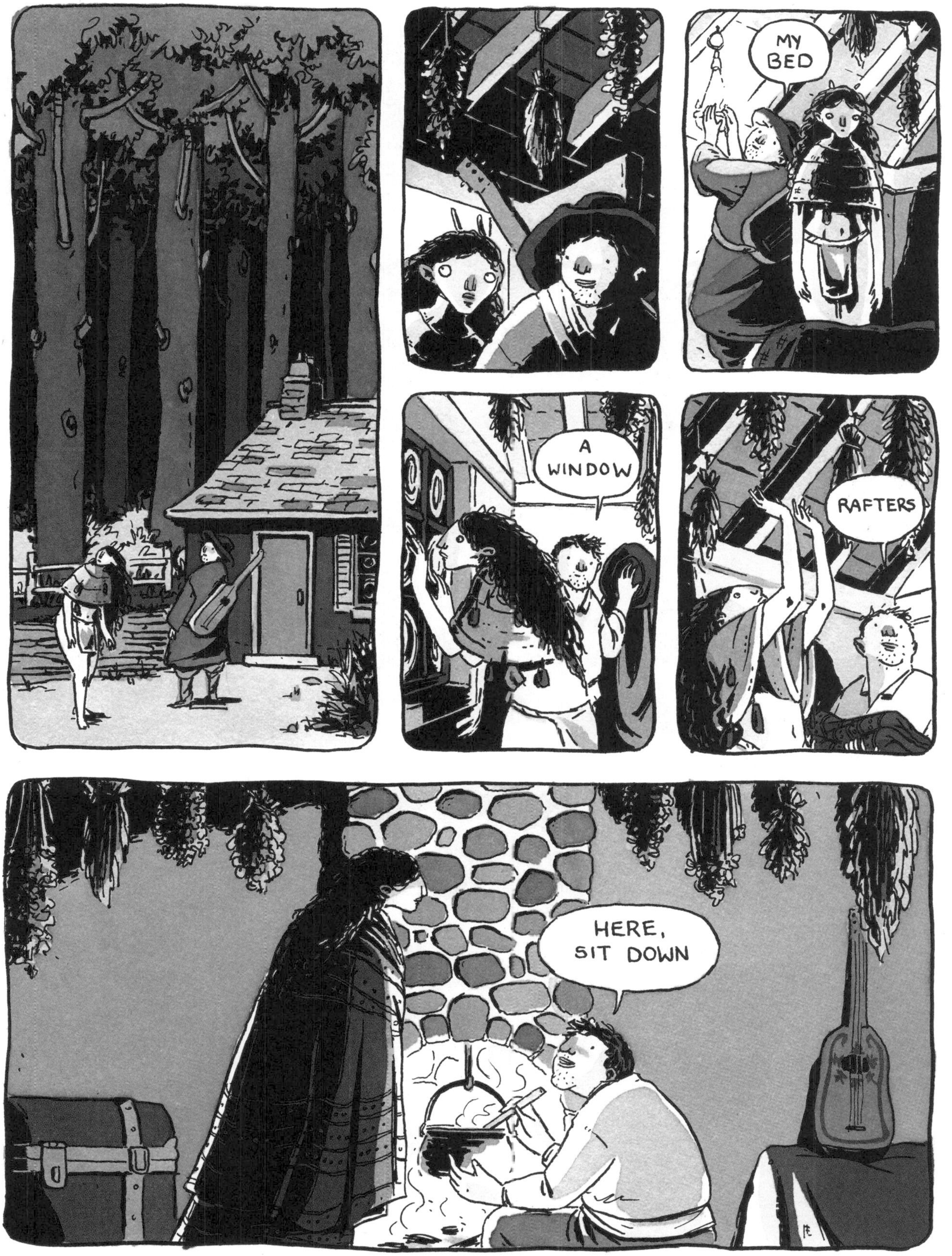
MY BED
A WINDOW
RAFTERS
HERE, SIT DOWN

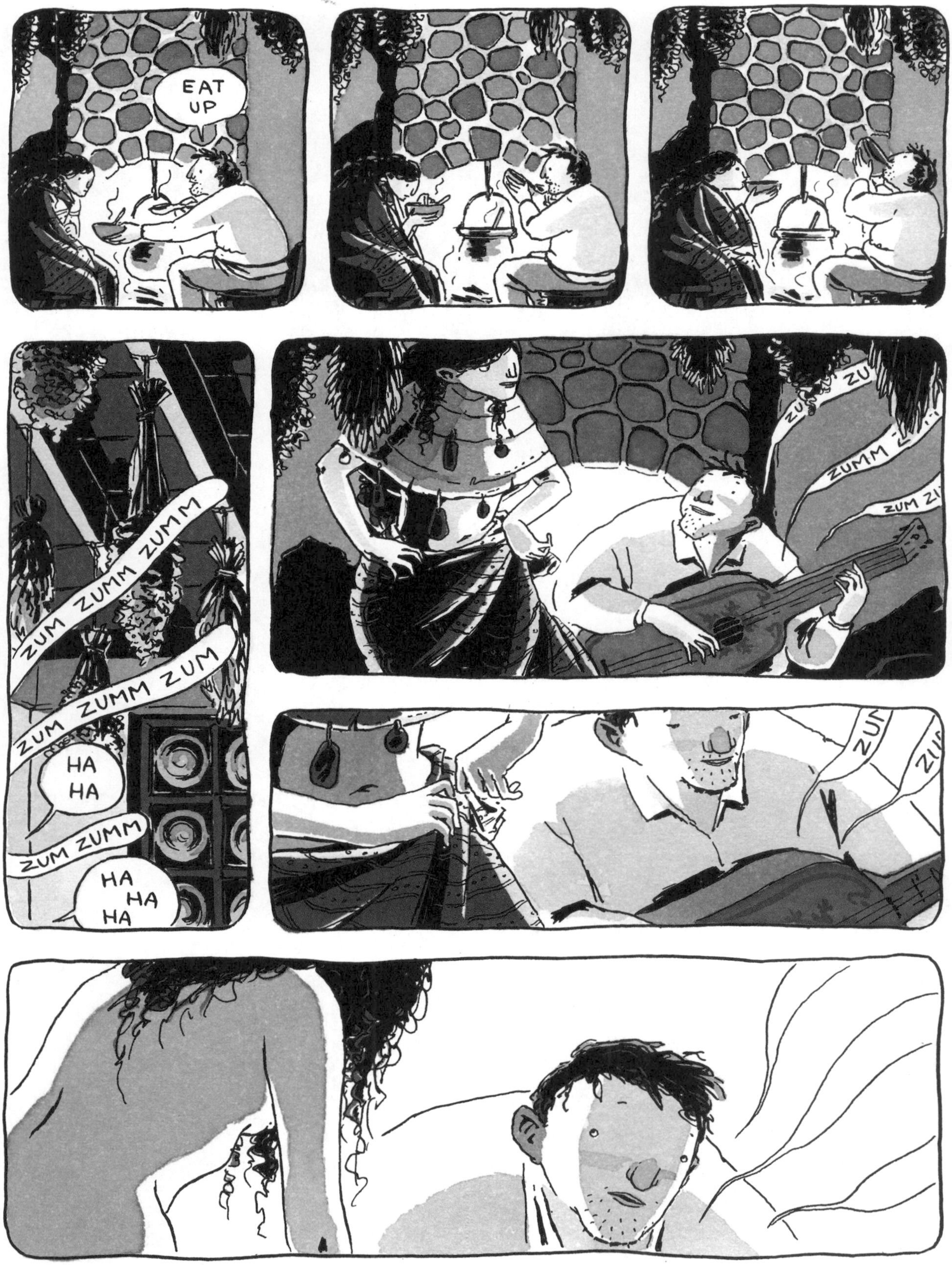
EAT UP
ZUM ZUMM ZUMM
ZUM ZUMM ZUM
HA HA
ZUM ZUMM
HA HA HA
ZUMM
ZUMM
ZUM ZU

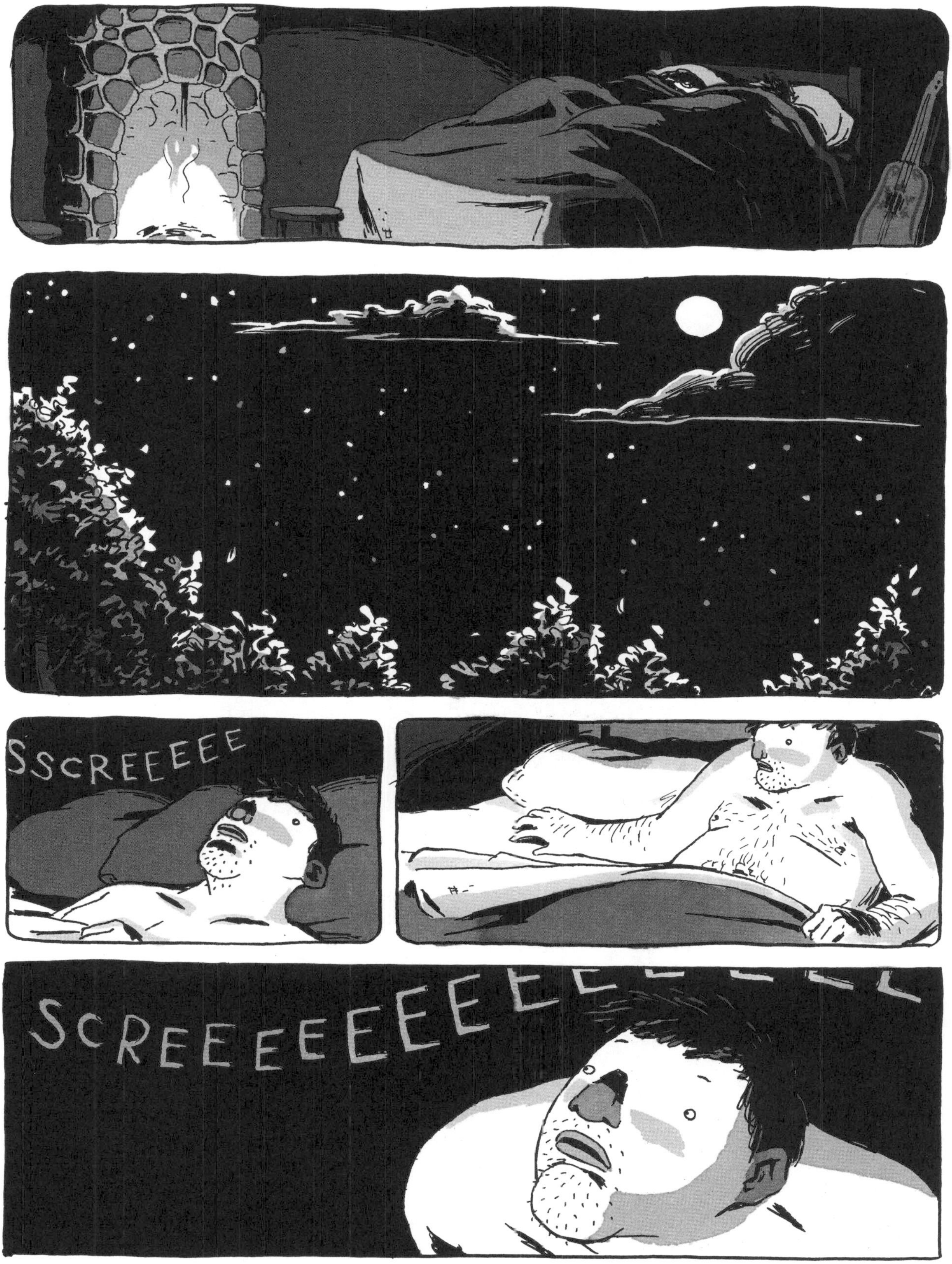
SSCREEEEE
SCREEEEEEEEEEEE

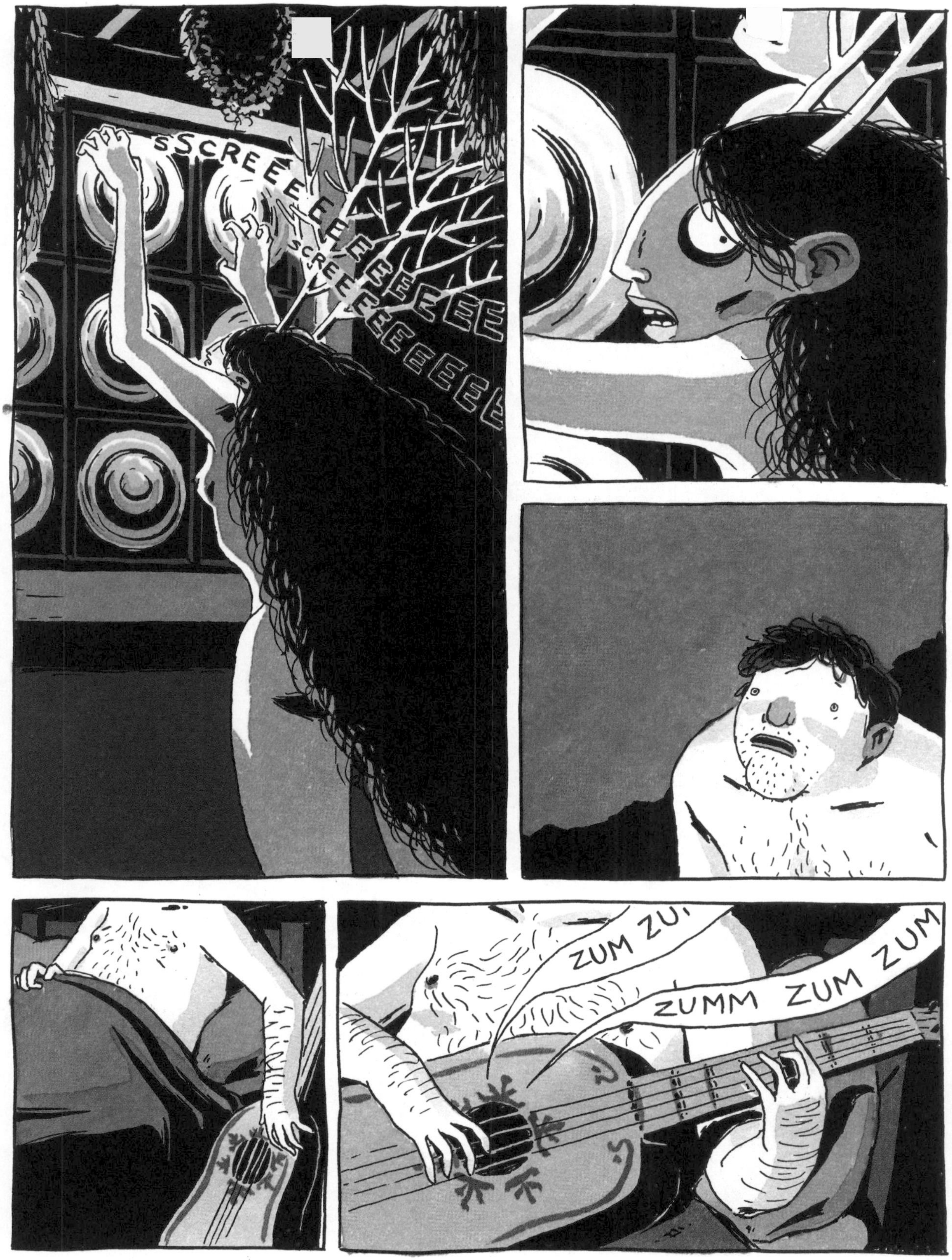
sSCREEEEEEEEEE
SCREEEEEEEEEEE
ZUM ZU
ZUMM ZUM ZUM

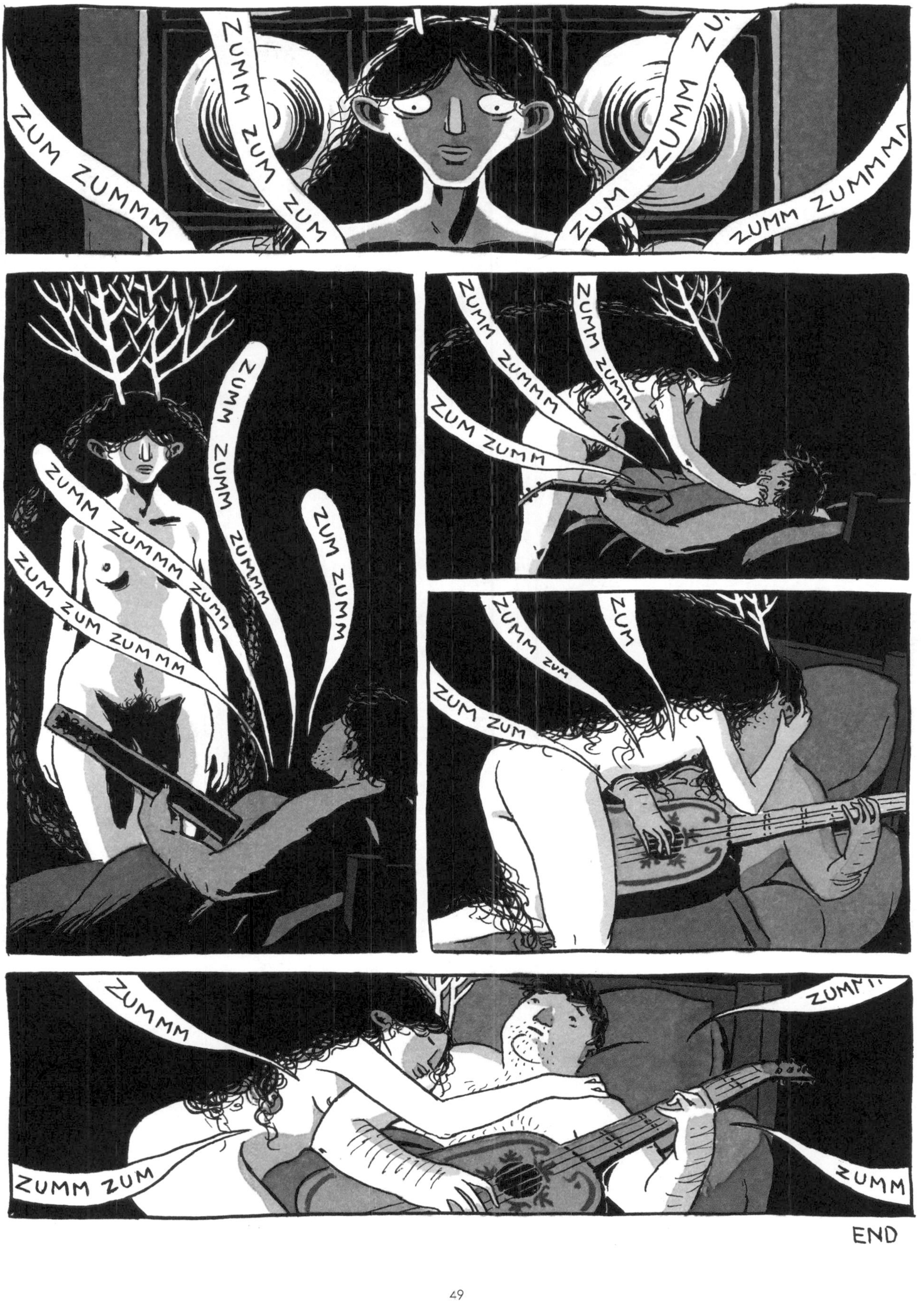
ZUM ZUMMM
ZUMM ZUM ZUM
ZUM ZUMM ZU
ZUMM ZUMMM
ZUMM ZUMMM ZUMM
ZUMM ZUMM ZUMMM
ZUM ZUM ZUMMM
ZUM ZUMM
ZUMM ZUMMM
ZUMM ZUMM
ZUM ZUMM
ZUMM ZUM
ZUM
ZUM ZUM
ZUMMM
ZUMM ZUM
ZUMM

END

DARLING, I'VE REALIZED I DON'T LOVE YOU.

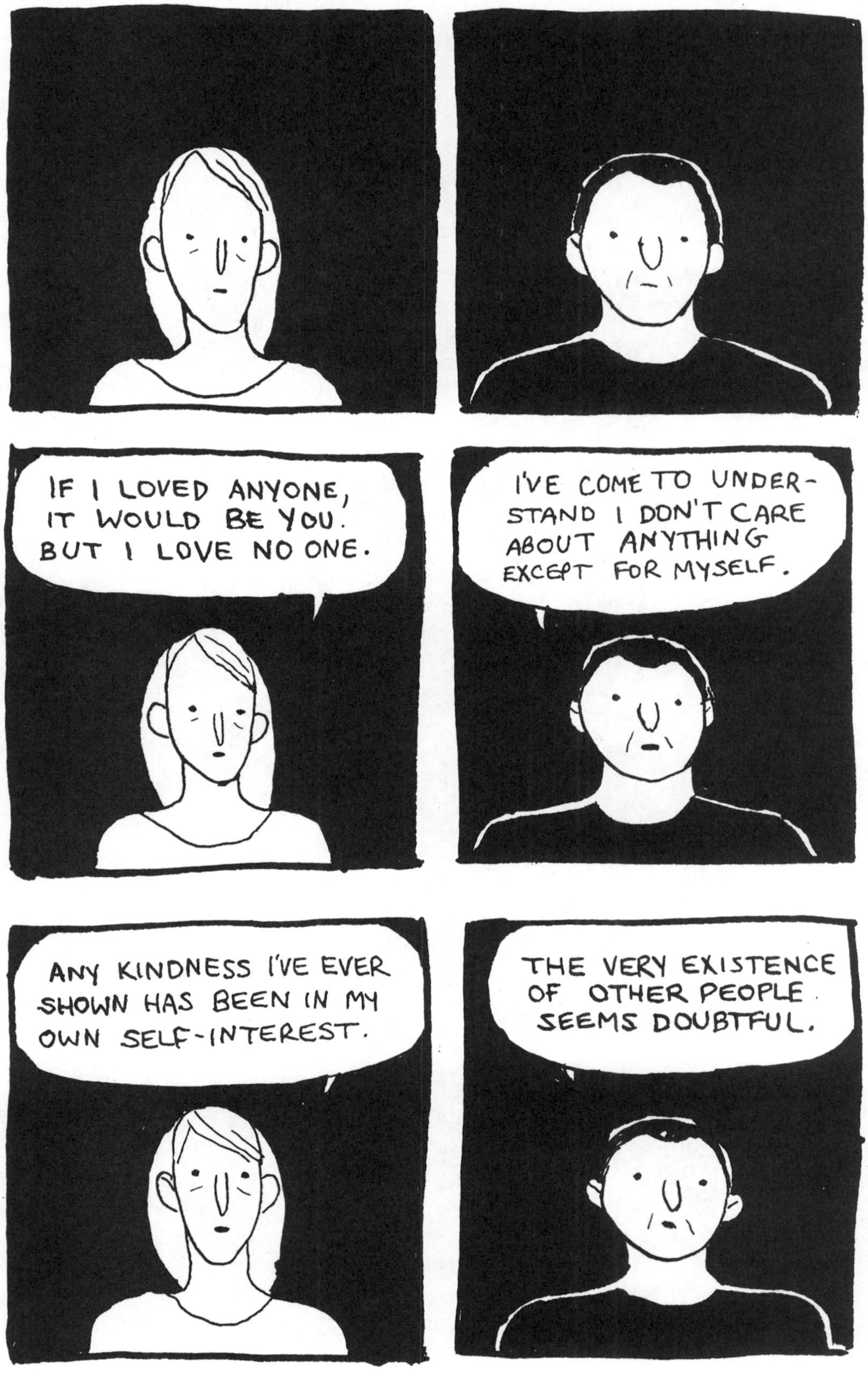
IF I LOVED ANYONE, IT WOULD BE YOU. BUT I LOVE NO ONE.
I'VE COME TO UNDER-STAND I DON'T CARE ABOUT ANYTHING EXCEPT FOR MYSELF.
ANY KINDNESS I'VE EVER SHOWN HAS BEEN IN MY OWN SELF-INTEREST.
THE VERY EXISTENCE OF OTHER PEOPLE SEEMS DOUBTFUL.

I WANTED MORE FROM LIFE THAN THIS
LET'S HAVE A BABY.

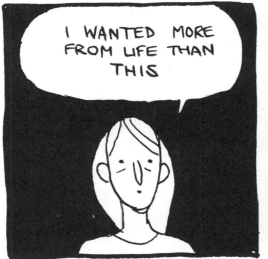

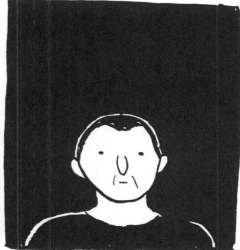

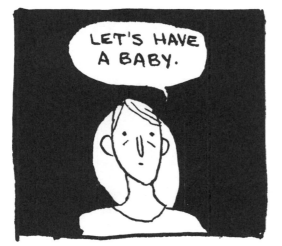

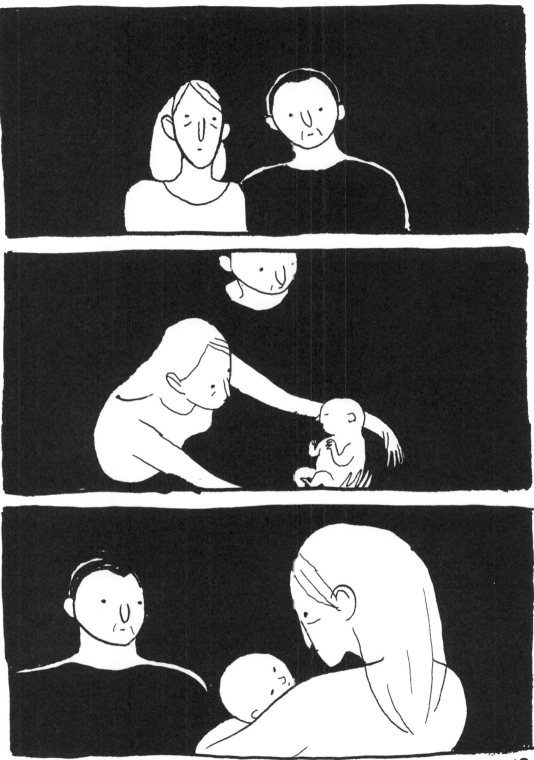

END

53

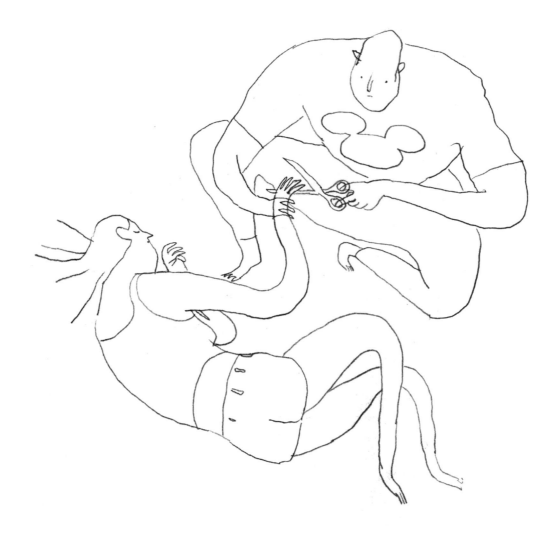

SNIP

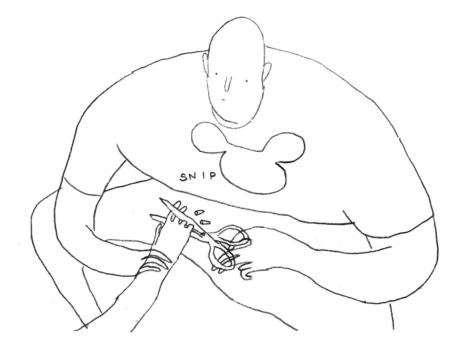

THE EMOTION ROOM

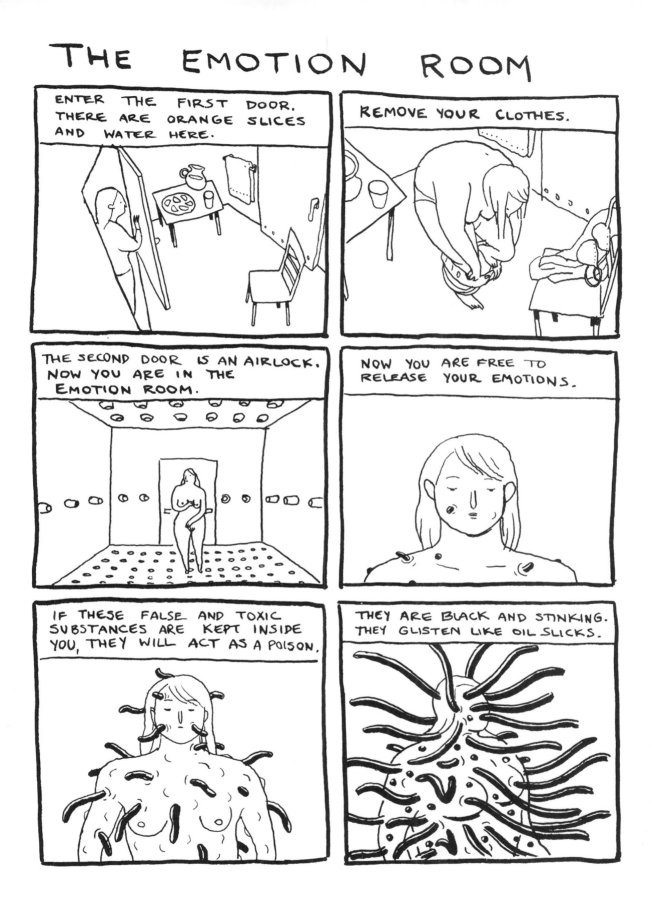

ENTER THE FIRST DOOR. THERE ARE ORANGE SLICES AND WATER HERE.

REMOVE YOUR CLOTHES.

THE SECOND DOOR IS AN AIRLOCK. NOW YOU ARE IN THE EMOTION ROOM.

NOW YOU ARE FREE TO RELEASE YOUR EMOTIONS.

IF THESE FALSE AND TOXIC SUBSTANCES ARE KEPT INSIDE YOU, THEY WILL ACT AS A POISON.

THEY ARE BLACK AND STINKING. THEY GLISTEN LIKE OIL SLICKS.

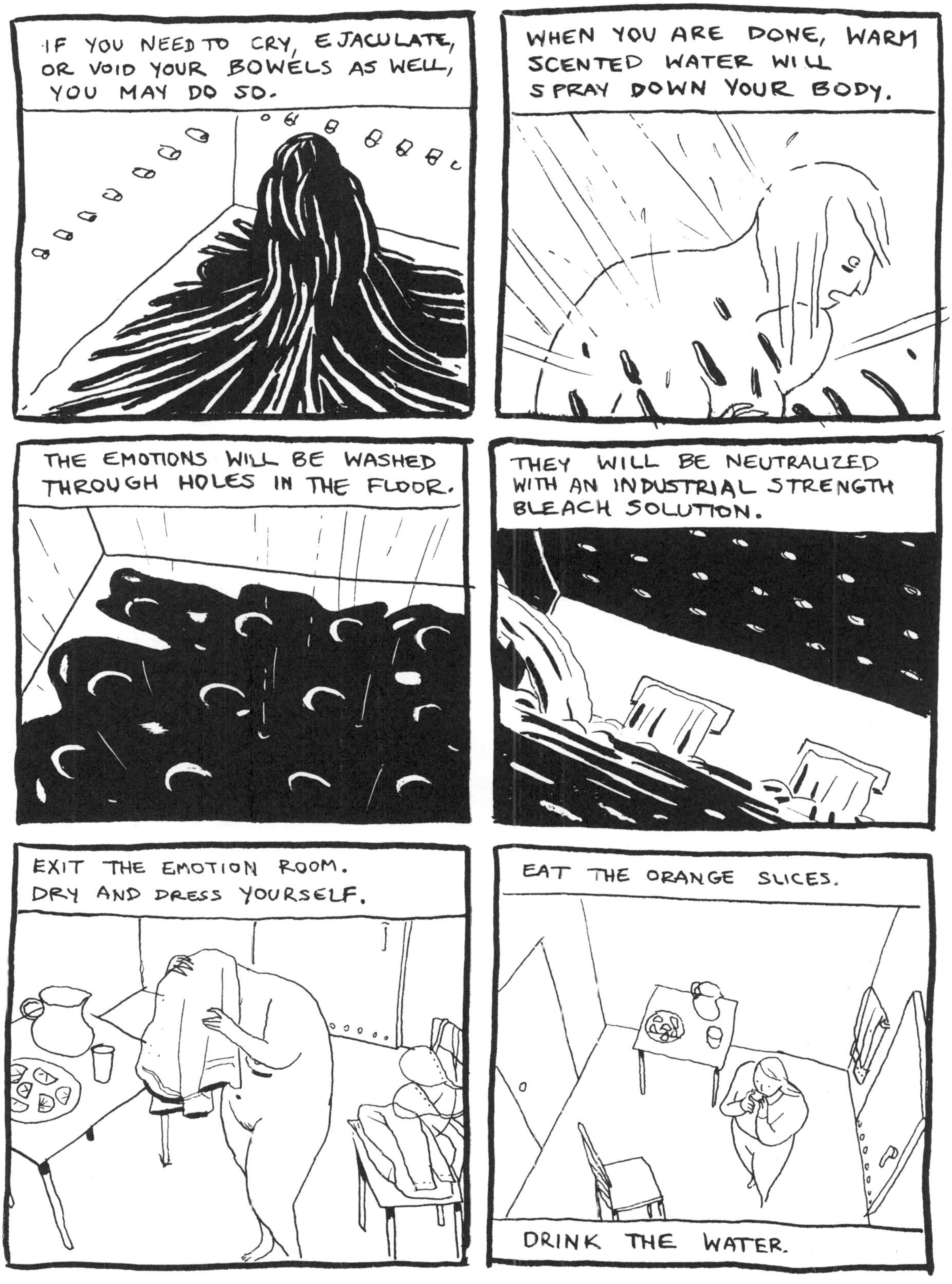
IF YOU NEED TO CRY, EJACULATE, OR VOID YOUR BOWELS AS WELL, YOU MAY DO SO.
WHEN YOU ARE DONE, WARM SCENTED WATER WILL SPRAY DOWN YOUR BODY.
THE EMOTIONS WILL BE WASHED THROUGH HOLES IN THE FLOOR.
THEY WILL BE NEUTRALIZED WITH AN INDUSTRIAL STRENGTH BLEACH SOLUTION.
EXIT THE EMOTION ROOM. DRY AND DRESS YOURSELF.
EAT THE ORANGE SLICES.
DRINK THE WATER.

END

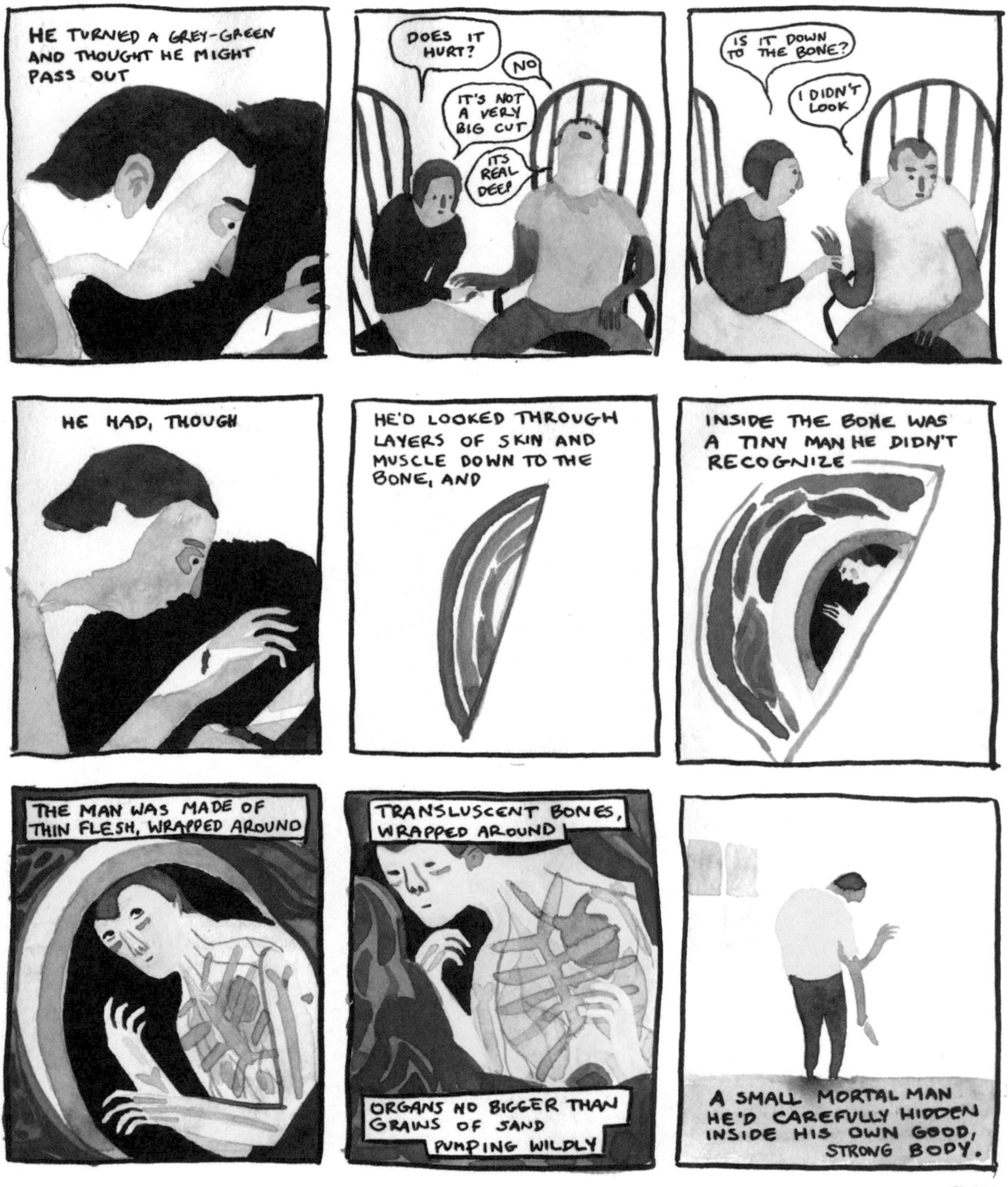
HE TURNED A GREY-GREEN AND THOUGHT HE MIGHT PASS OUT
DOES IT HURT?
NO
IT'S NOT A VERY BIG CUT
ITS REAL DEEP
IS IT DOWN TO THE BONE?
I DIDN'T LOOK
HE HAD, THOUGH
HE'D LOOKED THROUGH LAYERS OF SKIN AND MUSCLE DOWN TO THE BONE, AND
INSIDE THE BONE WAS A TINY MAN HE DIDN'T RECOGNIZE
THE MAN WAS MADE OF THIN FLESH, WRAPPED AROUND
TRANSLUSCENT BONES, WRAPPED AROUND
ORGANS NO BIGGER THAN GRAINS OF SAND
PUMPING WILDLY
A SMALL MORTAL MAN HE'D CAREFULLY HIDDEN INSIDE HIS OWN GOOD, STRONG BODY.

END

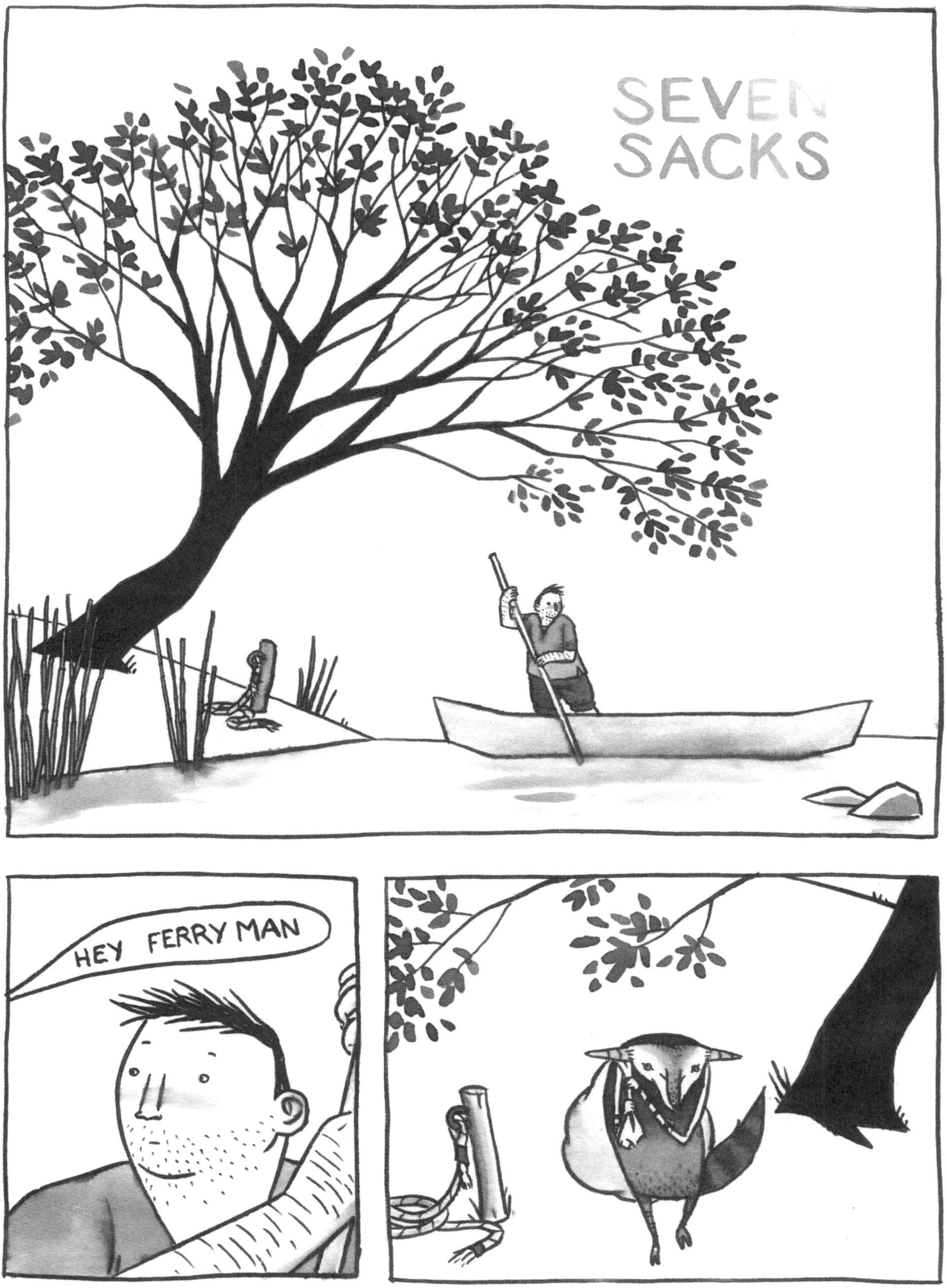
SEVEN SACKS
HEY FERRY MAN

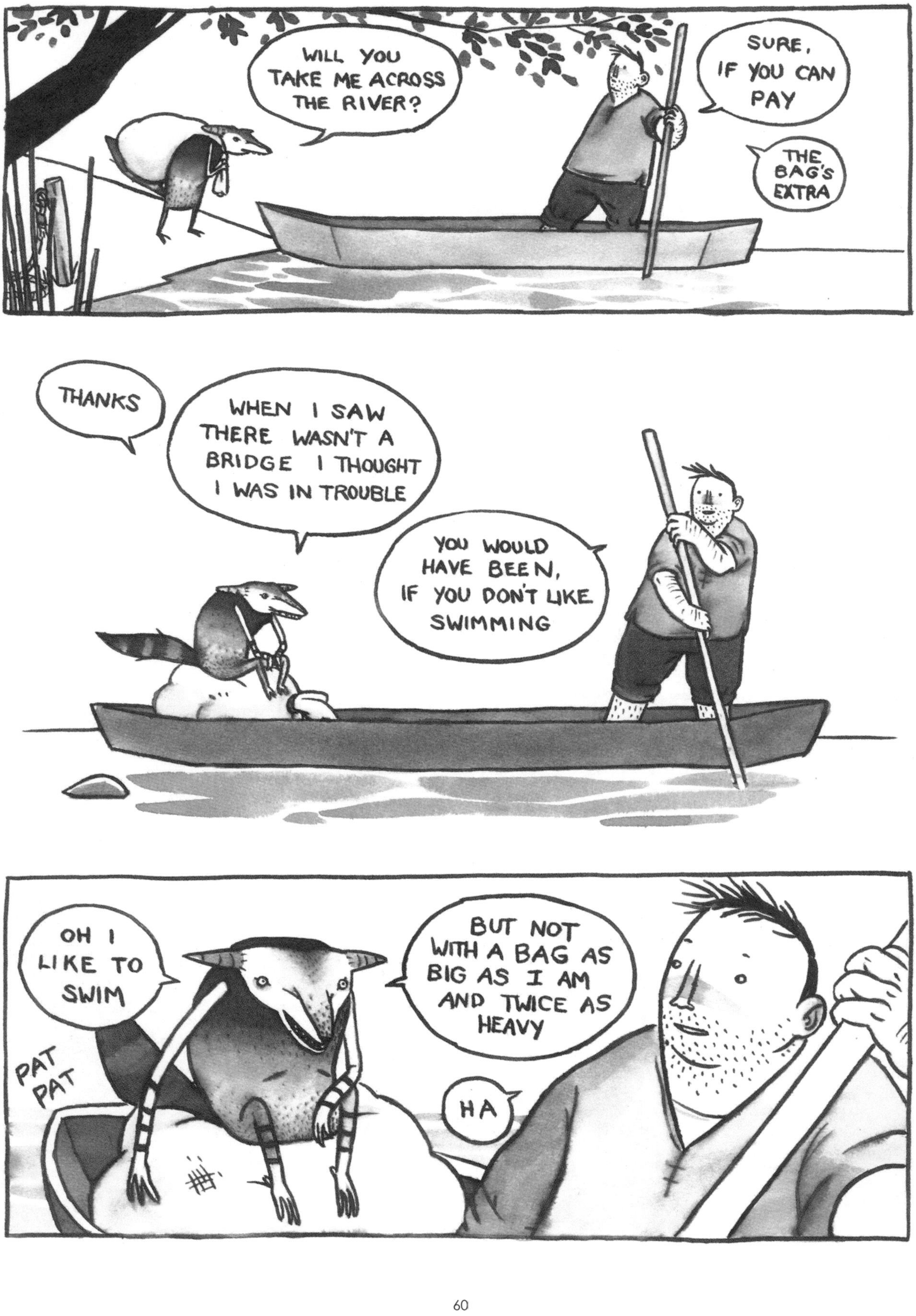
WILL YOU TAKE ME ACROSS THE RIVER?
SURE, IF YOU CAN PAY
THE BAG'S EXTRA
THANKS
WHEN I SAW THERE WASN'T A BRIDGE I THOUGHT I WAS IN TROUBLE
YOU WOULD HAVE BEEN, IF YOU DON'T LIKE SWIMMING
OH I LIKE TO SWIM
BUT NOT WITH A BAG AS BIG AS I AM AND TWICE AS HEAVY
PAT PAT
HA

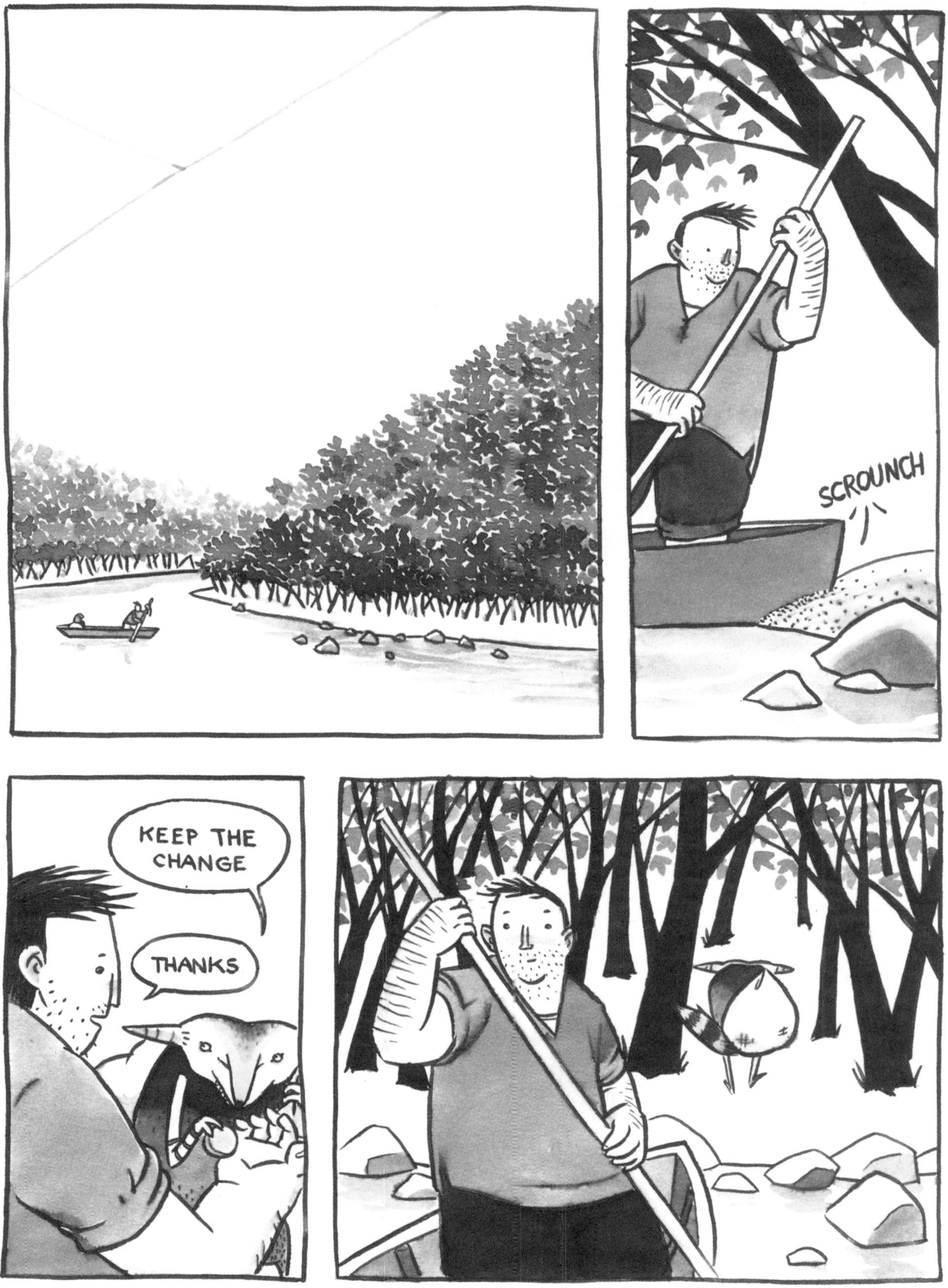
SCROUNCH
KEEP THE CHANGE
THANKS

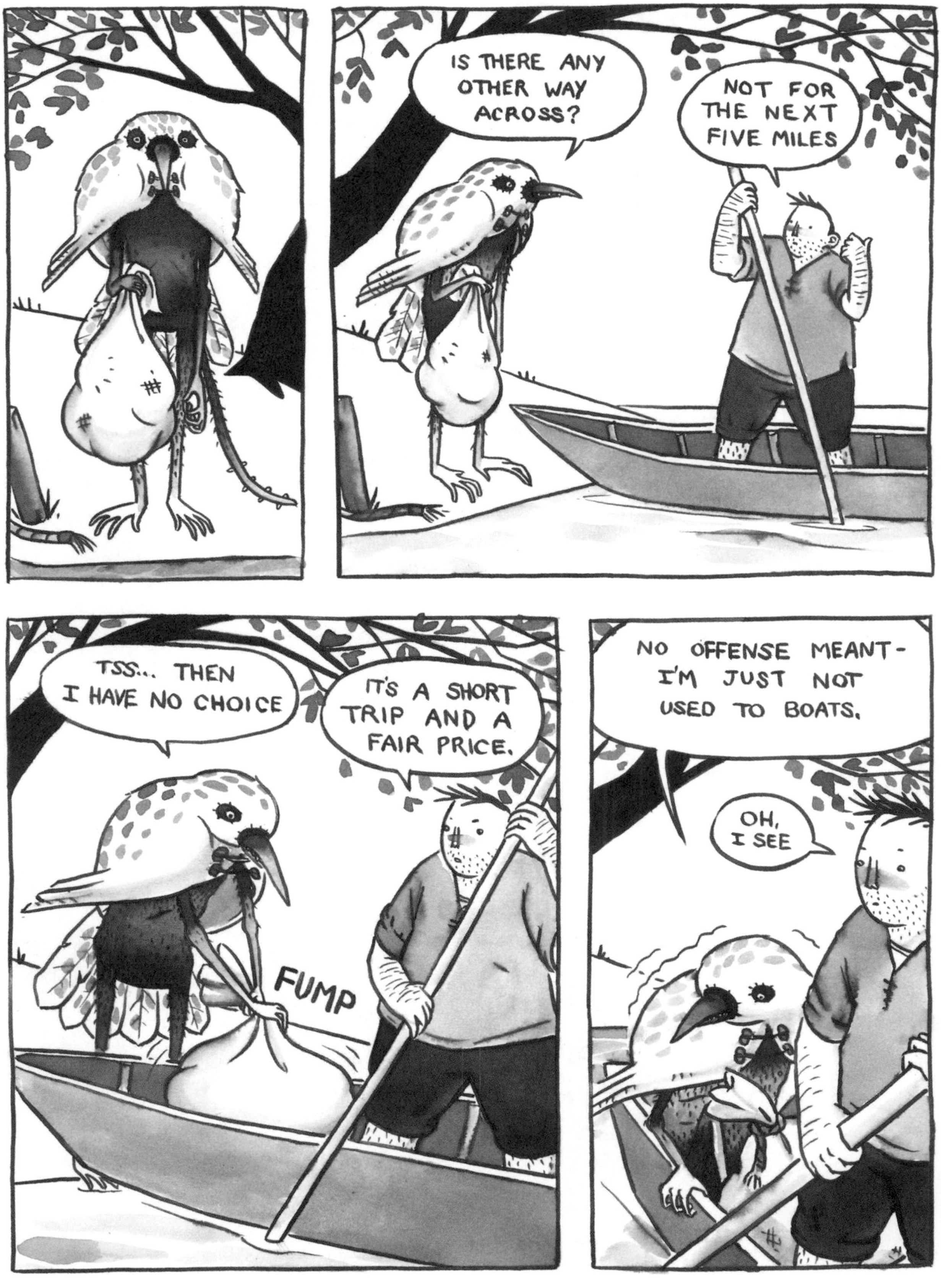
IS THERE ANY OTHER WAY ACROSS?
NOT FOR THE NEXT FIVE MILES
TSS... THEN I HAVE NO CHOICE
IT'S A SHORT TRIP AND A FAIR PRICE.
FUMP
NO OFFENSE MEANT- I'M JUST NOT USED TO BOATS.
OH, I SEE

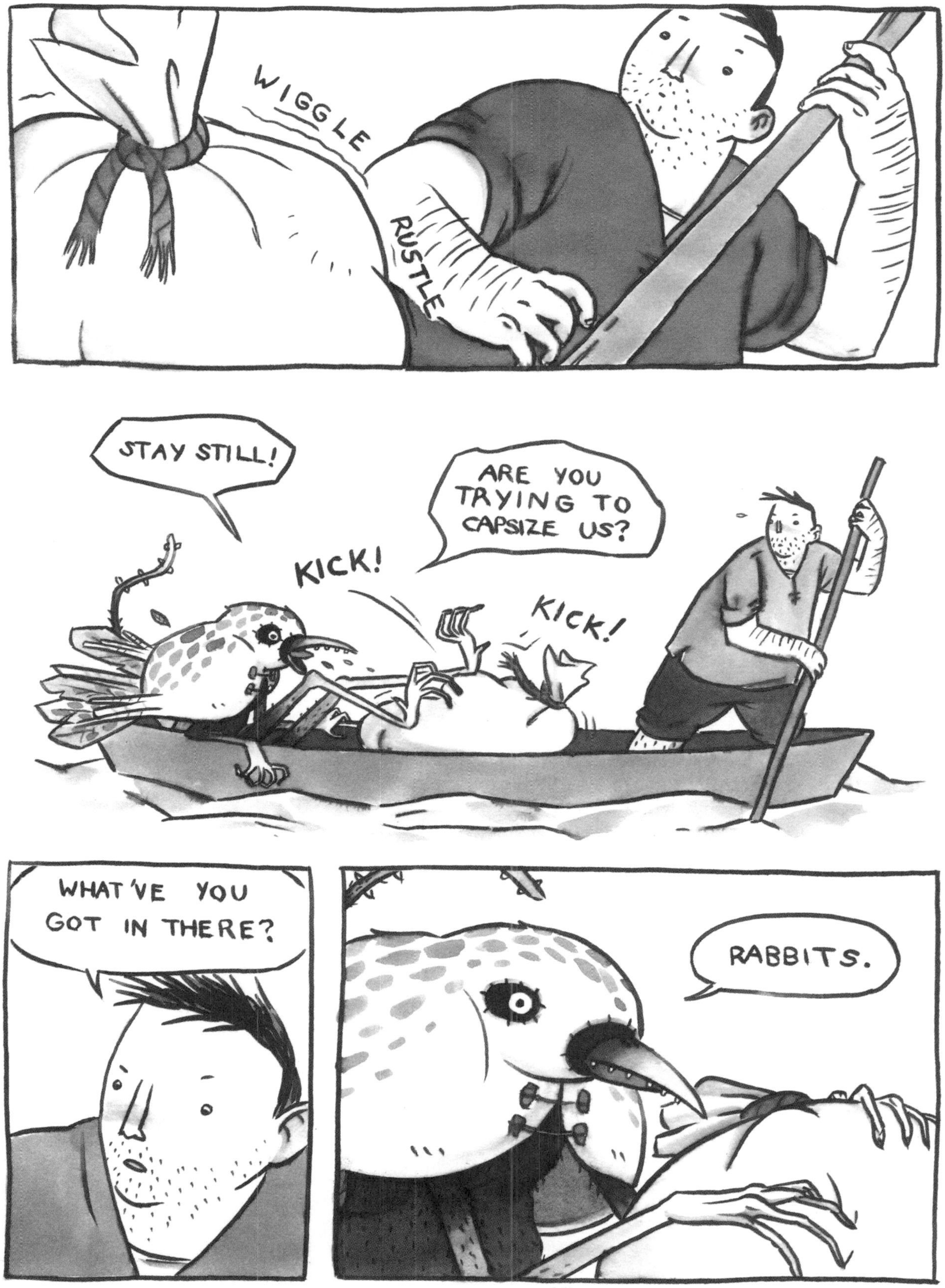
WIGGLE
RUSTLE
STAY STILL!
ARE YOU TRYING TO CAPSIZE US?
KICK!
KICK!
WHAT'VE YOU GOT IN THERE?
RABBITS.

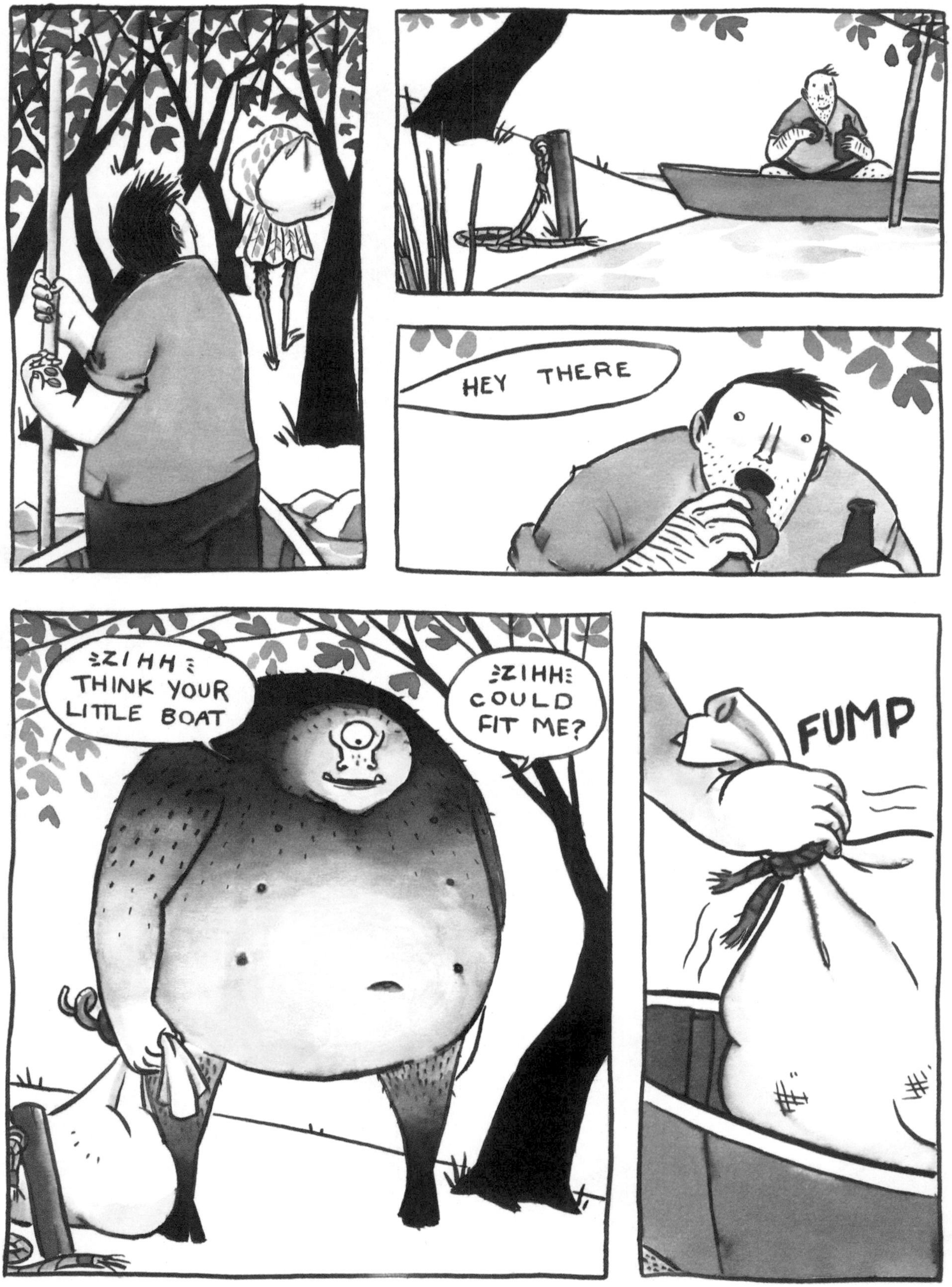
HEY THERE
ZIHH
THINK YOUR
LITTLE BOAT
ZIHH
COULD
FIT ME?
FUMP

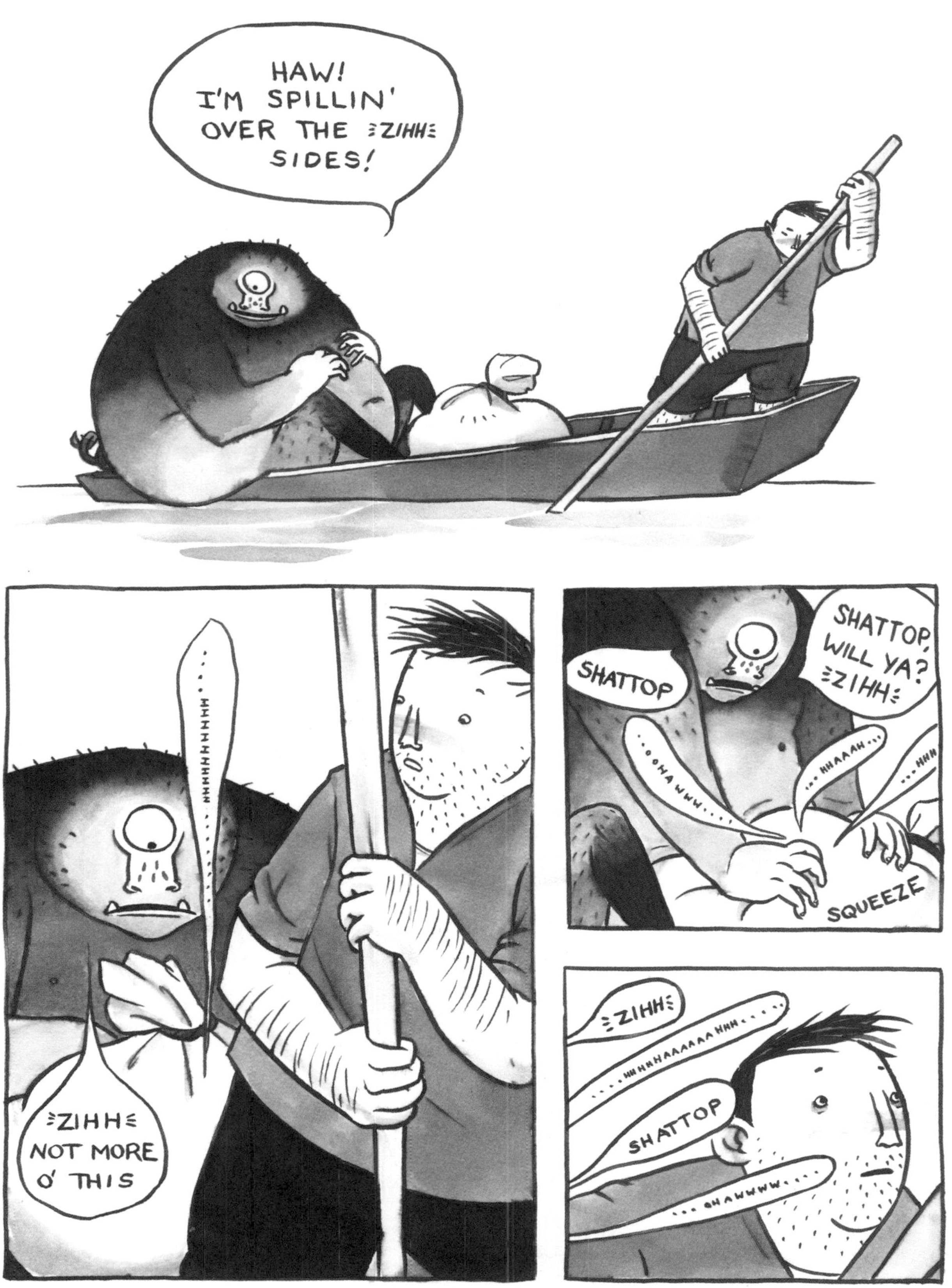
HAW! I'M SPILLIN' OVER THE ≡ZIHH≡ SIDES!
≡ZIHH≡ NOT MORE O' THIS
SHATTOP
SHATTOP, WILL YA? ≡ZIHH≡
SQUEEZE
≡ZIHH≡
SHATTOP

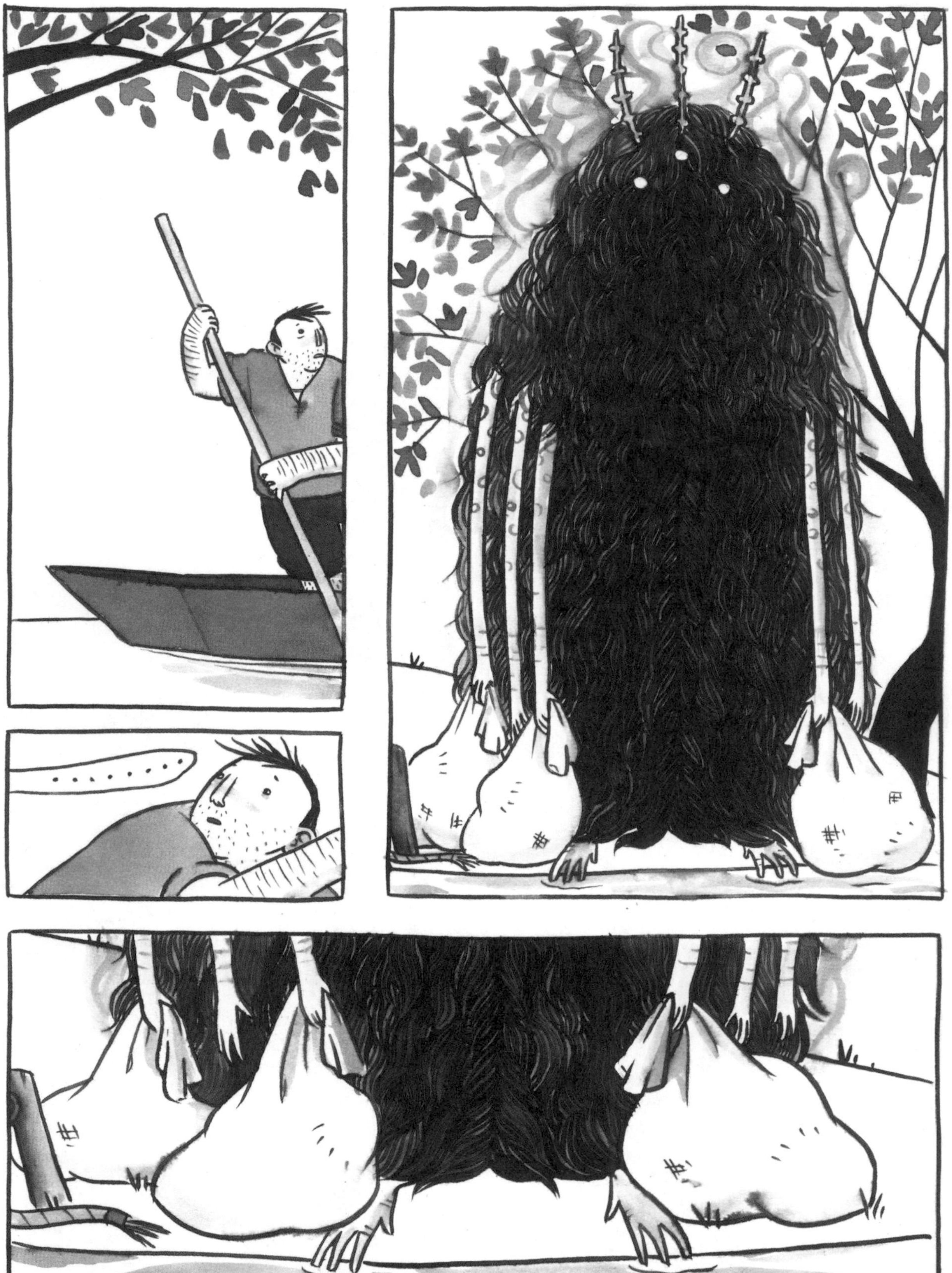

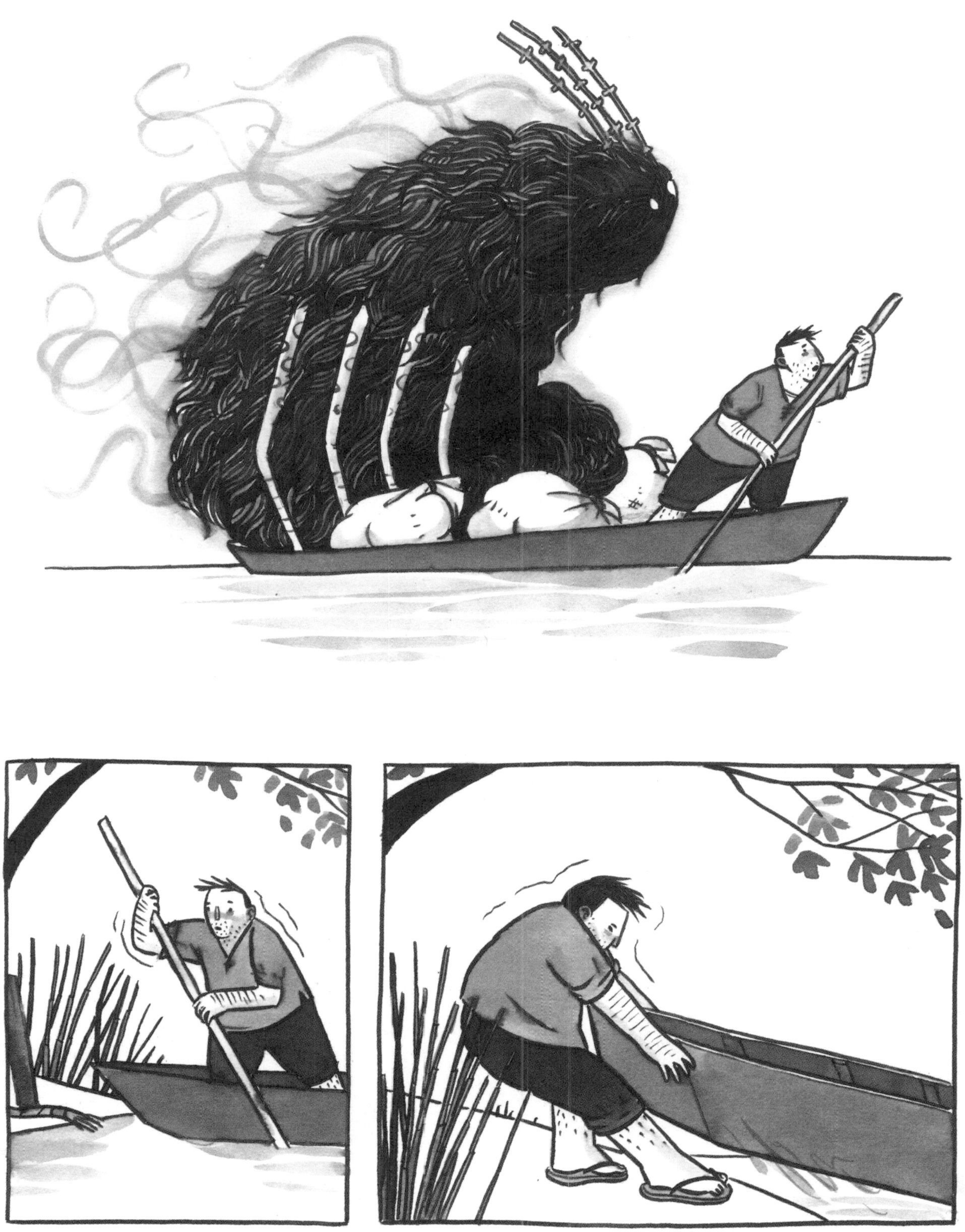

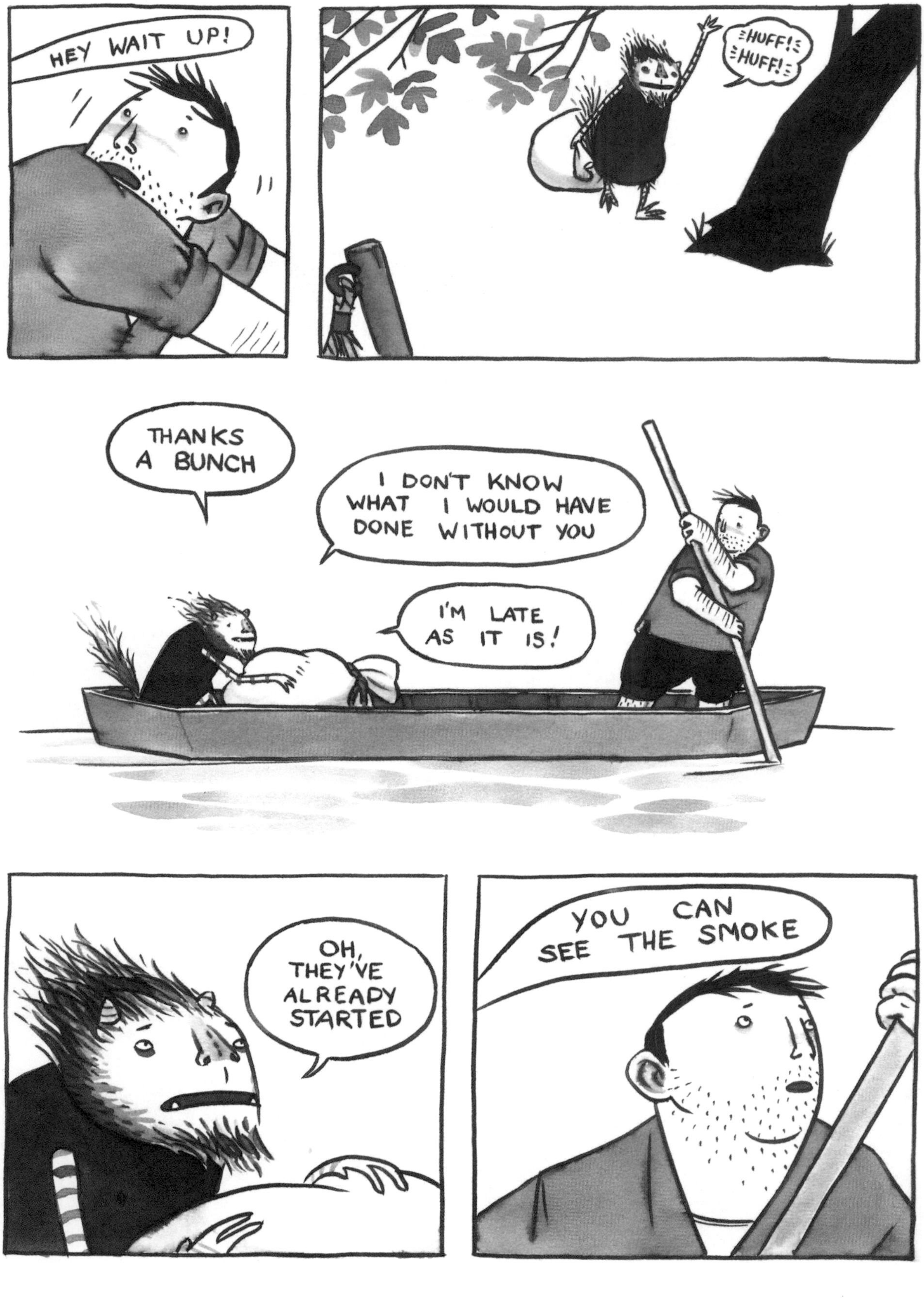
HEY WAIT UP!
HUFF! HUFF!
THANKS A BUNCH
I DON'T KNOW WHAT I WOULD HAVE DONE WITHOUT YOU
I'M LATE AS IT IS!
OH, THEY'VE ALREADY STARTED
YOU CAN SEE THE SMOKE

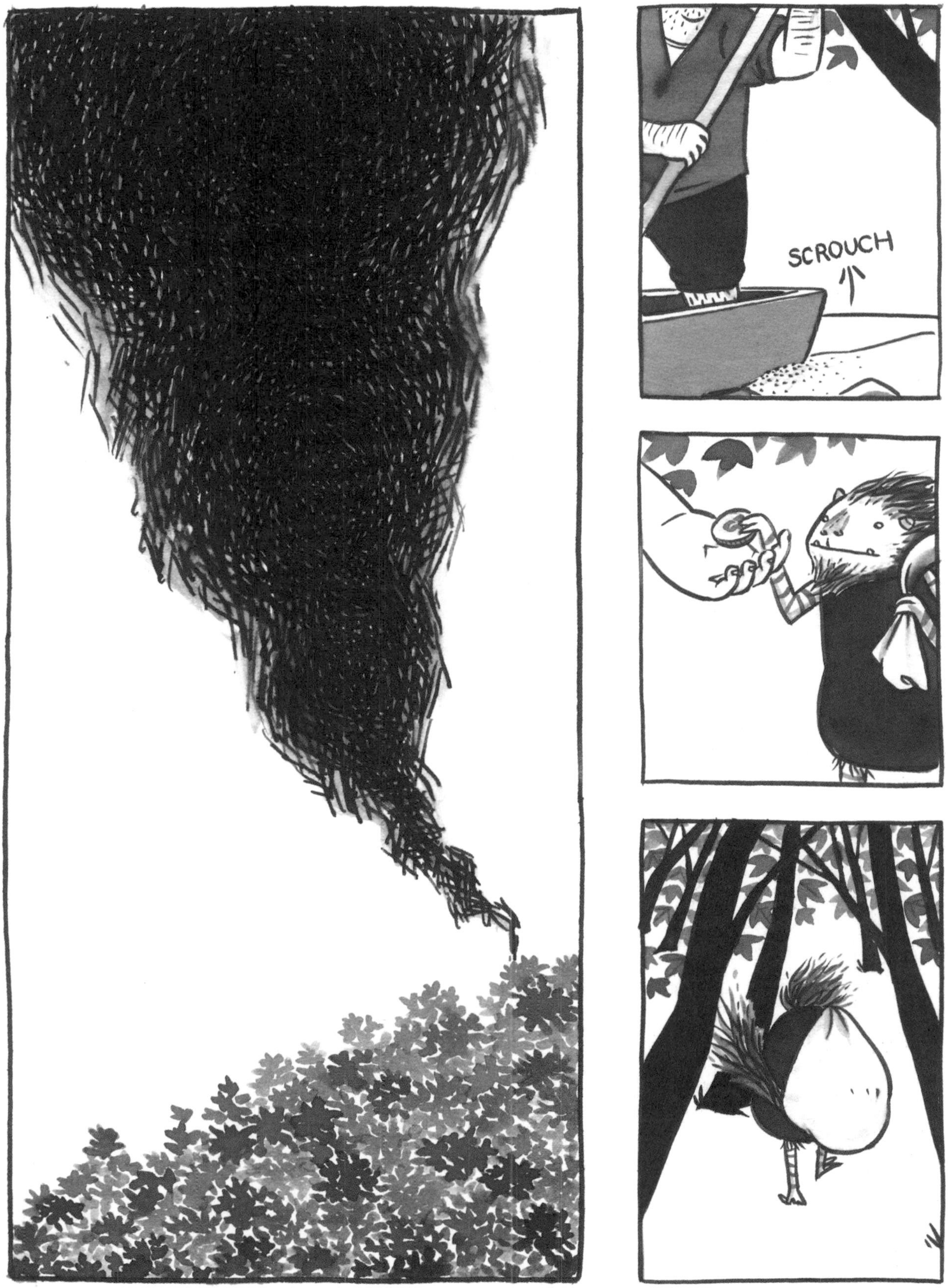
SCROUCH

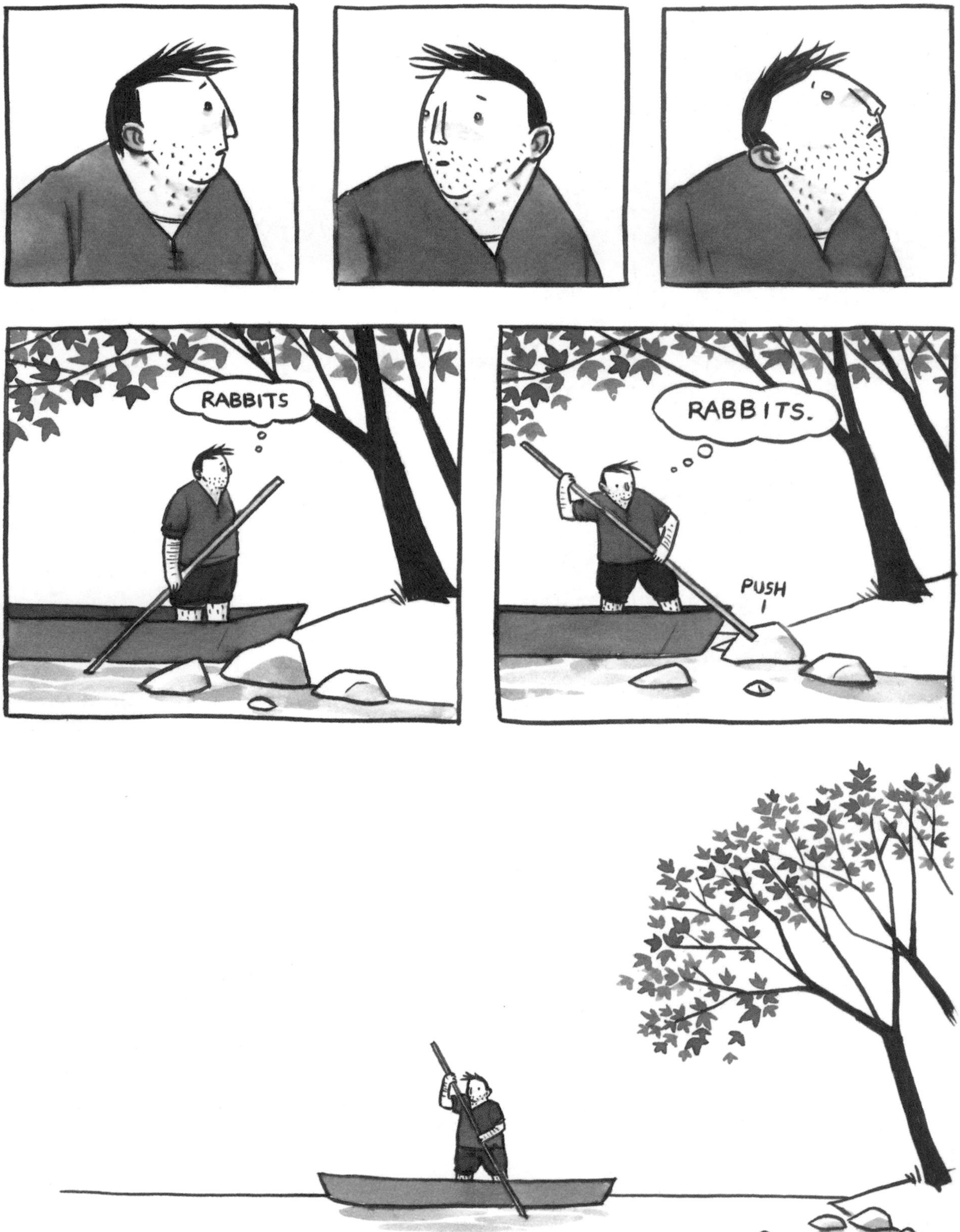
RABBITS
RABBITS.
PUSH
END

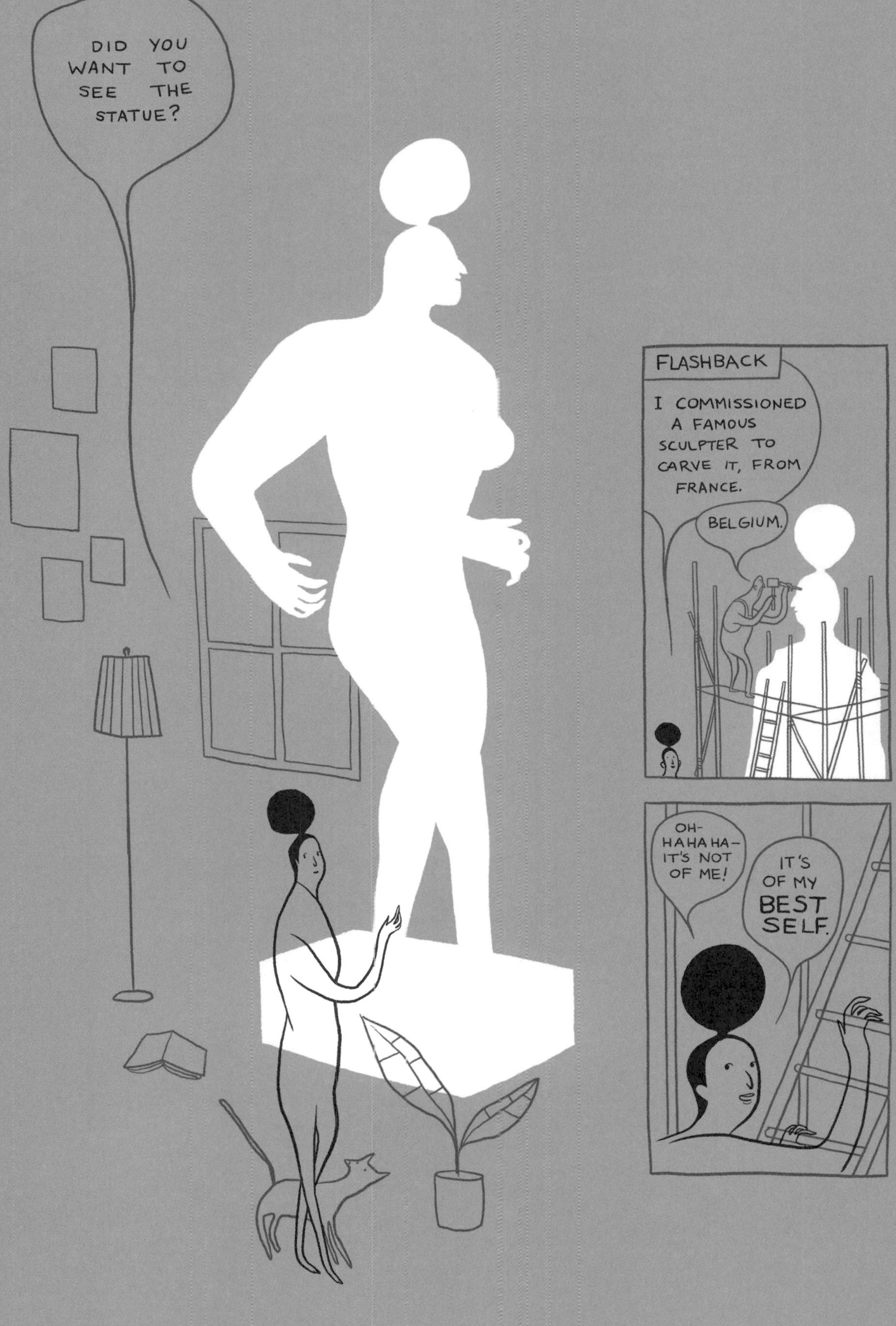
DID YOU WANT TO SEE THE STATUE?
FLASHBACK
I COMMISSIONED A FAMOUS SCULPTER TO CARVE IT, FROM FRANCE.
BELGIUM.
OH- HAHAHA- IT'S NOT OF ME!
IT'S OF MY BEST SELF.

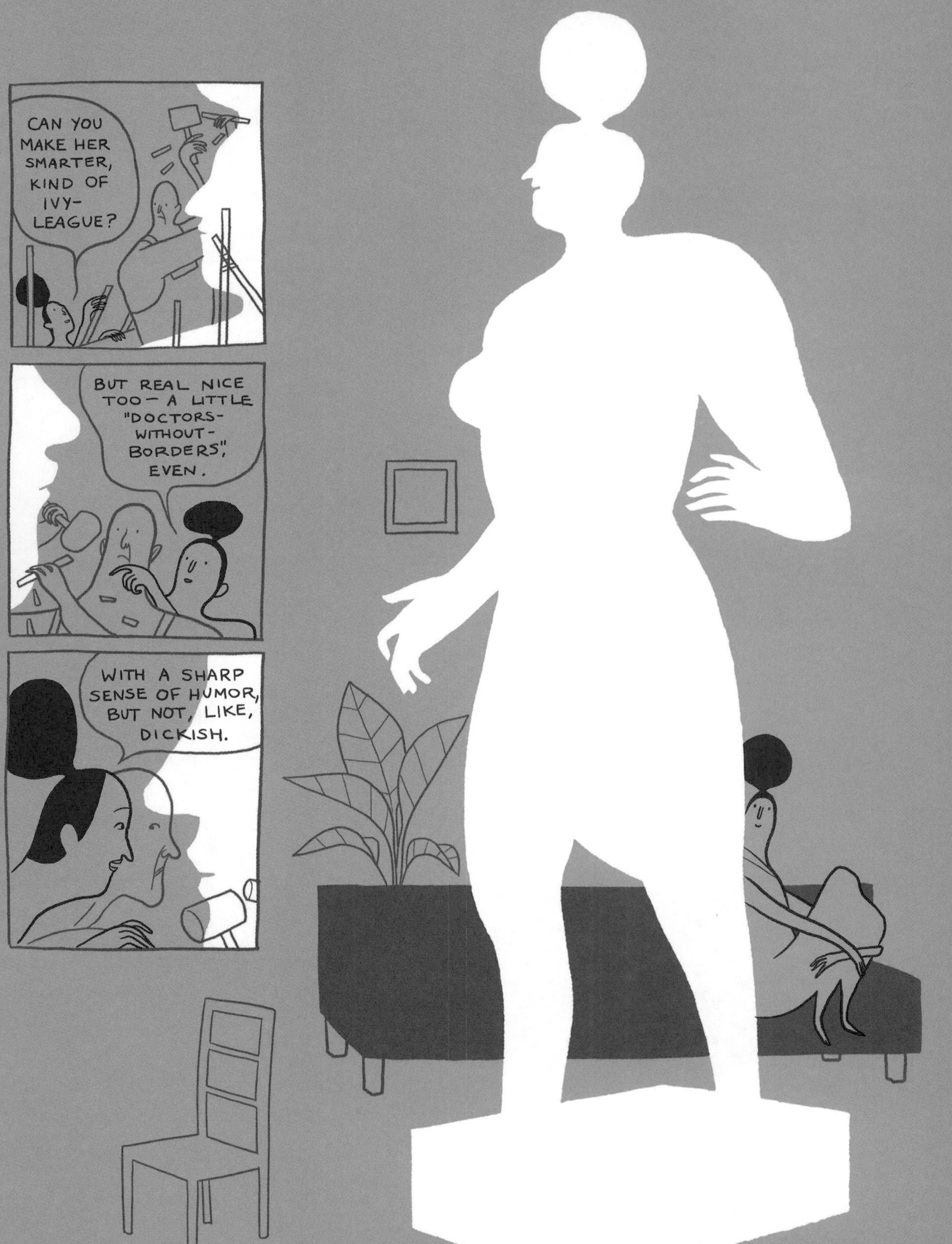
CAN YOU MAKE HER SMARTER, KIND OF IVY-LEAGUE?
BUT REAL NICE TOO— A LITTLE "DOCTORS-WITHOUT-BORDERS", EVEN.
WITH A SHARP SENSE OF HUMOR, BUT NOT, LIKE, DICKISH.
END

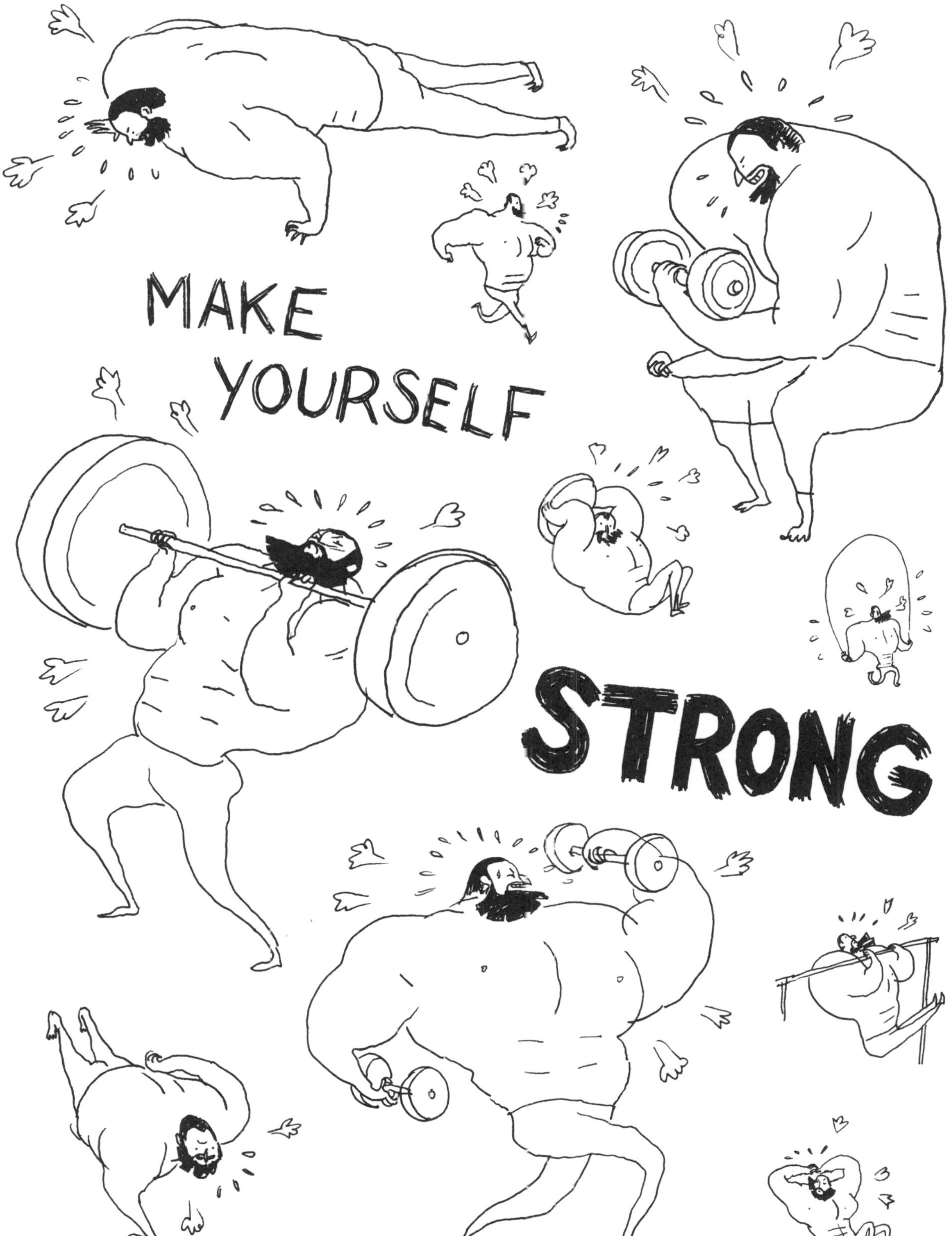
MAKE
YOURSELF
STRONG

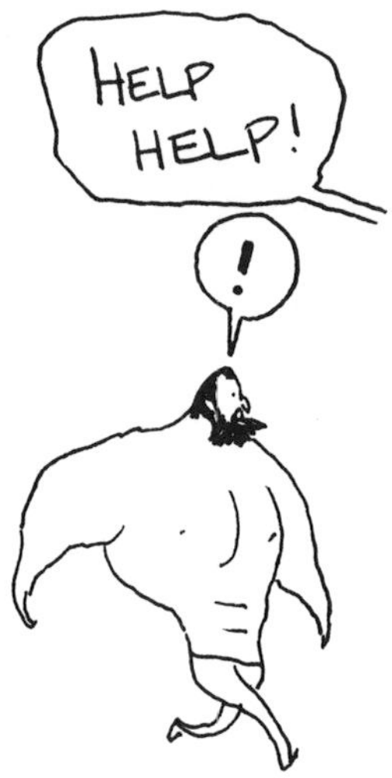
HELP
HELP!
!

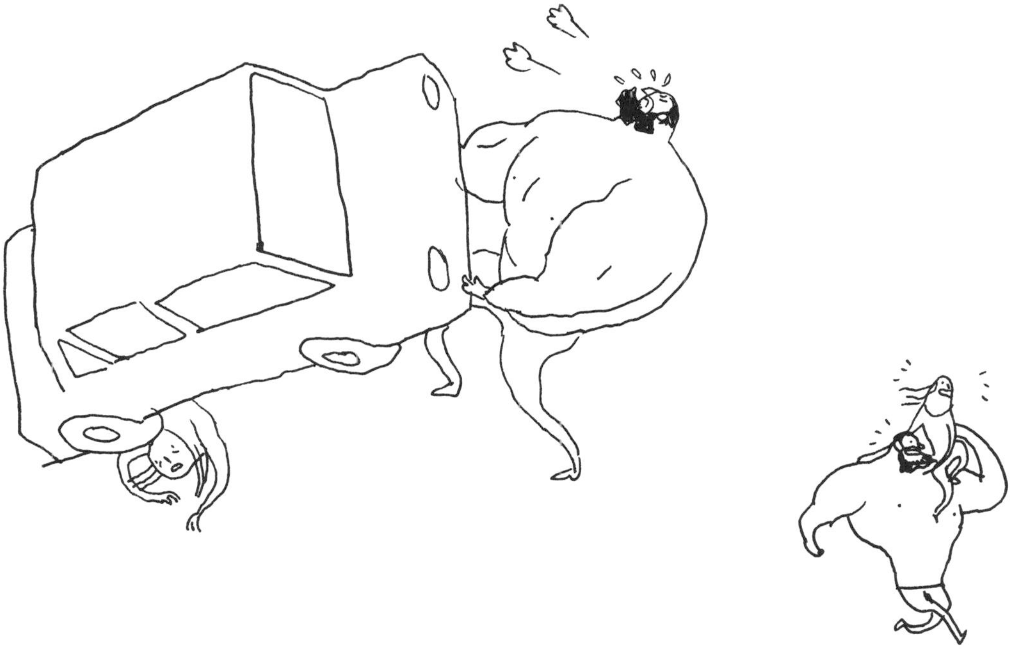

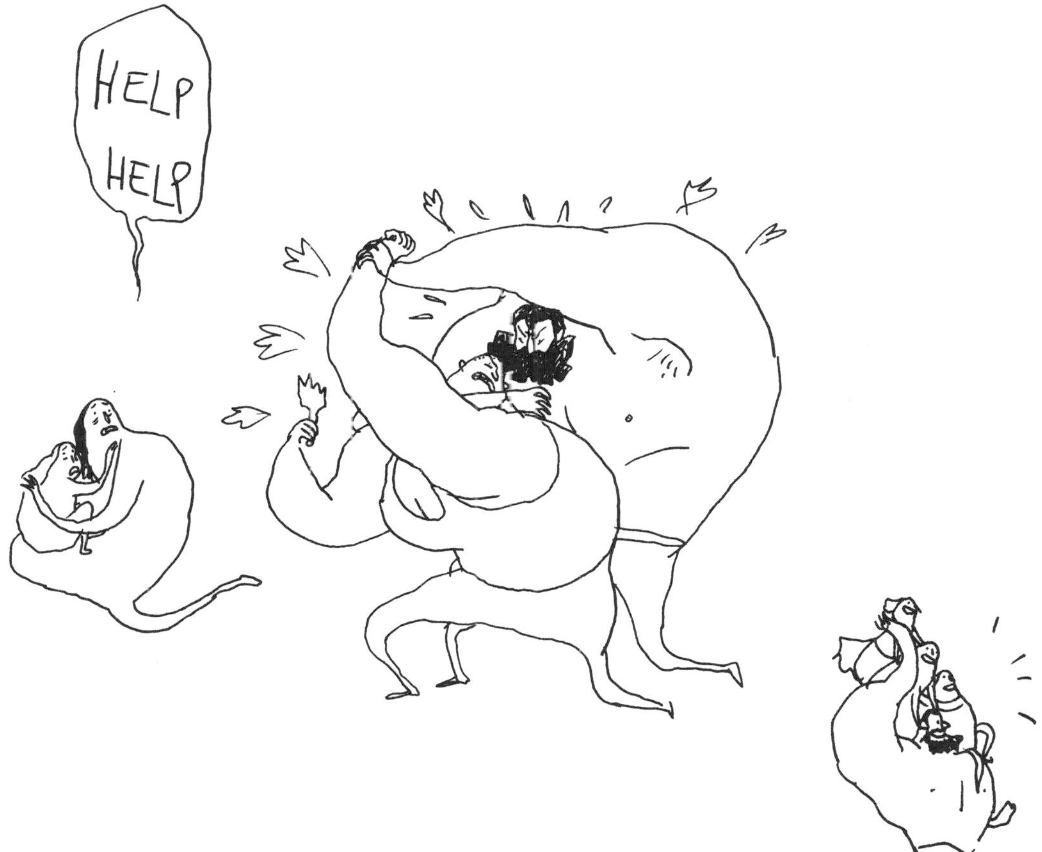
HELP
HELP

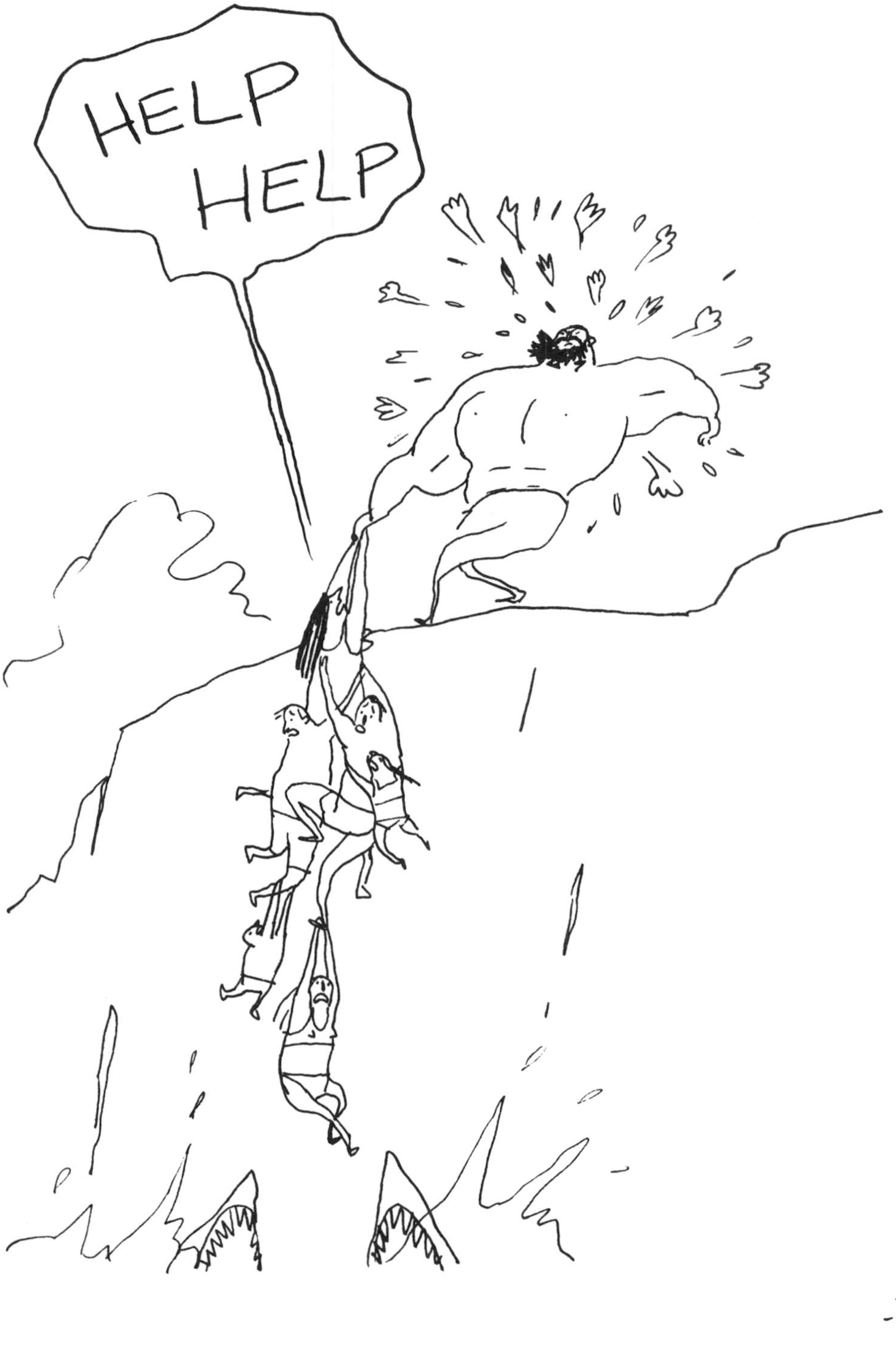
HELP
HELP

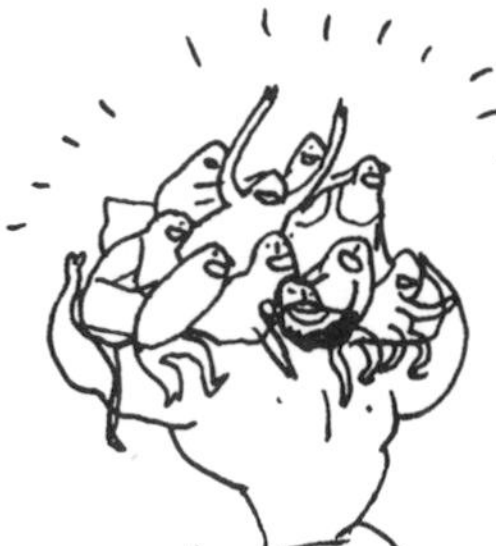

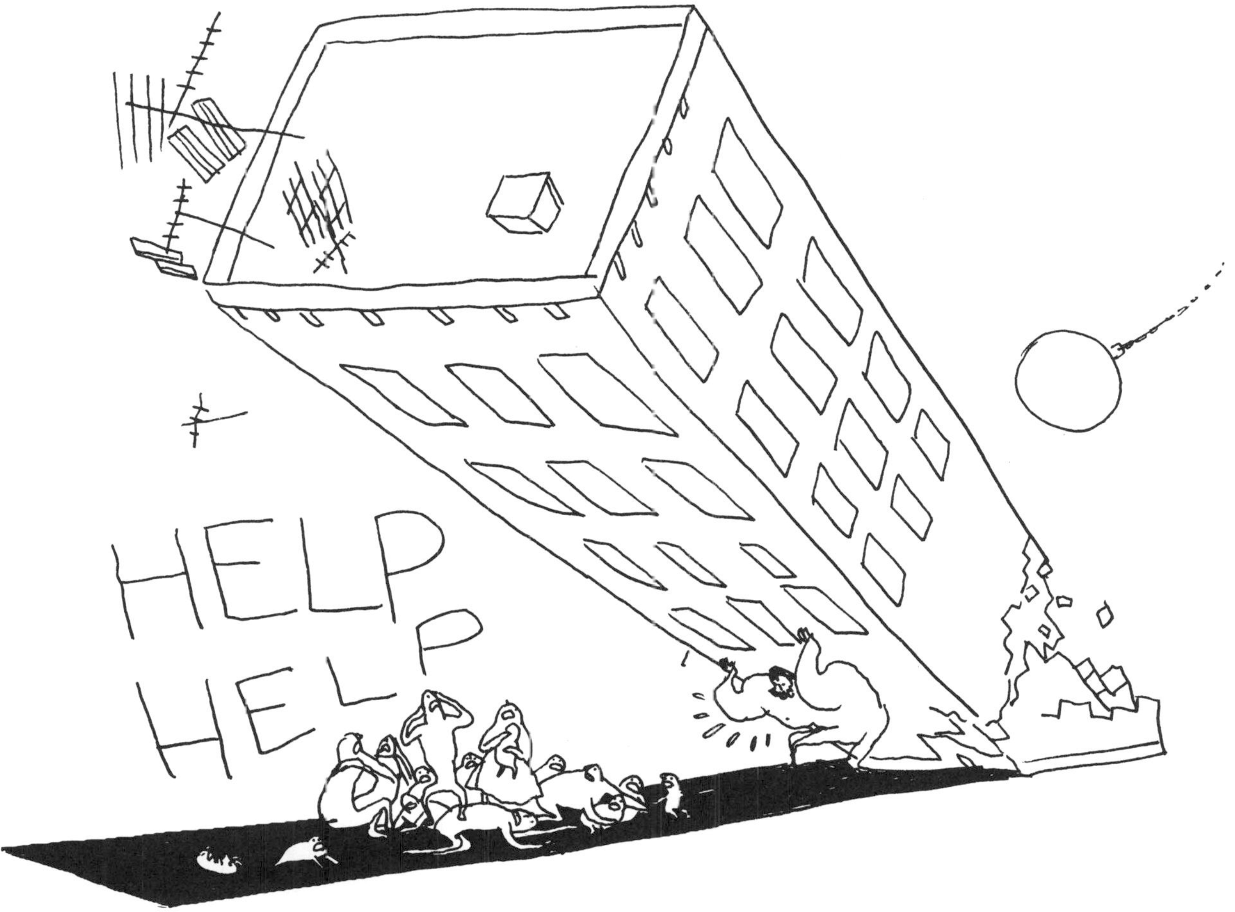
HELP
HELP

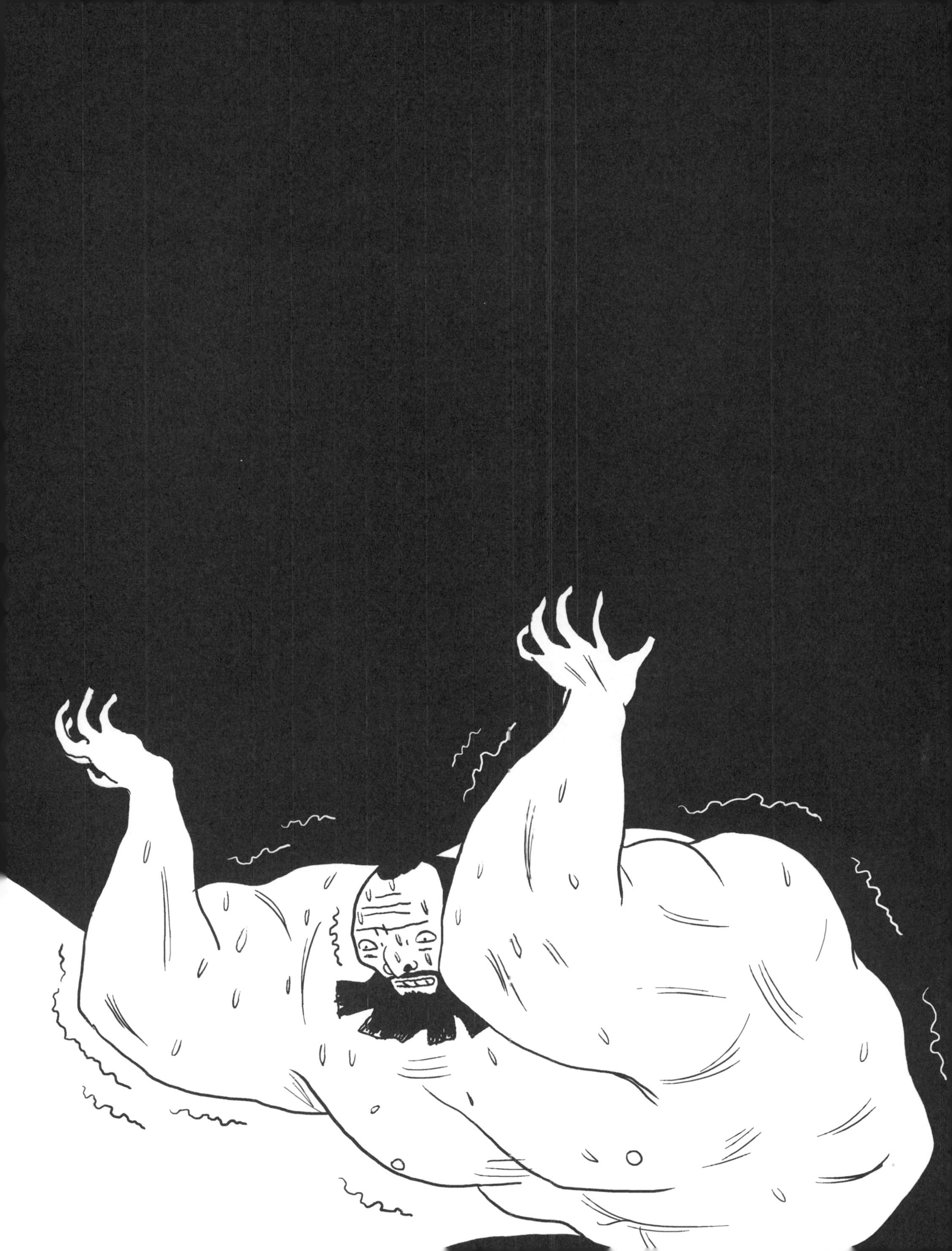

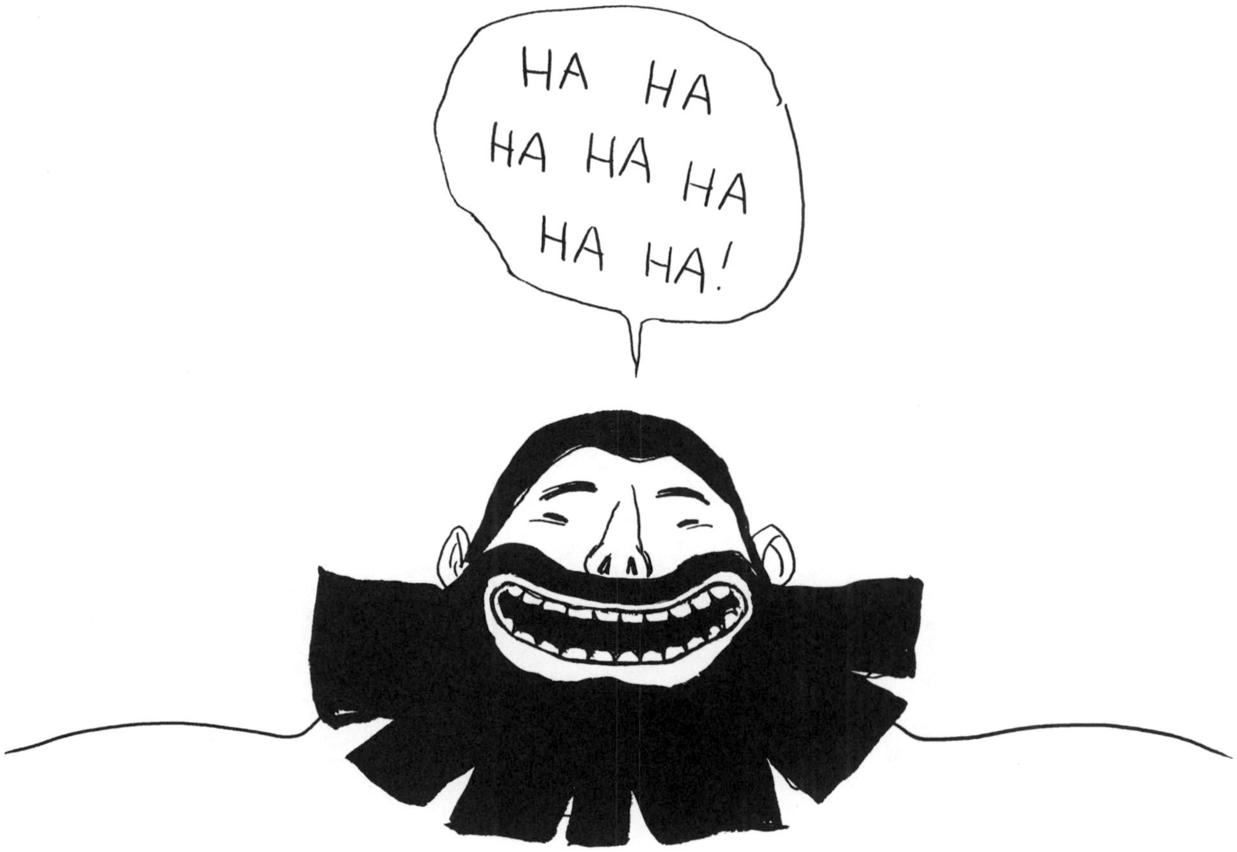
HA HA HA HA HA HA HA!

END

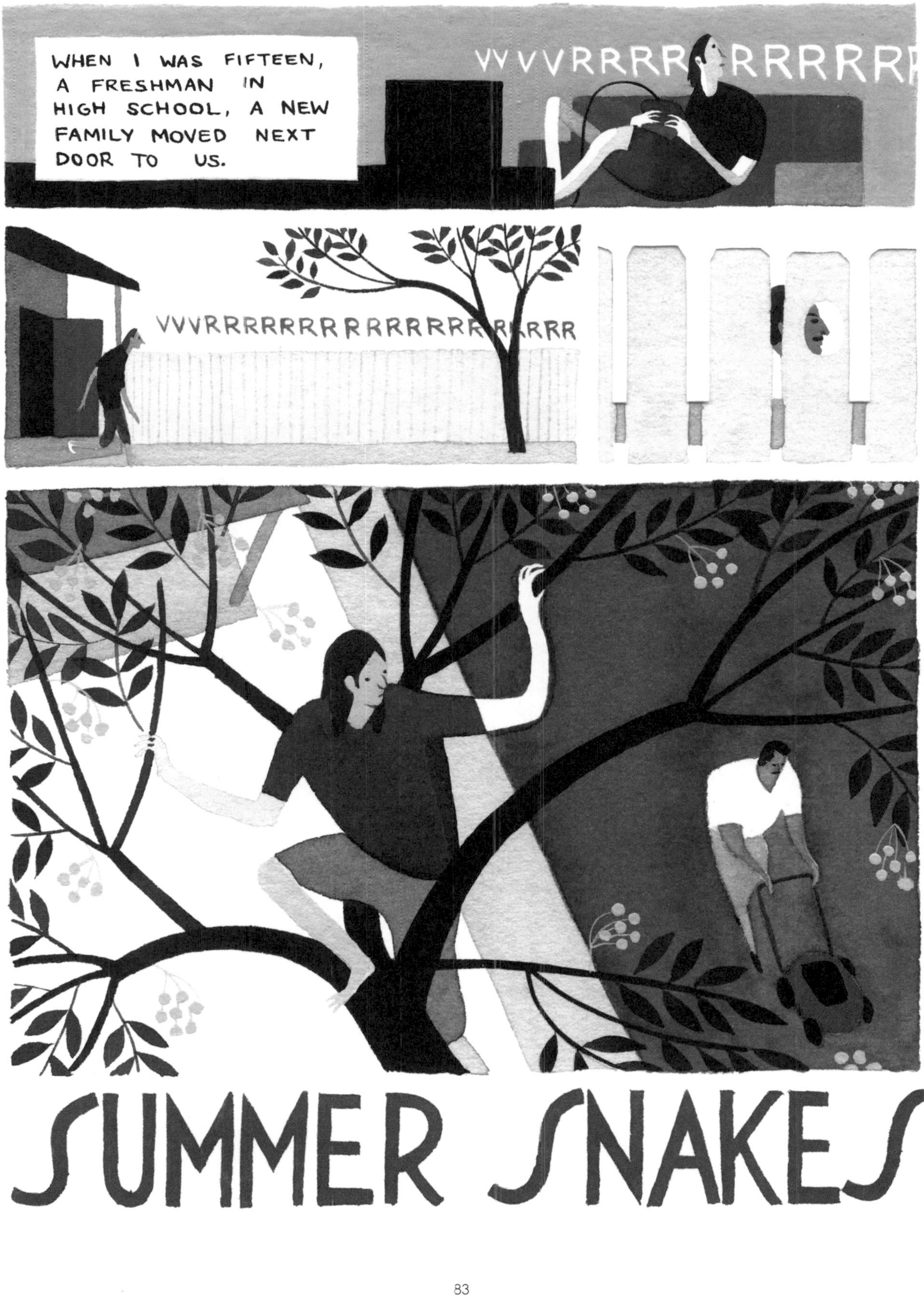

WHEN I WAS FIFTEEN, A FRESHMAN IN HIGH SCHOOL, A NEW FAMILY MOVED NEXT DOOR TO US.
VVVVRRRRRRRRRRRR
VVVRRRRRRRRRRRRRRRRRR

SUMMER SNAKES

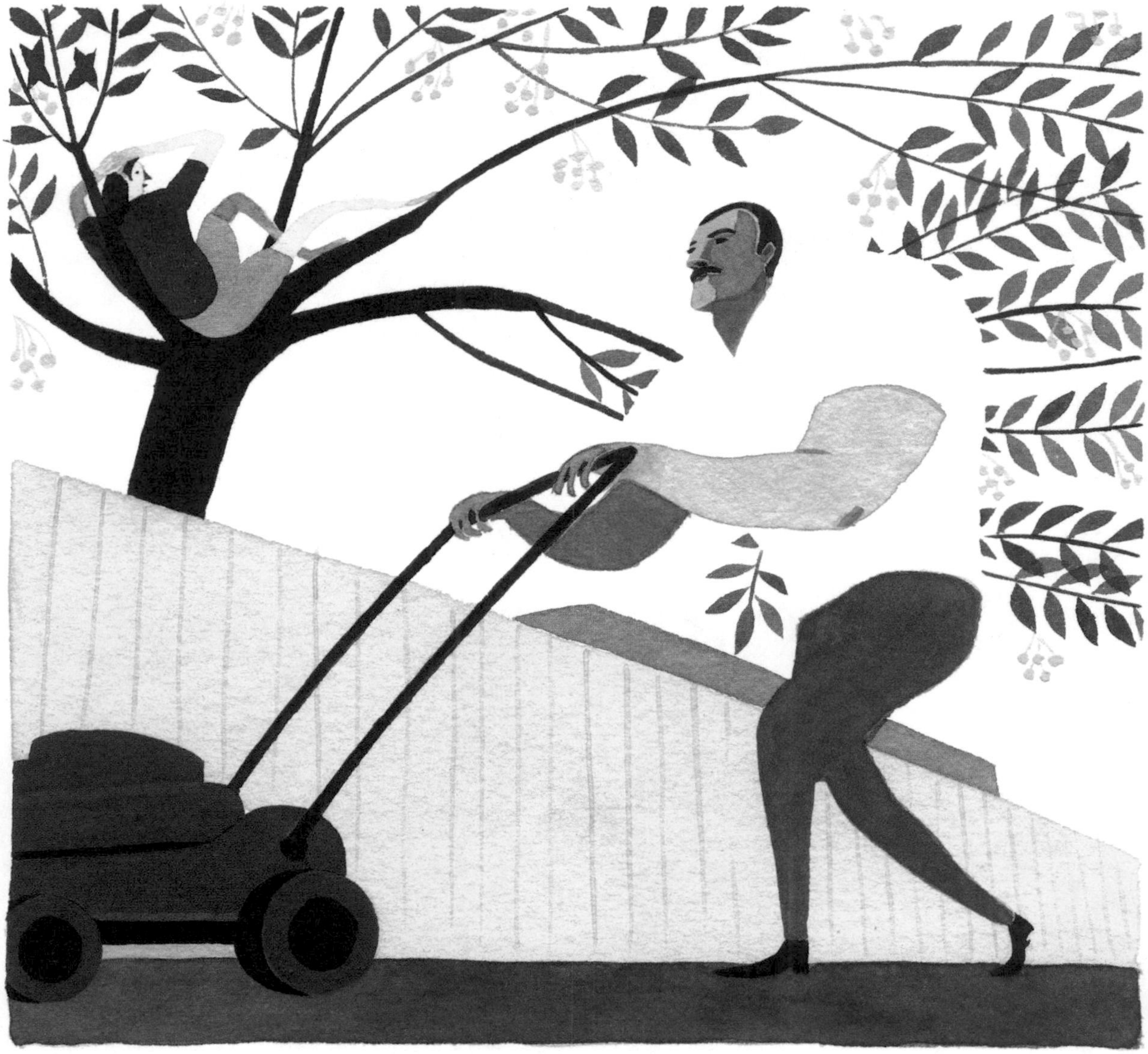

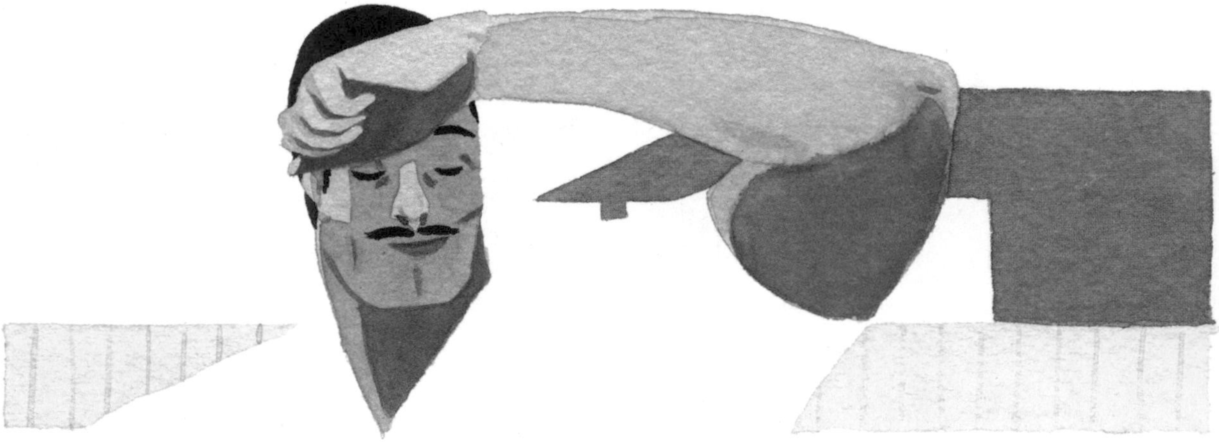

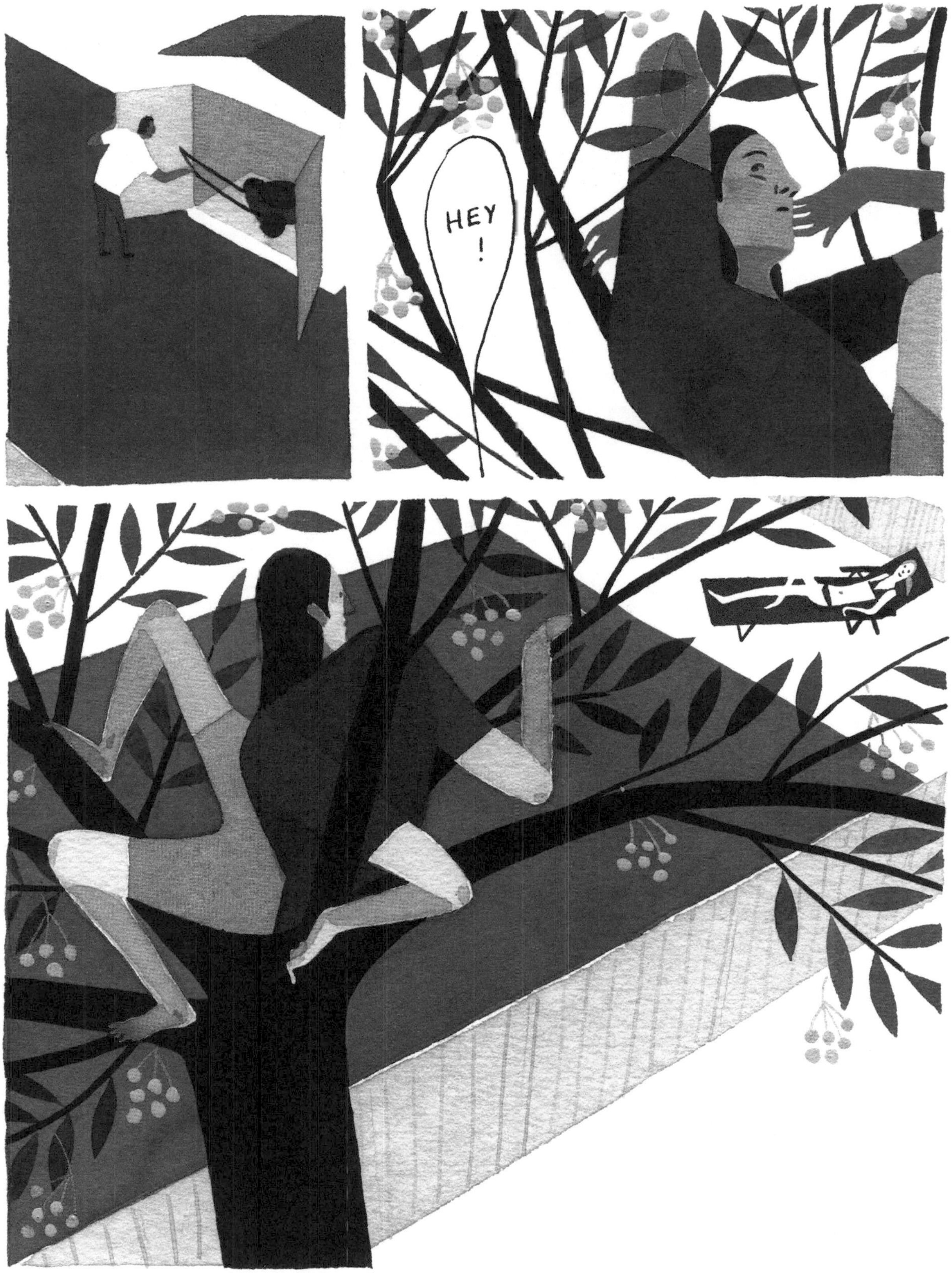
HEY!

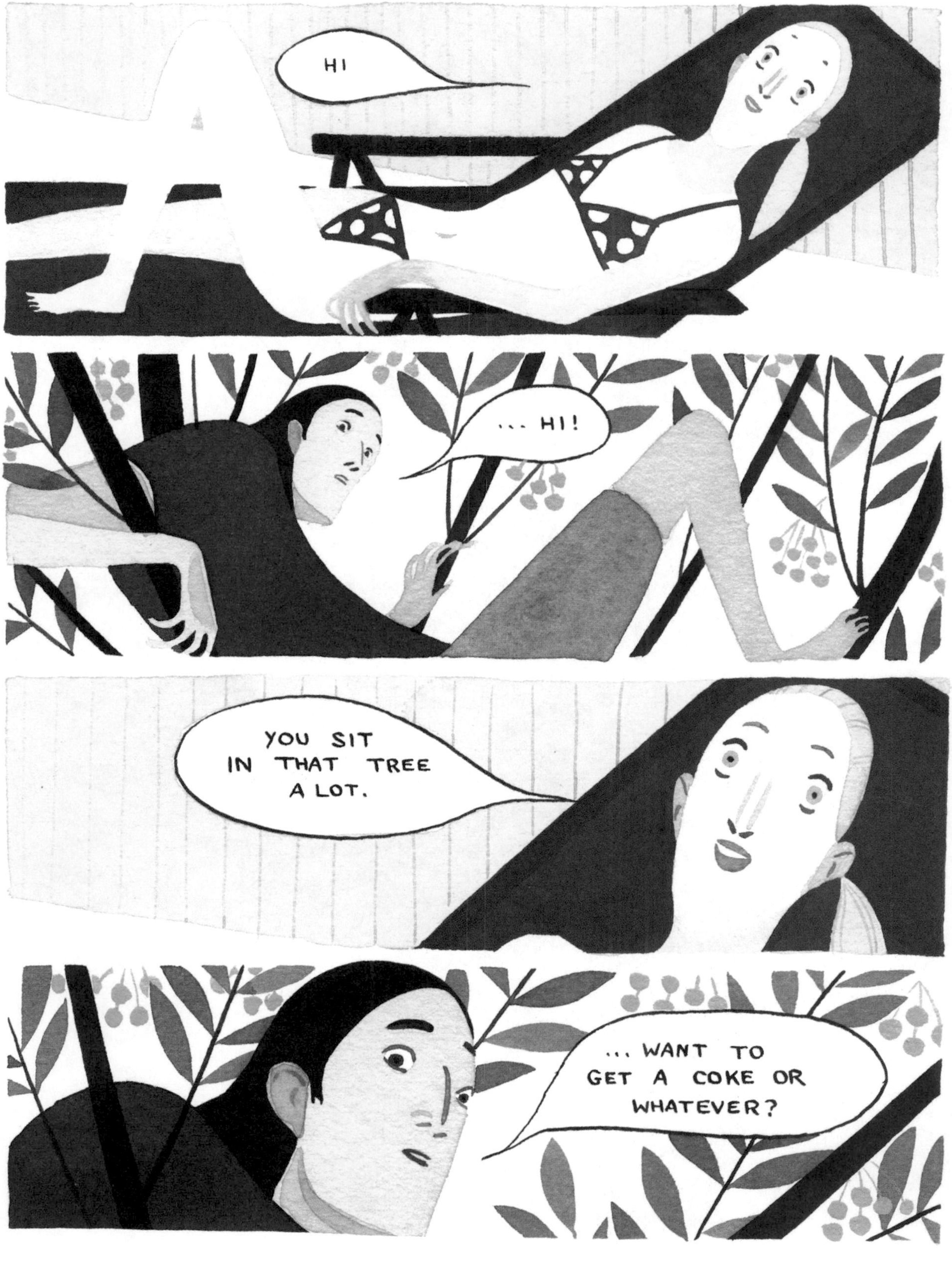
HI
... HI!
YOU SIT IN THAT TREE A LOT.
... WANT TO GET A COKE OR WHATEVER?

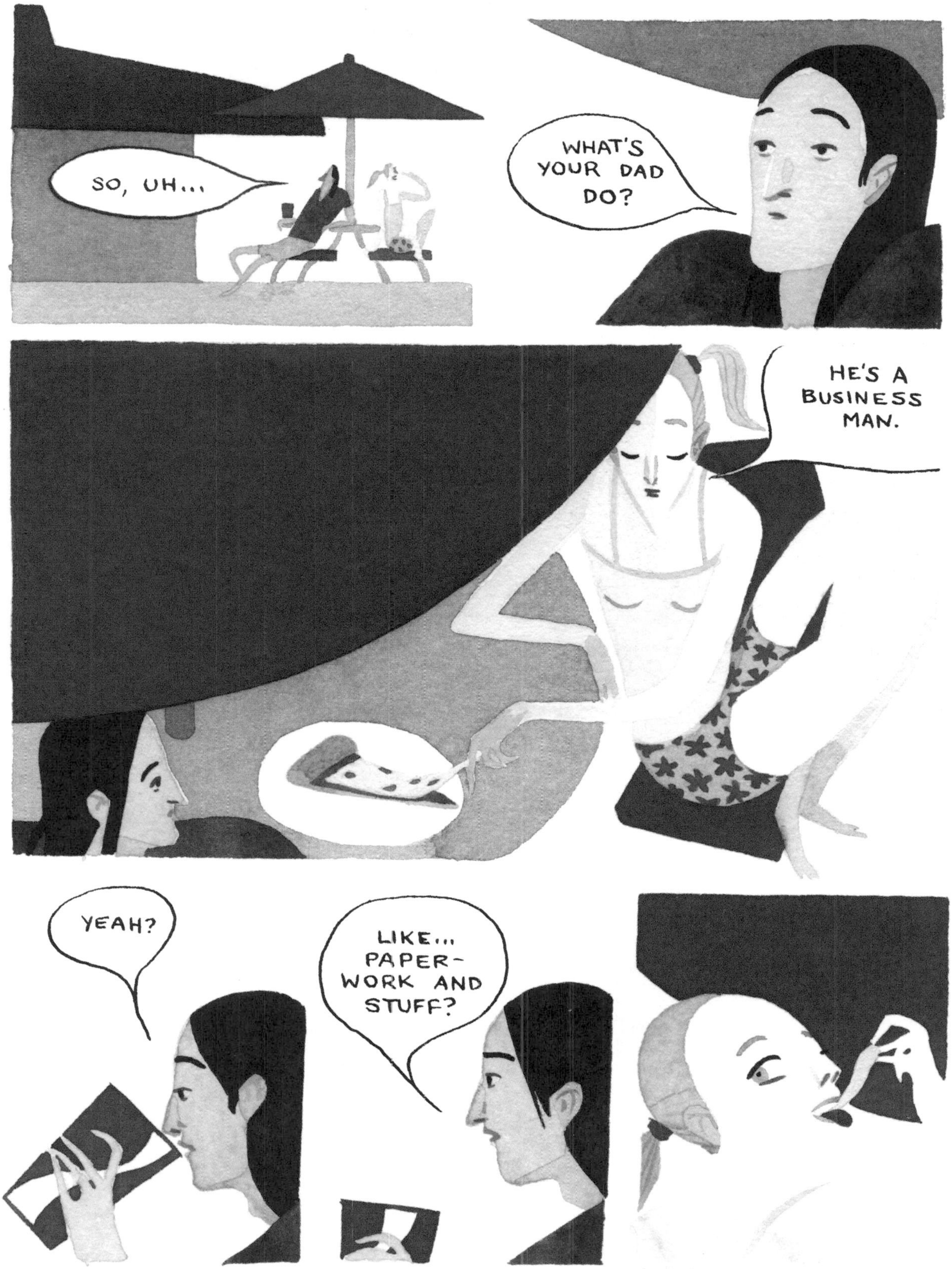
SO, UH...
WHAT'S YOUR DAD DO?
HE'S A BUSINESS MAN.
YEAH?
LIKE... PAPER-WORK AND STUFF?

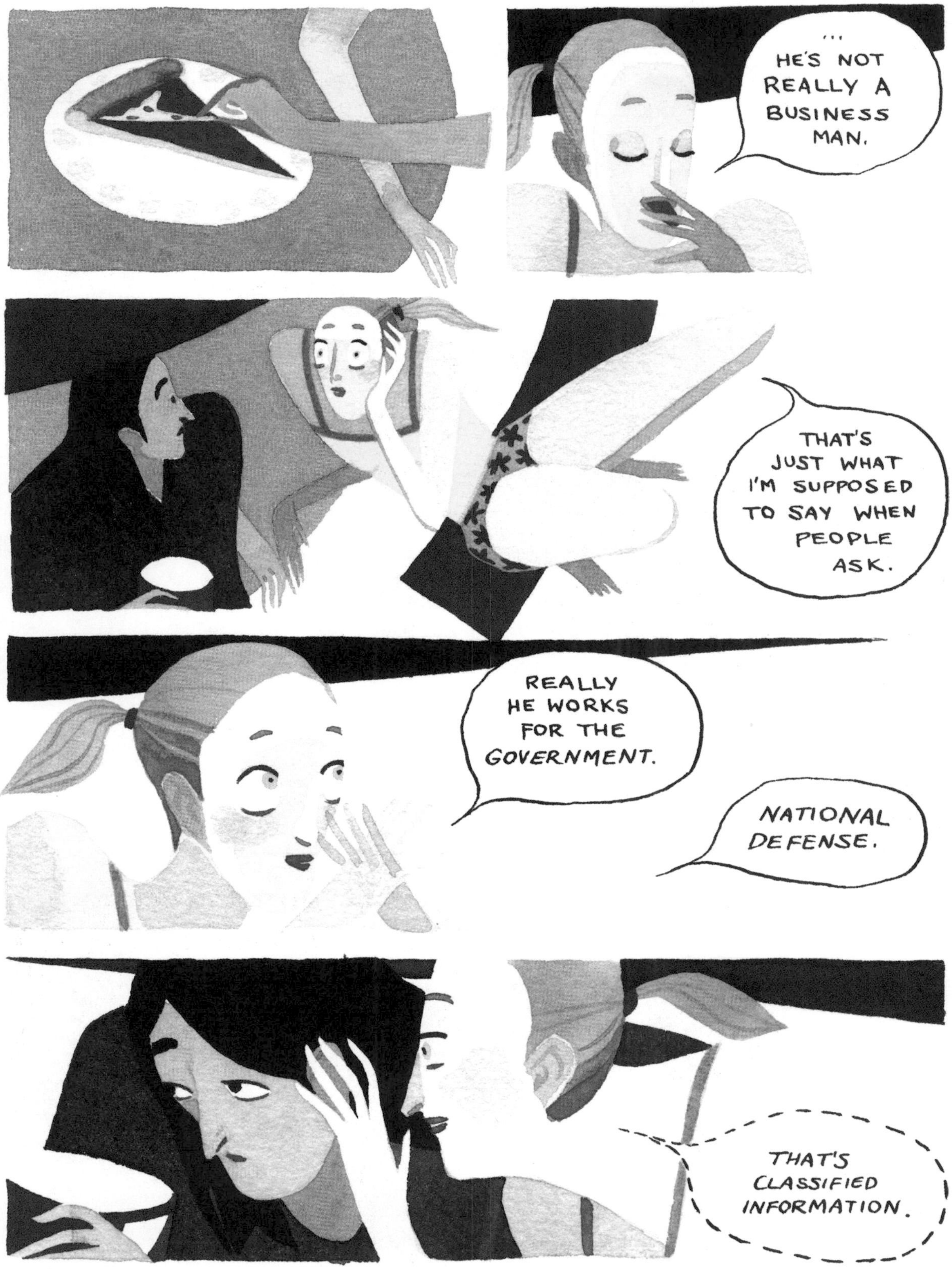
...
HE'S NOT REALLY A BUSINESS MAN.
THAT'S JUST WHAT I'M SUPPOSED TO SAY WHEN PEOPLE ASK.
REALLY HE WORKS FOR THE GOVERNMENT.
NATIONAL DEFENSE.
THAT'S CLASSIFIED INFORMATION.

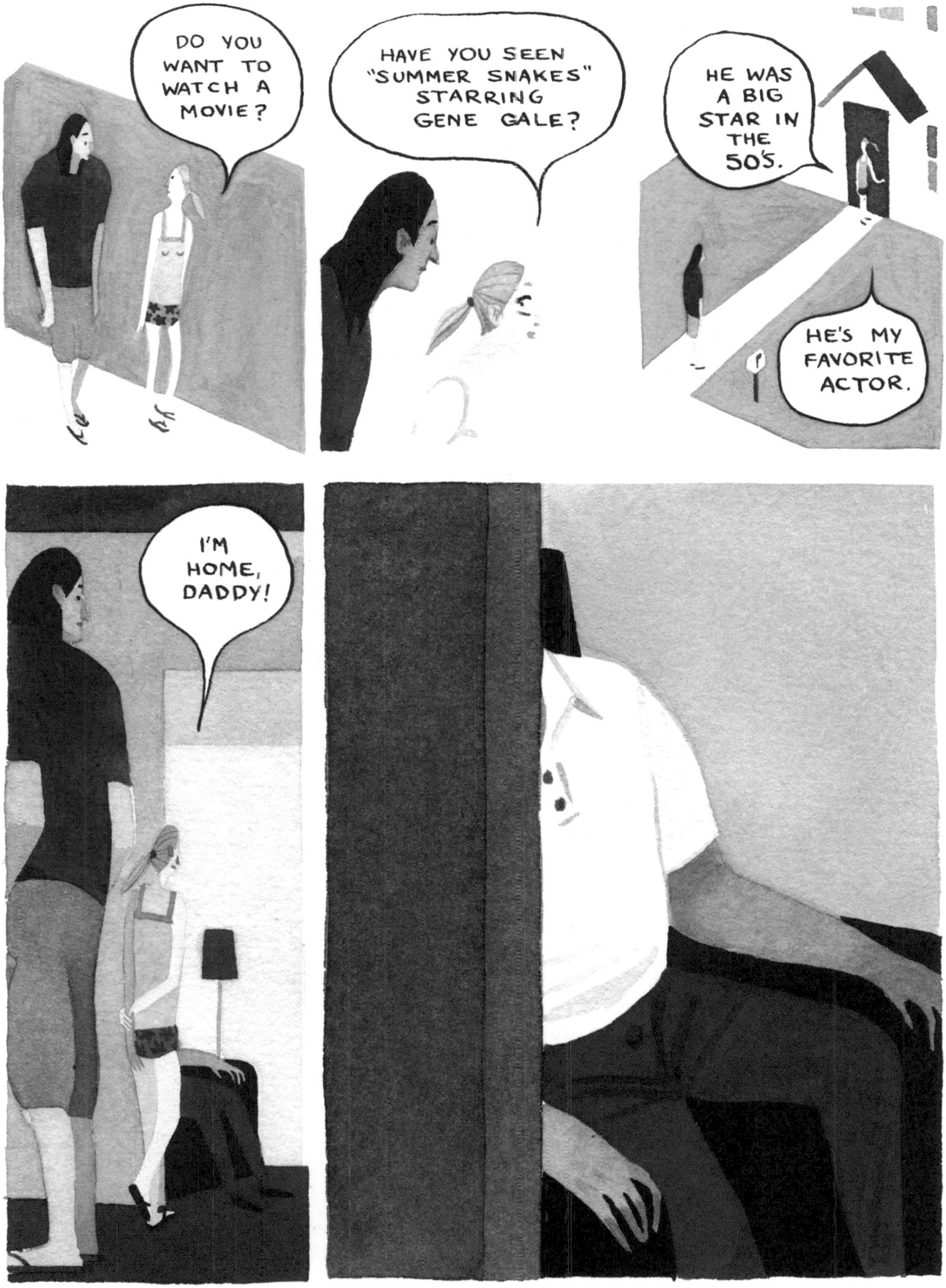
DO YOU WANT TO WATCH A MOVIE?
HAVE YOU SEEN "SUMMER SNAKES" STARRING GENE GALE?
HE WAS A BIG STAR IN THE 50'S.
HE'S MY FAVORITE ACTOR.
I'M HOME, DADDY!

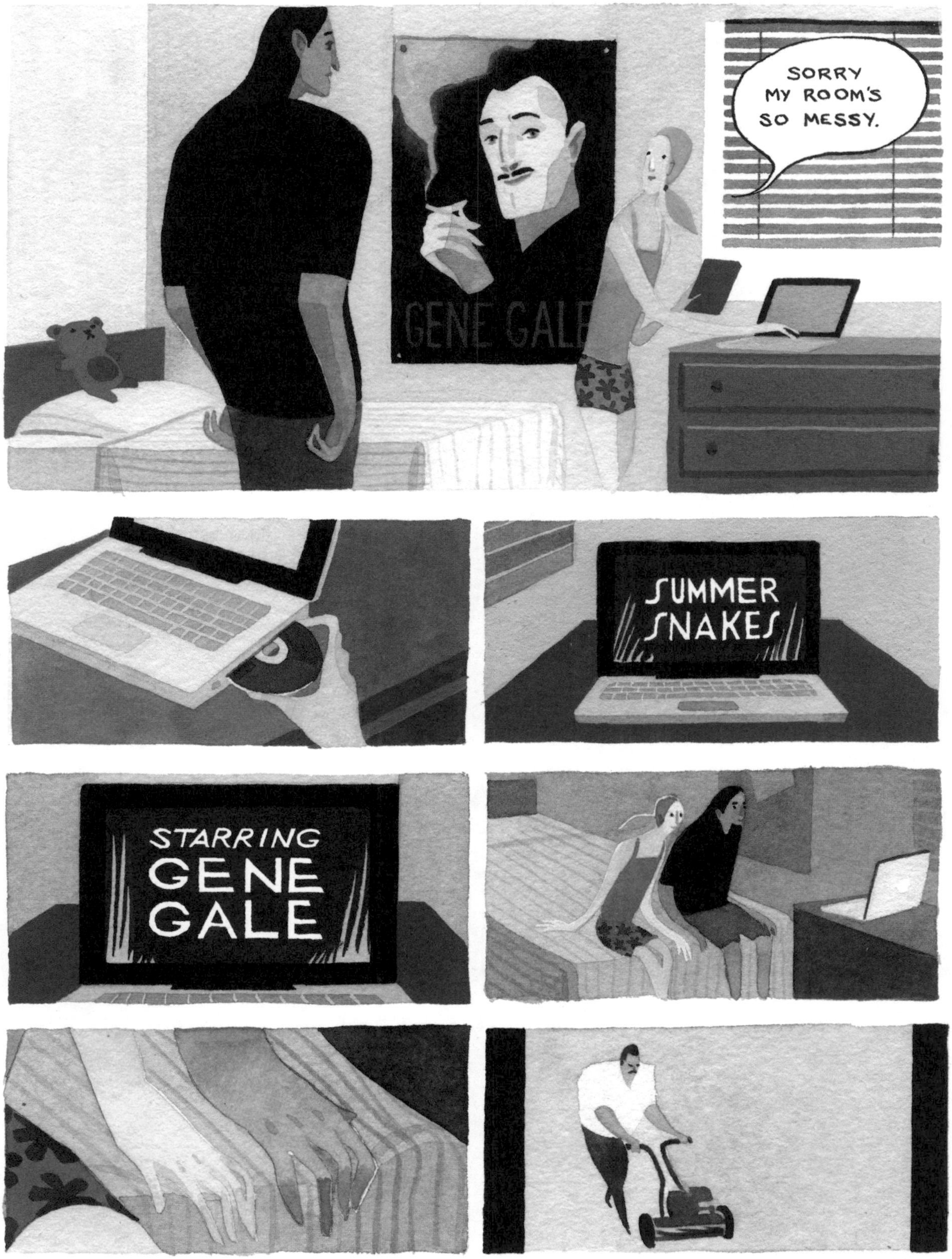
SORRY MY ROOM'S SO MESSY.
GENE GALE
SUMMER SNAKES
STARRING GENE GALE

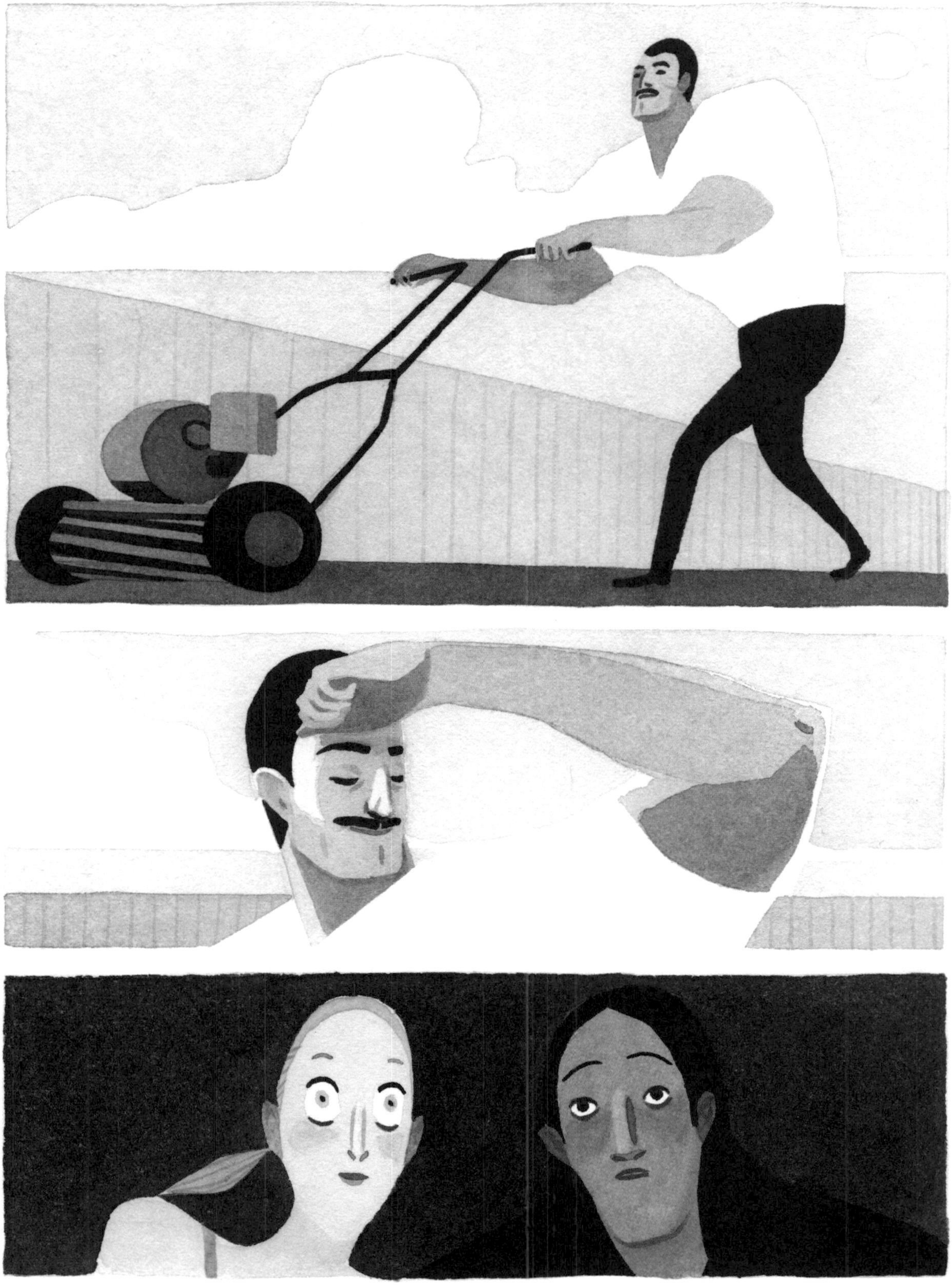

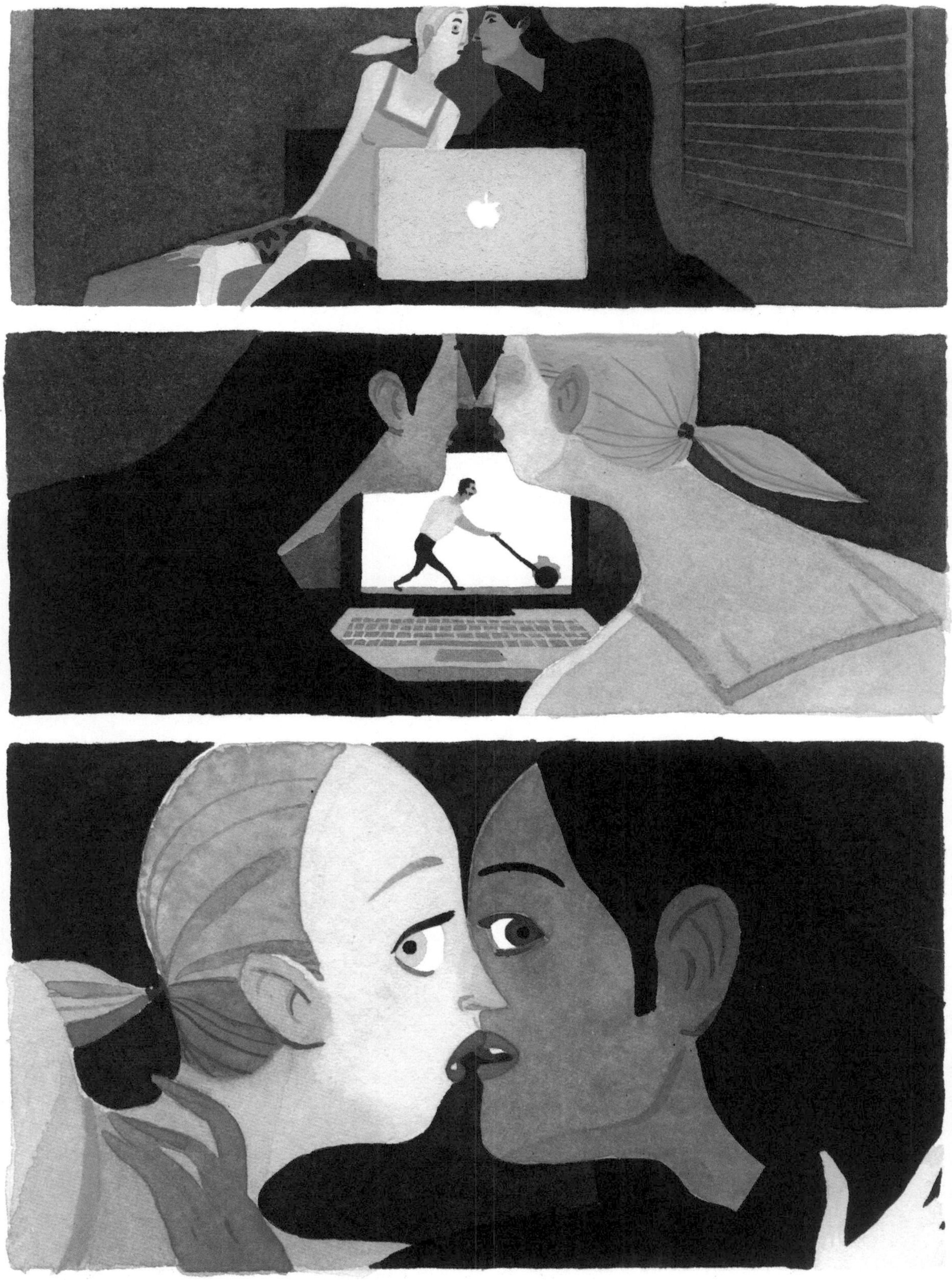
END

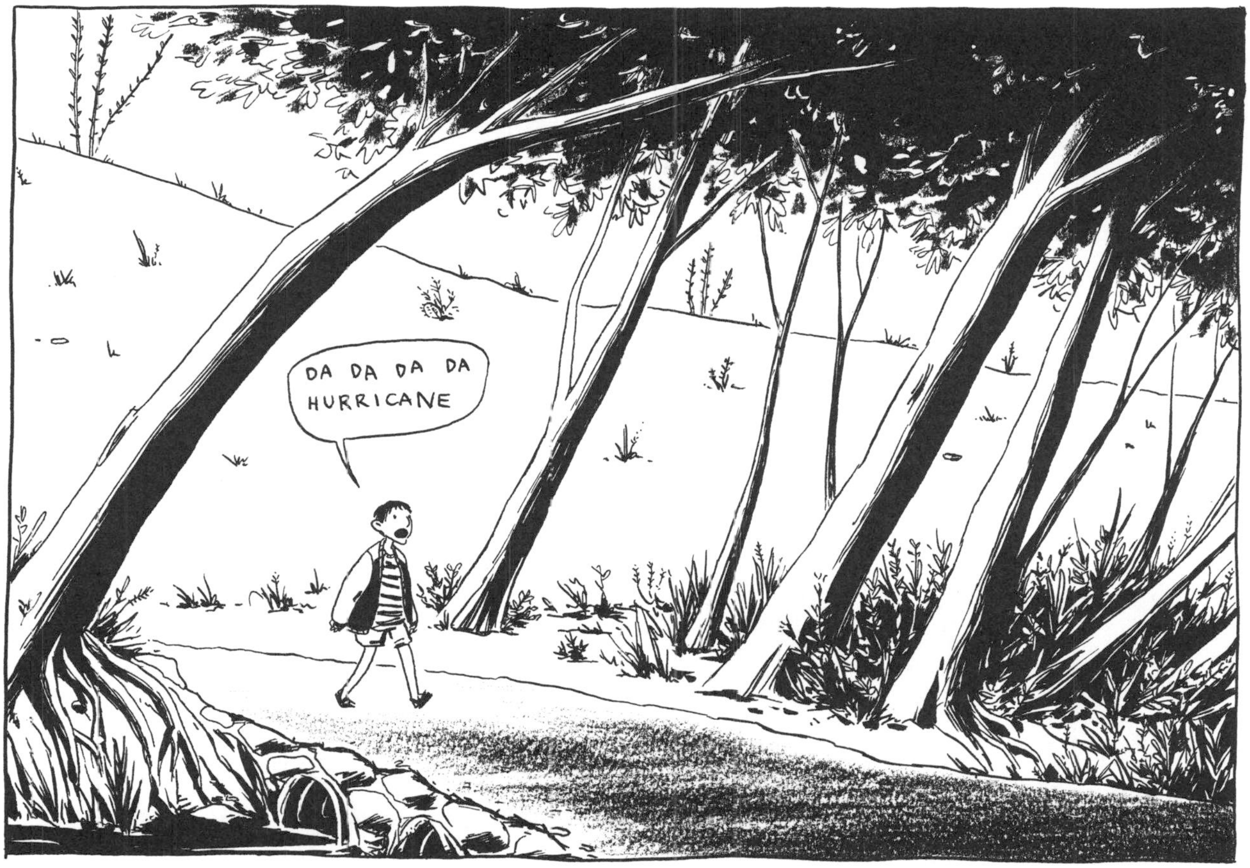
DA DA DA DA HURRICANE

THOMAS THE LEADER

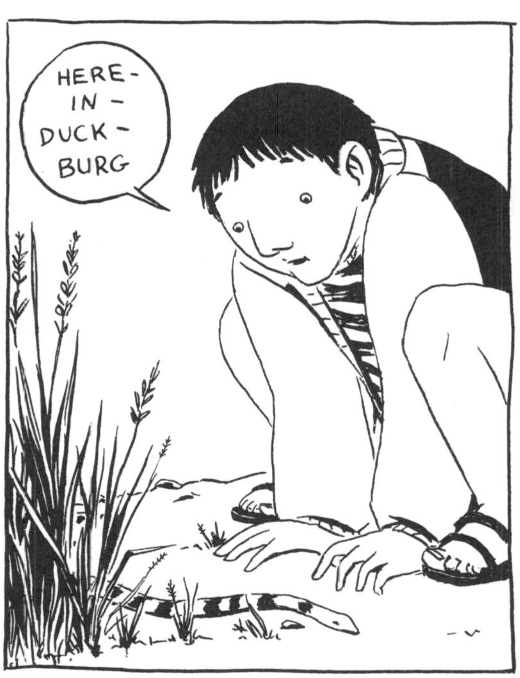
HERE- IN - DUCK - BURG

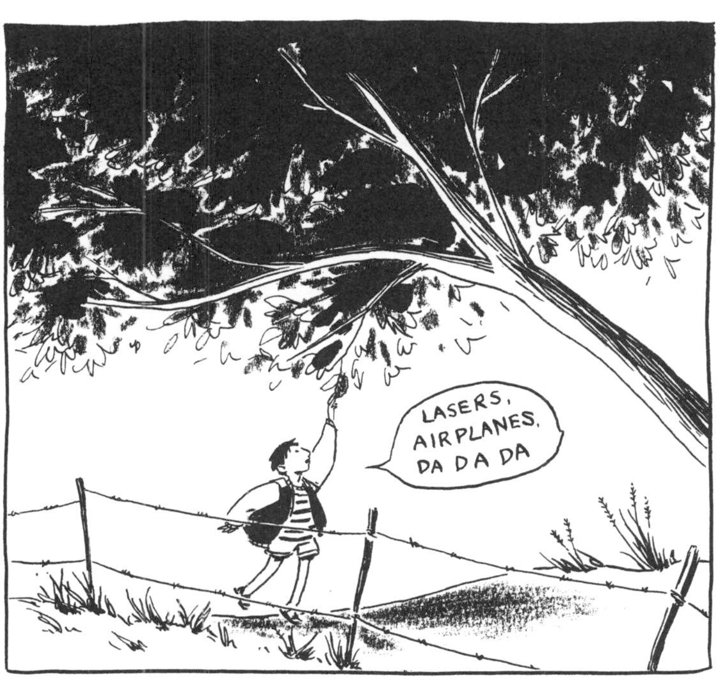
LASERS, AIRPLANES, DA DA DA

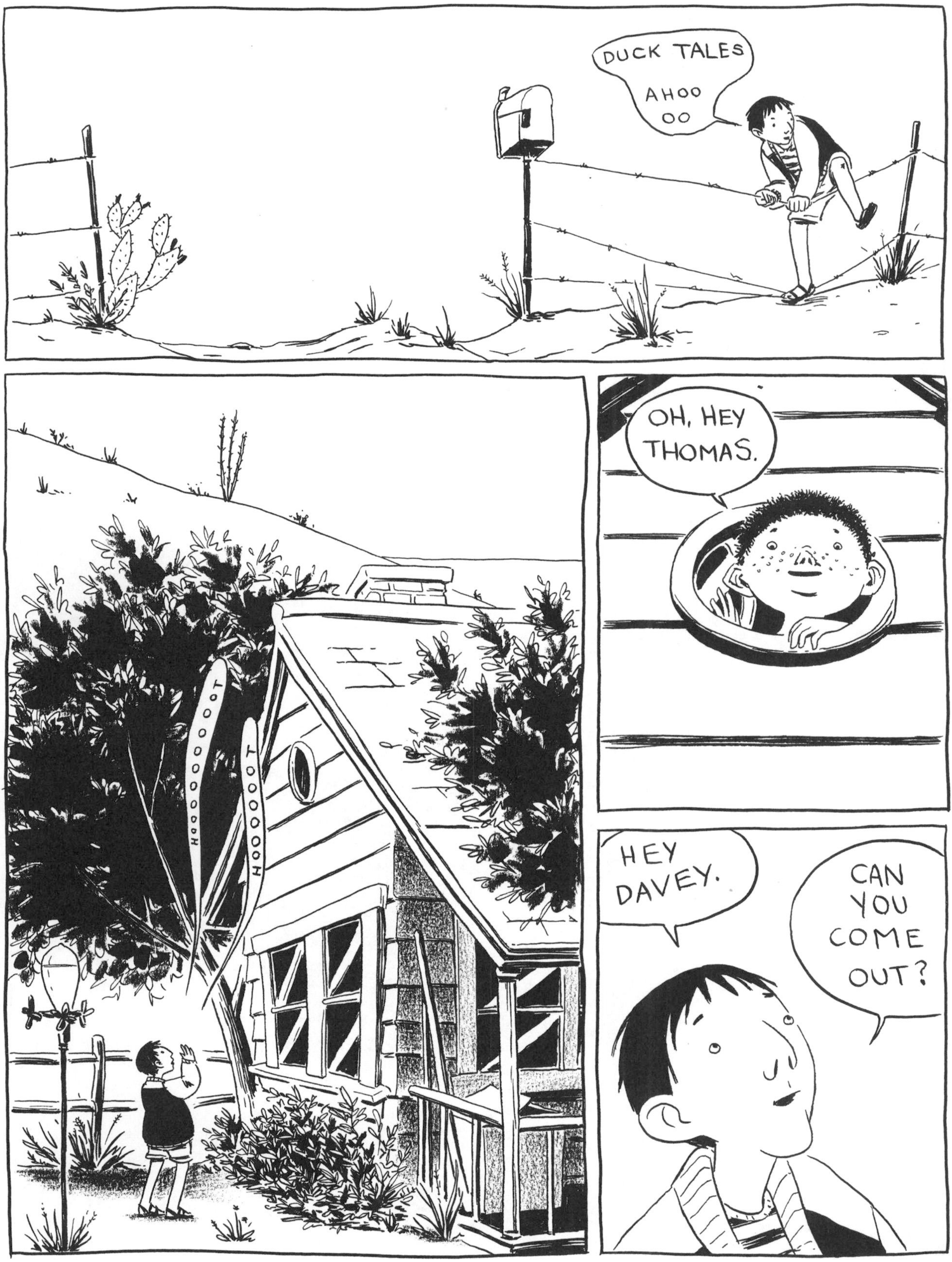
DUCK TALES AHOO OO
HOOOOOOOOT
HOOOOOOT
OH, HEY THOMAS.
HEY DAVEY.
CAN YOU COME OUT?

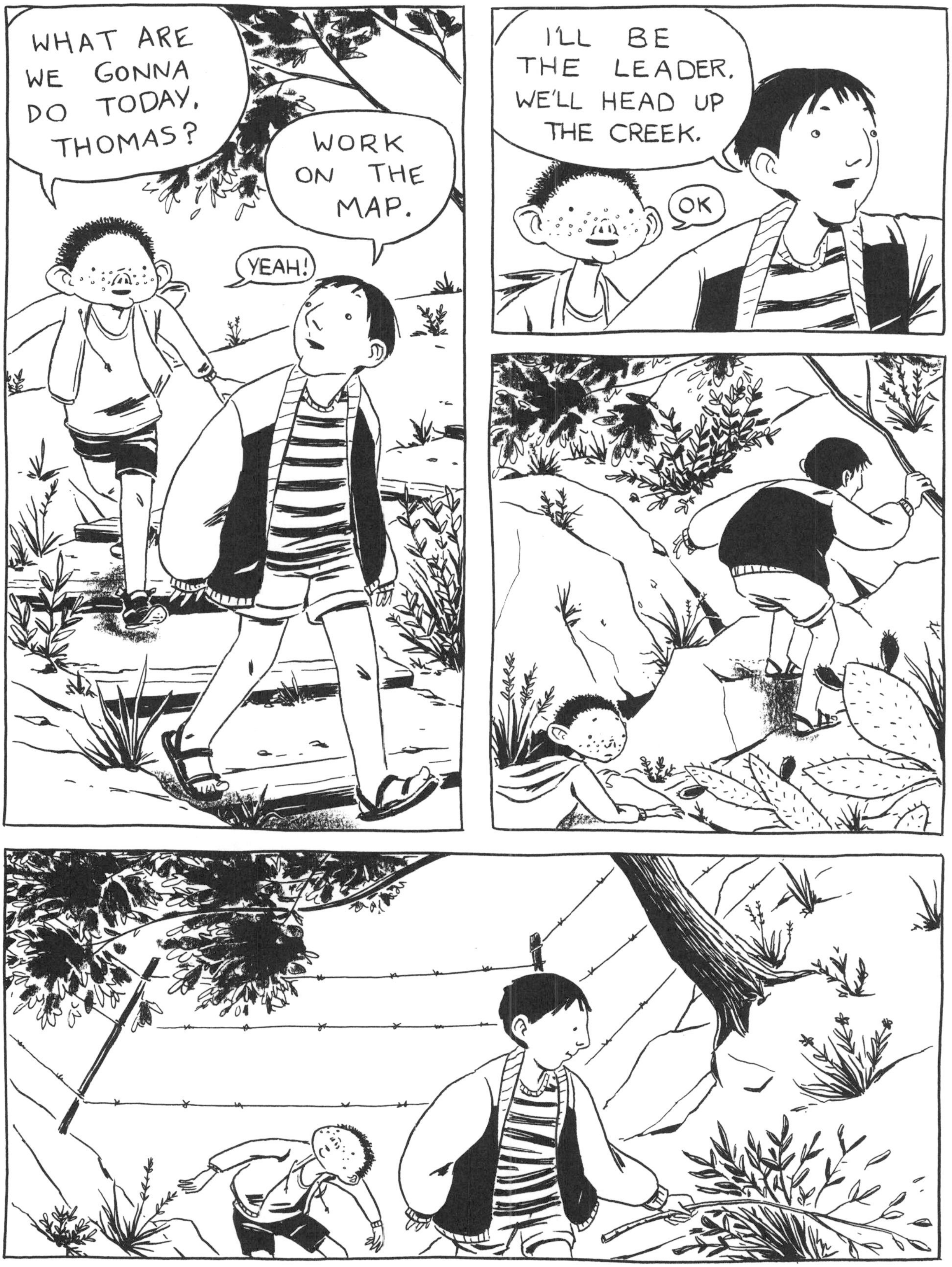
WHAT ARE WE GONNA DO TODAY, THOMAS?
WORK ON THE MAP.
YEAH!
I'LL BE THE LEADER. WE'LL HEAD UP THE CREEK.
OK

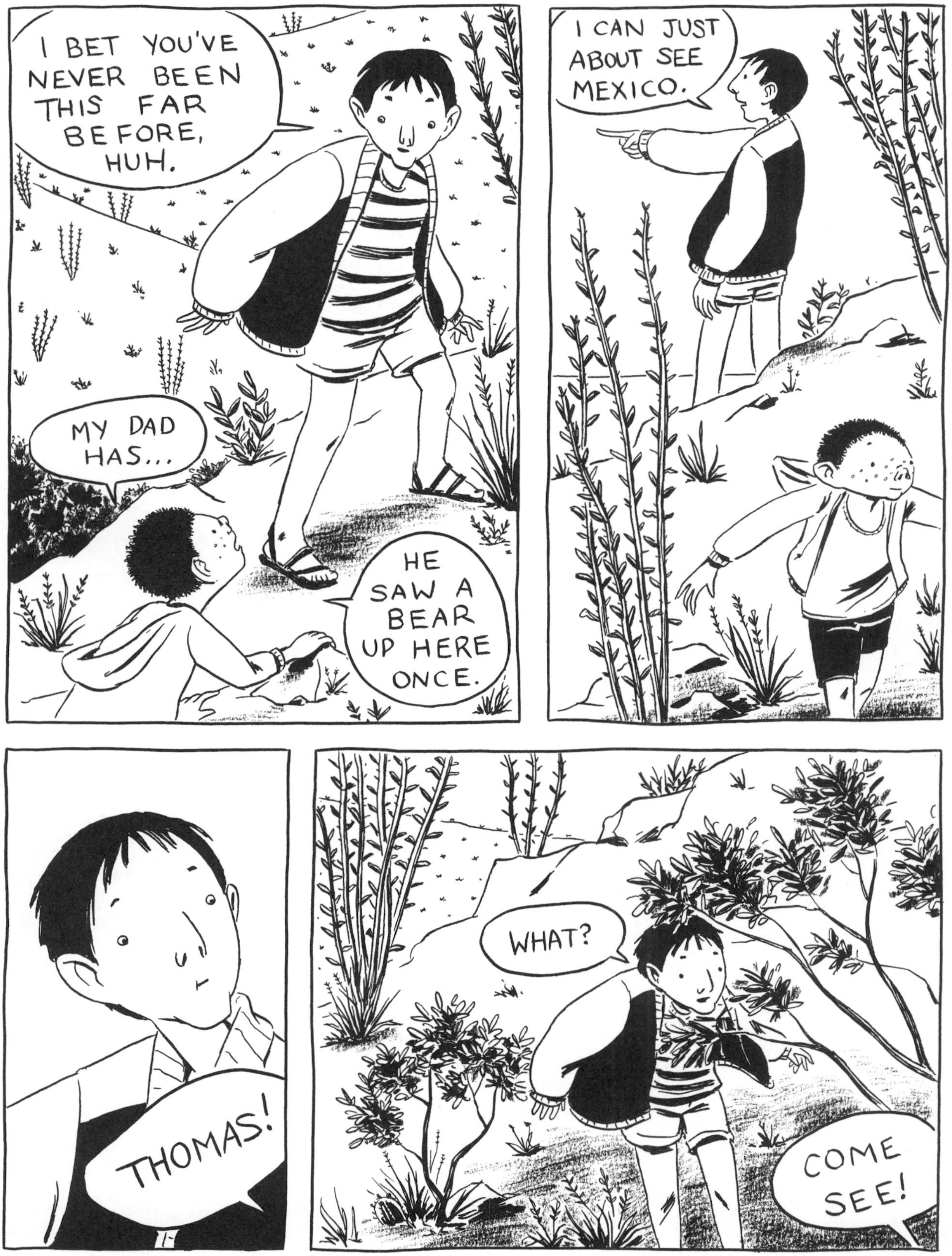
I BET YOU'VE NEVER BEEN THIS FAR BEFORE, HUH.
MY DAD HAS...
HE SAW A BEAR UP HERE ONCE.
I CAN JUST ABOUT SEE MEXICO.
THOMAS!
WHAT?
COME SEE!

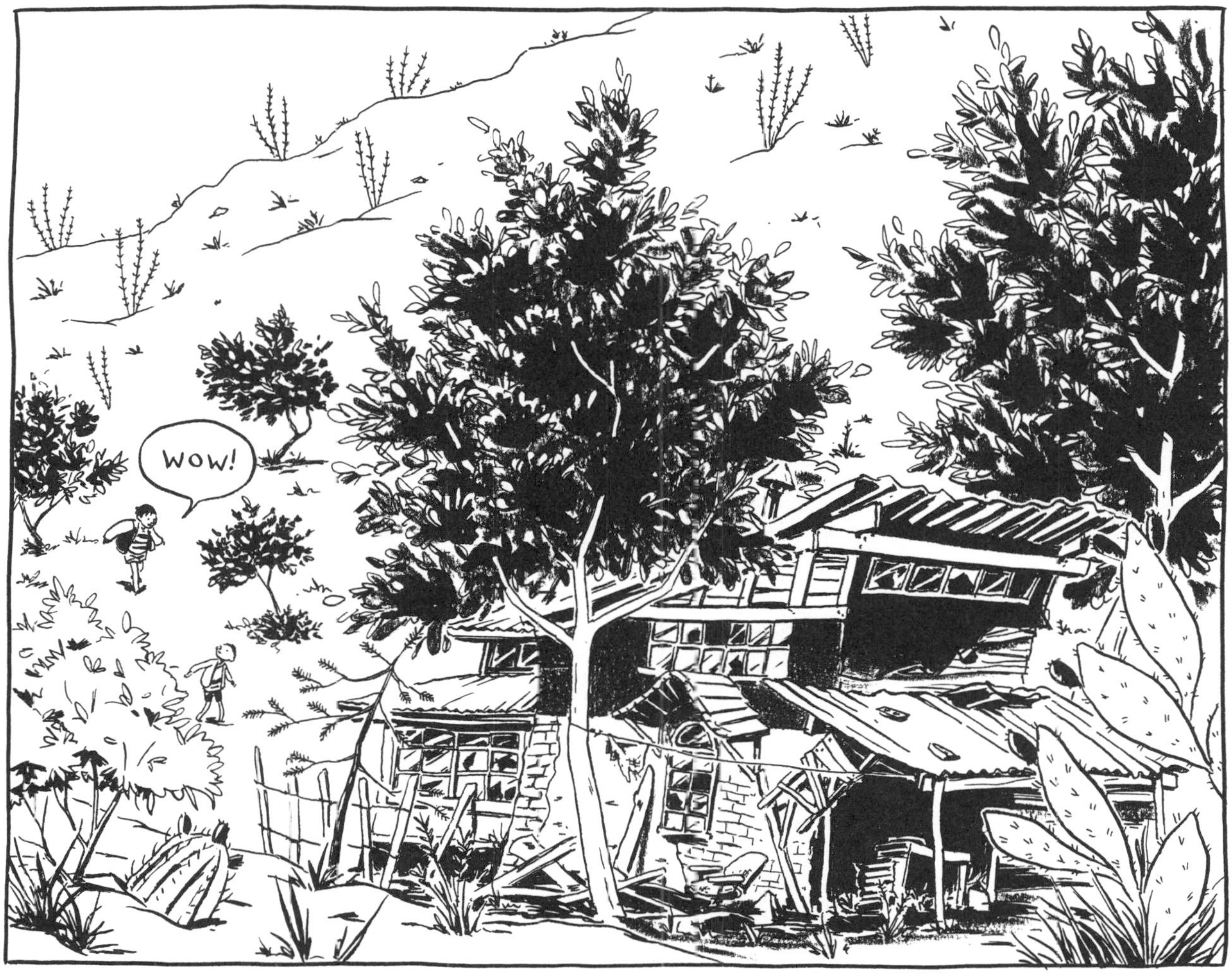
WOW!

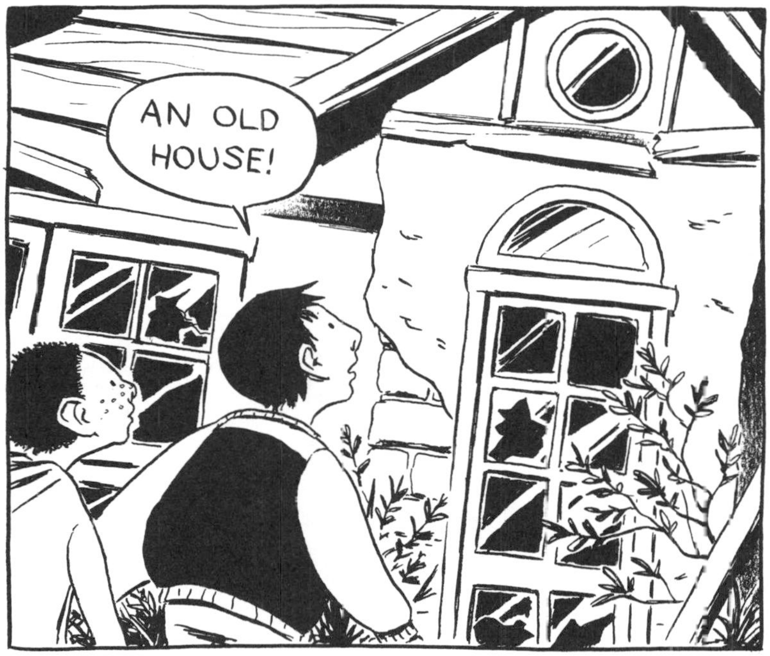
AN OLD HOUSE!

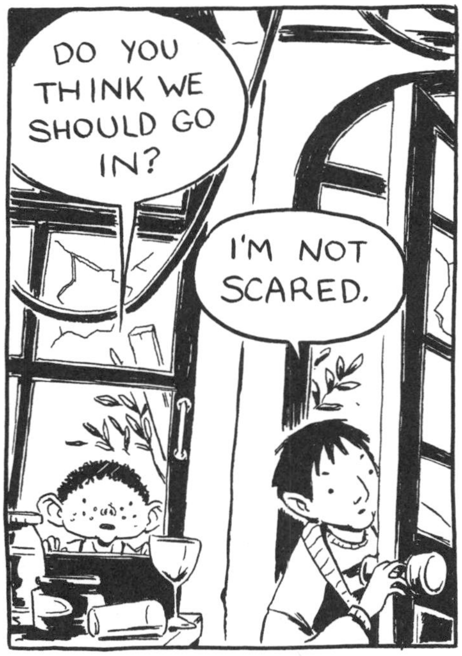
DO YOU THINK WE SHOULD GO IN?
I'M NOT SCARED.

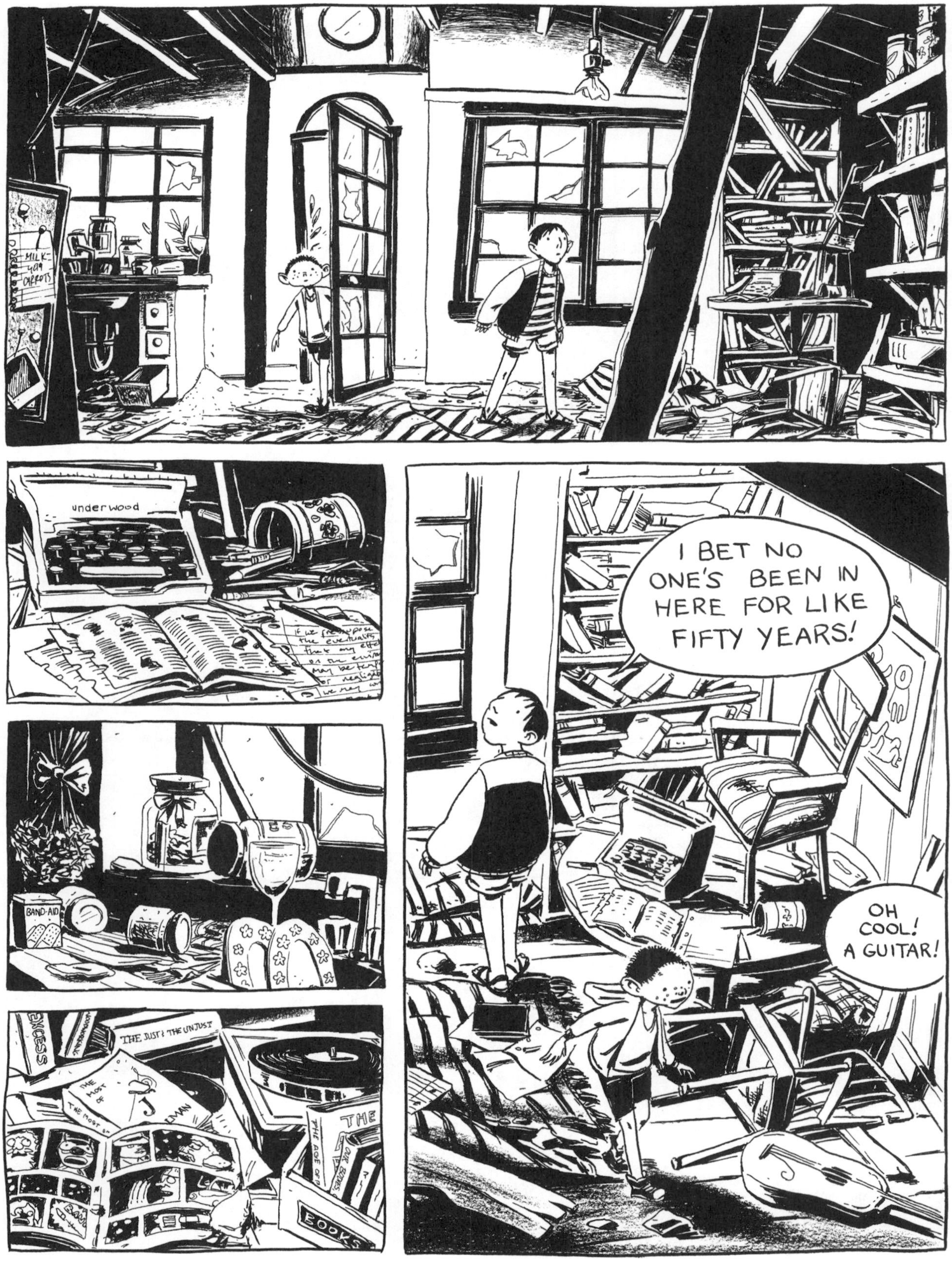
underwood
BAND-AID
EXCESS
THE JUST & THE UNJUST
BOOKS
I BET NO ONE'S BEEN IN HERE FOR LIKE FIFTY YEARS!
OH COOL! A GUITAR!

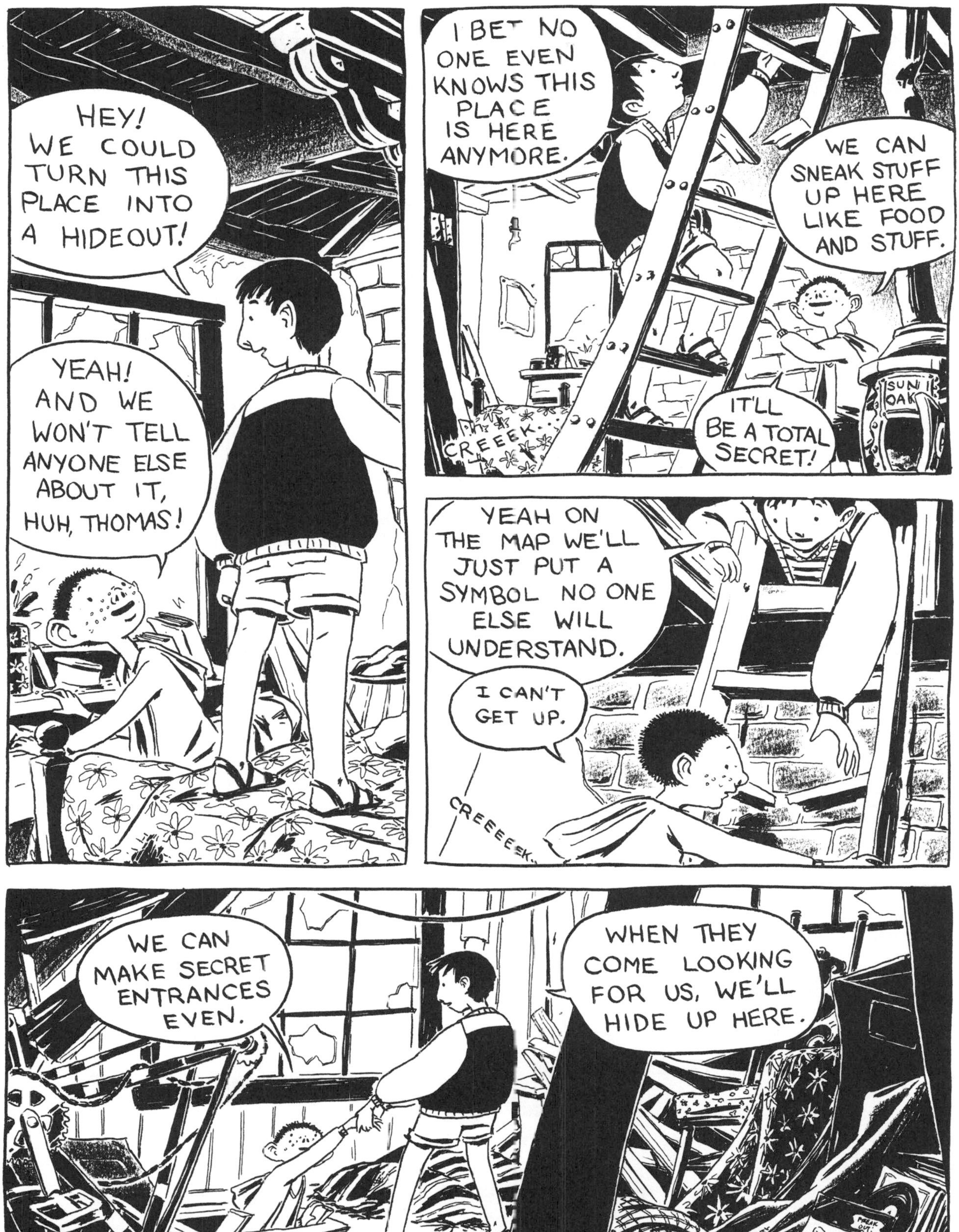
HEY! WE COULD TURN THIS PLACE INTO A HIDEOUT!
YEAH! AND WE WON'T TELL ANYONE ELSE ABOUT IT, HUH, THOMAS!
I BET NO ONE EVEN KNOWS THIS PLACE IS HERE ANYMORE.
WE CAN SNEAK STUFF UP HERE LIKE FOOD AND STUFF.
CREEEK.
IT'LL BE A TOTAL SECRET!
YEAH ON THE MAP WE'LL JUST PUT A SYMBOL NO ONE ELSE WILL UNDERSTAND.
I CAN'T GET UP.
CREEEEEEK.
WE CAN MAKE SECRET ENTRANCES EVEN.
WHEN THEY COME LOOKING FOR US, WE'LL HIDE UP HERE.

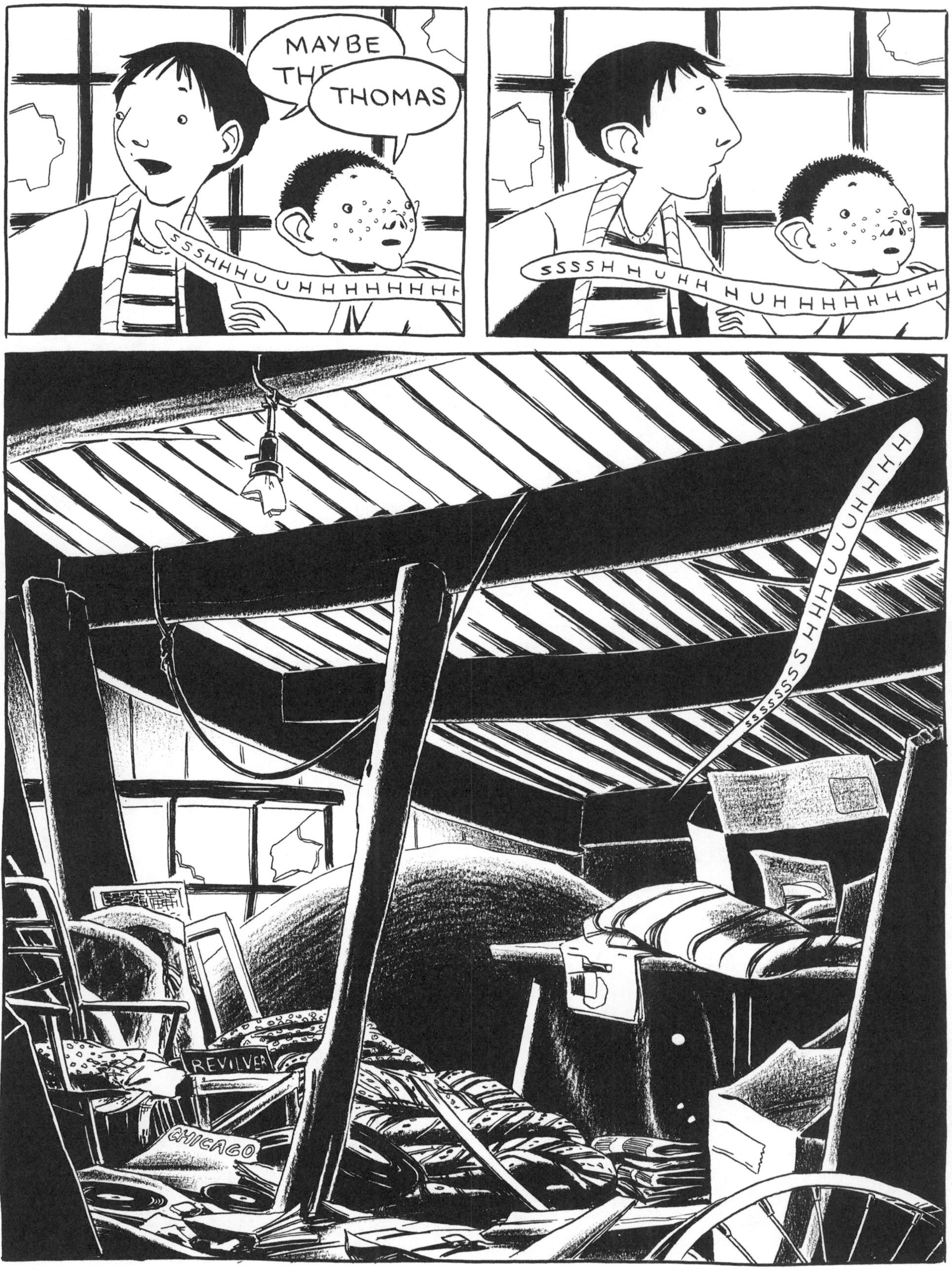
MAYBE TH
THOMAS
SSSHHHUUHHHHHHHH
SSSSH H U HH HUH HHHHHHHH
SSSSSSSSHHHUUUHHHH
REVILVER
CHICAGO

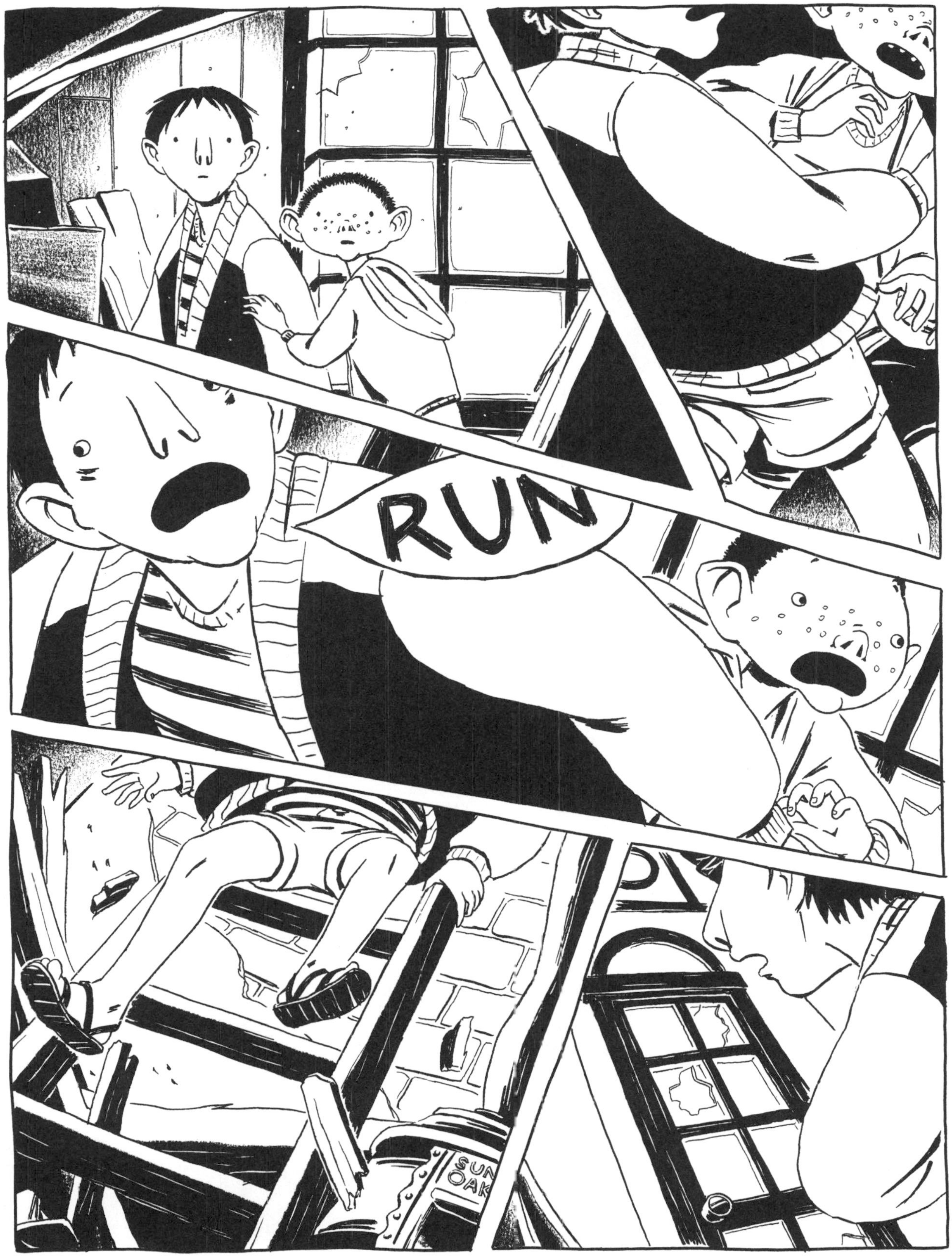
RUN
SUN
OAK

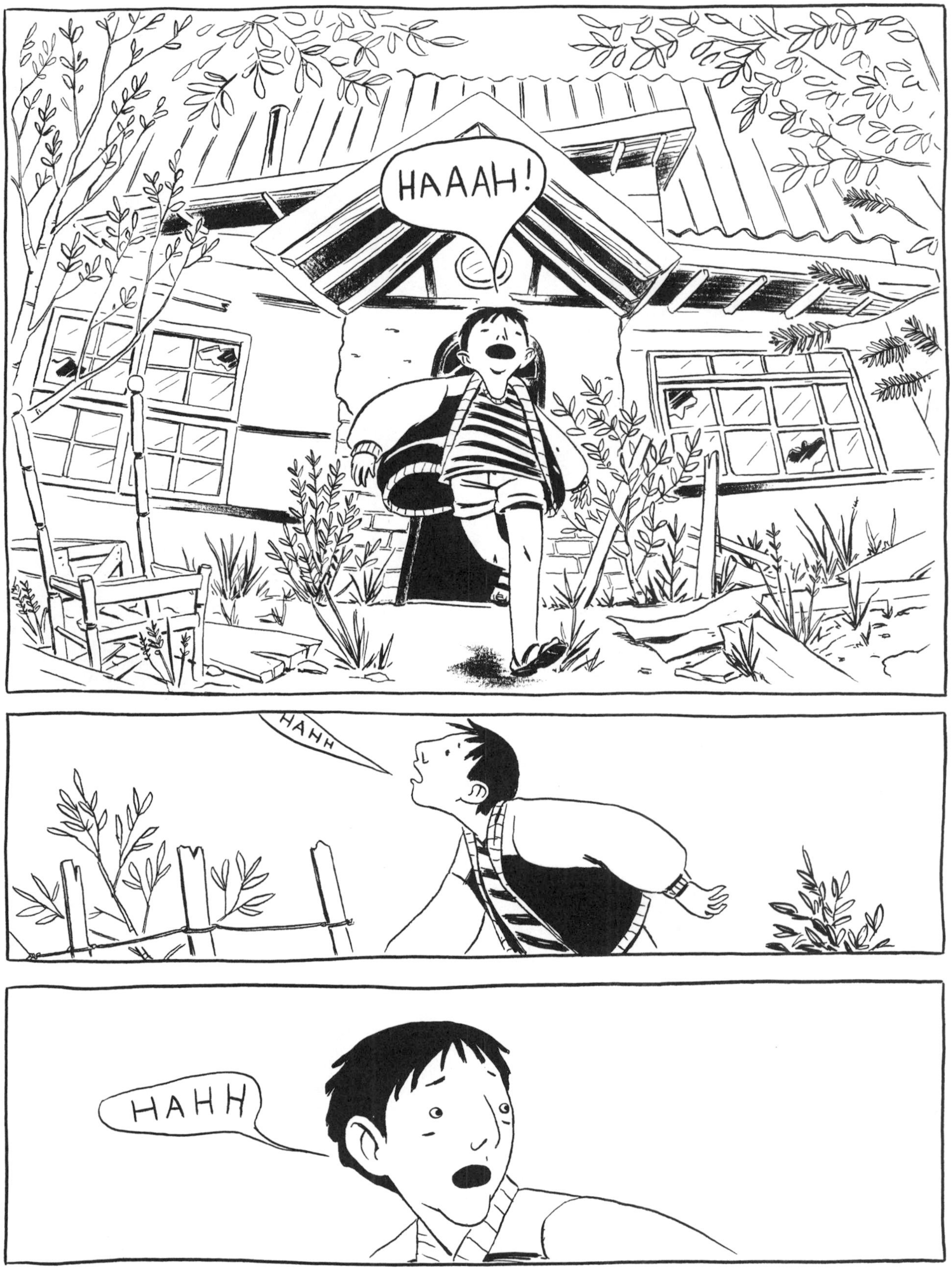
HAAAH!
HAHH
HAHH

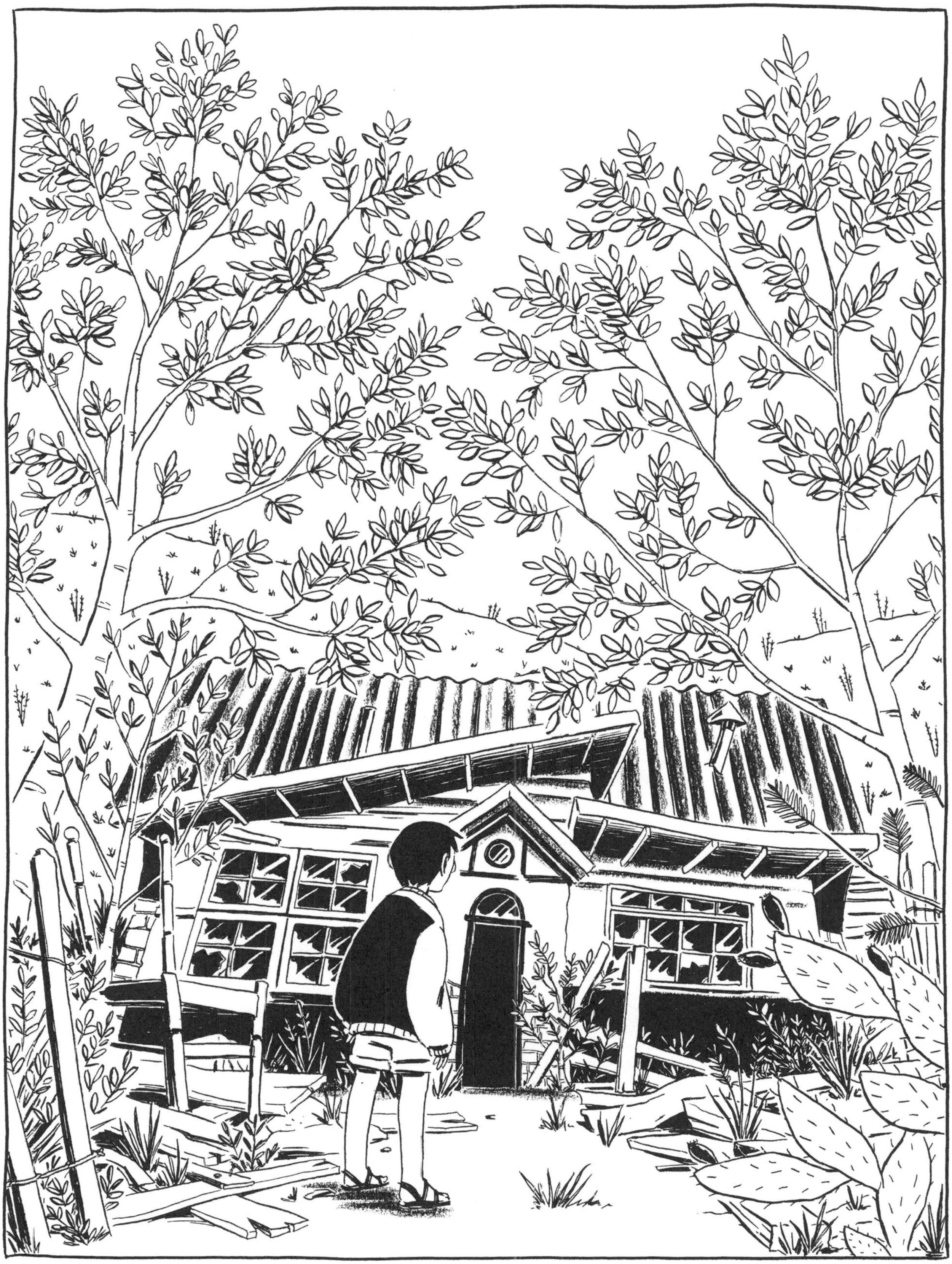

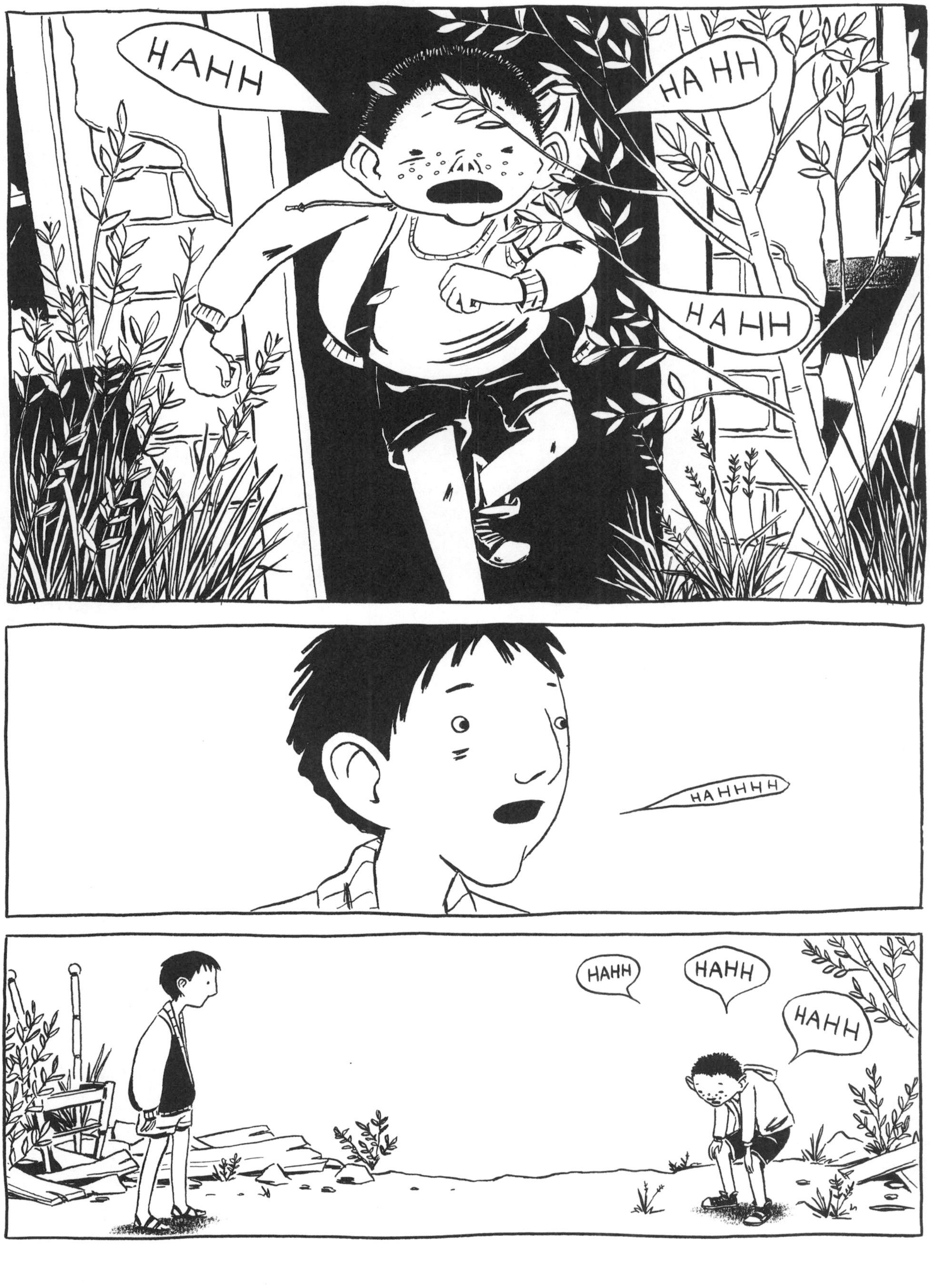
HAHH
HAHH
HAHH
HAHHHH
HAHH
HAHH
HAHH

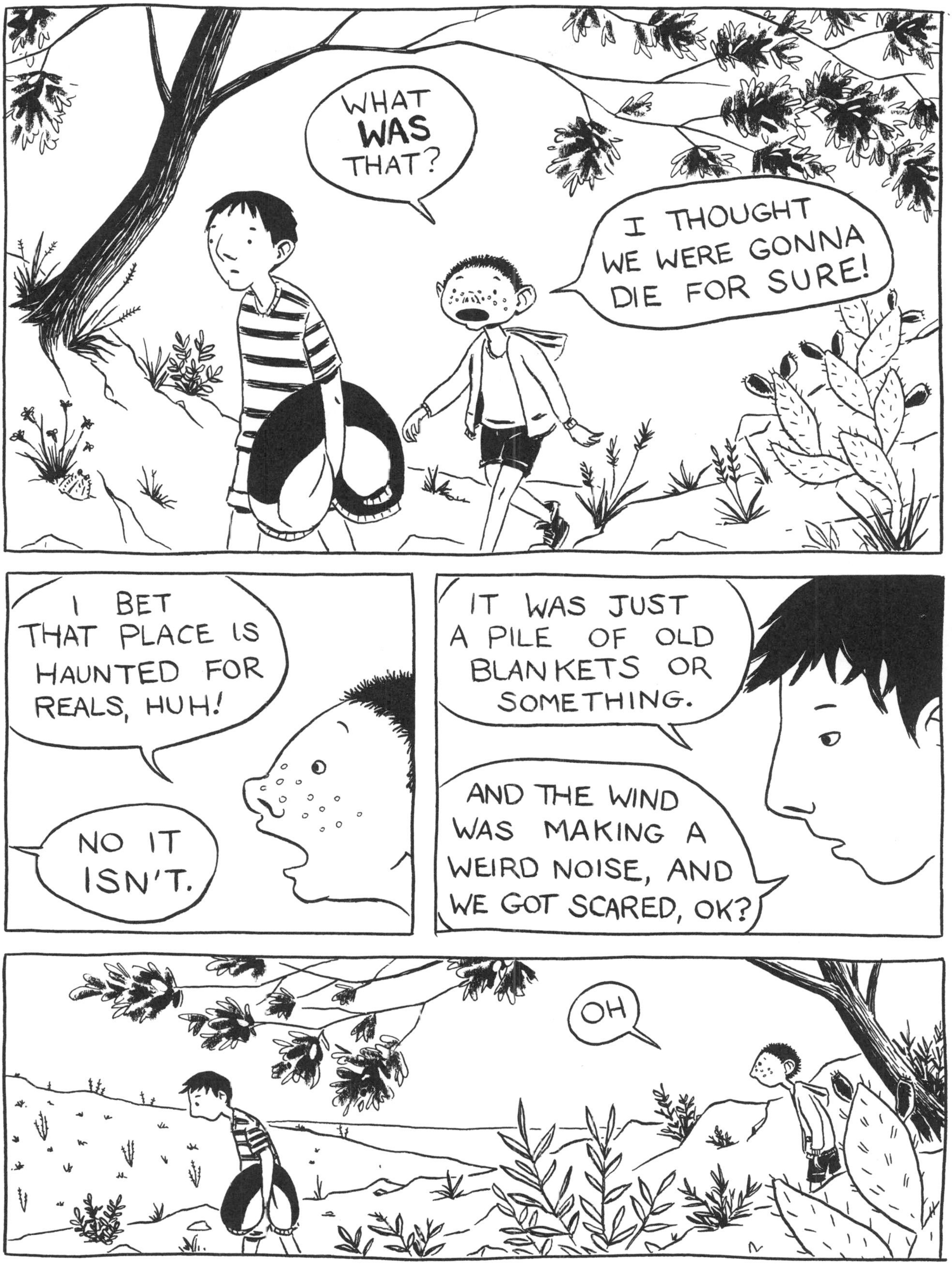
WHAT WAS THAT?
I THOUGHT WE WERE GONNA DIE FOR SURE!
I BET THAT PLACE IS HAUNTED FOR REALS, HUH!
NO IT ISN'T.
IT WAS JUST A PILE OF OLD BLANKETS OR SOMETHING.
AND THE WIND WAS MAKING A WEIRD NOISE, AND WE GOT SCARED, OK?
OH

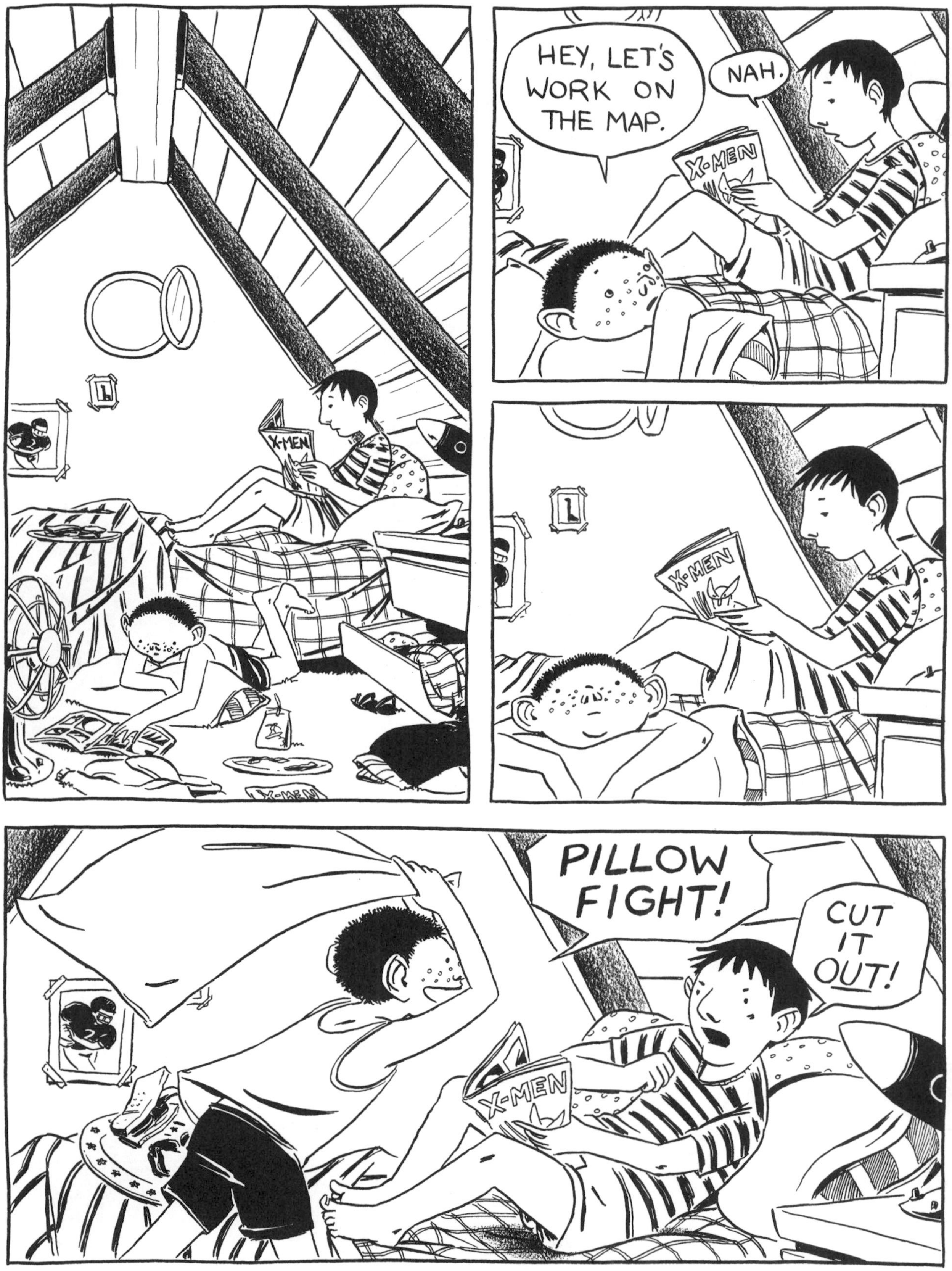
X-MEN
X-MEN
HEY, LET'S WORK ON THE MAP.
NAH.
X-MEN
X-MEN
PILLOW FIGHT!
CUT IT OUT!
X-MEN

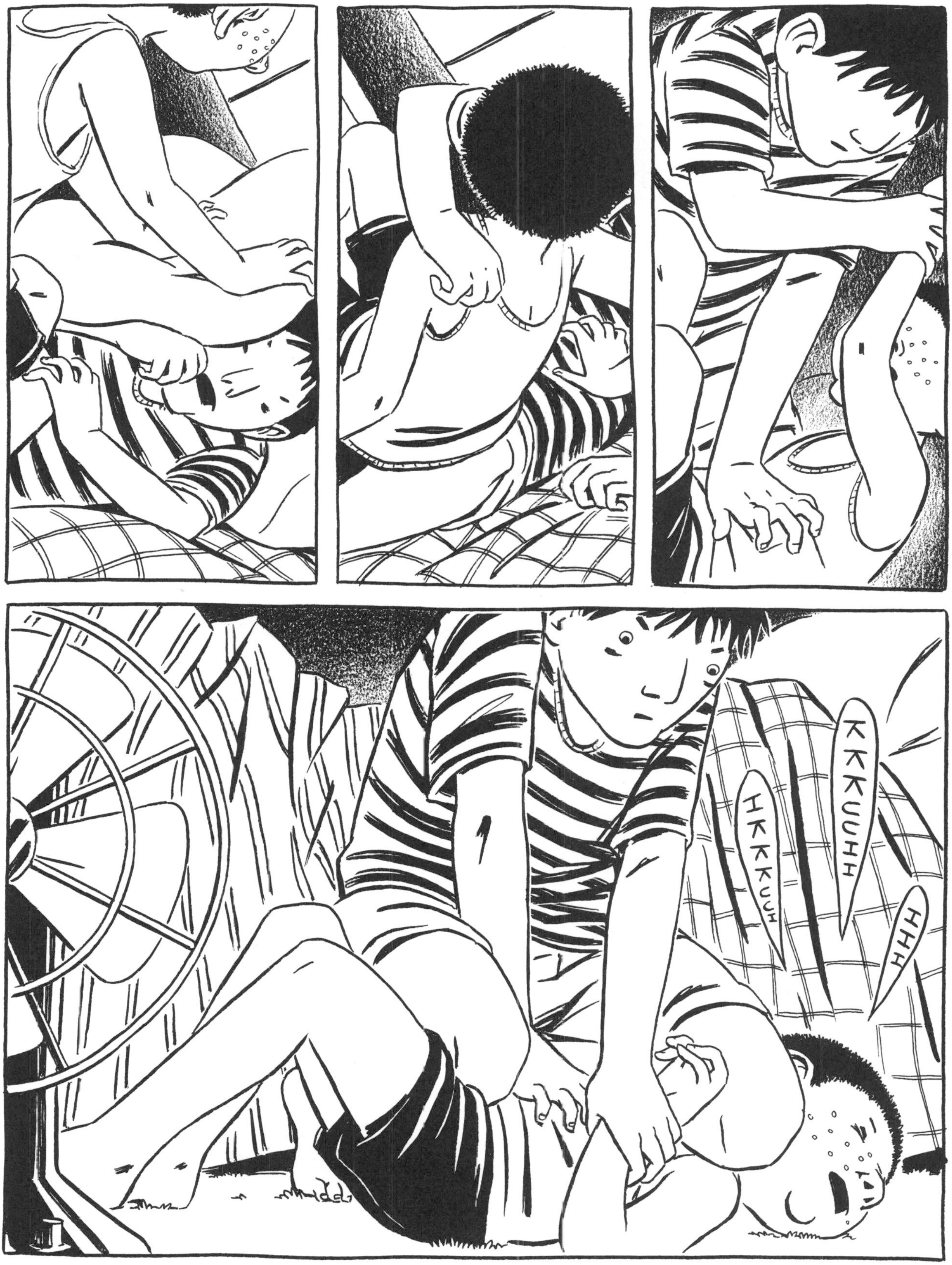
KKKUUHH
HKKKUUH
HHH

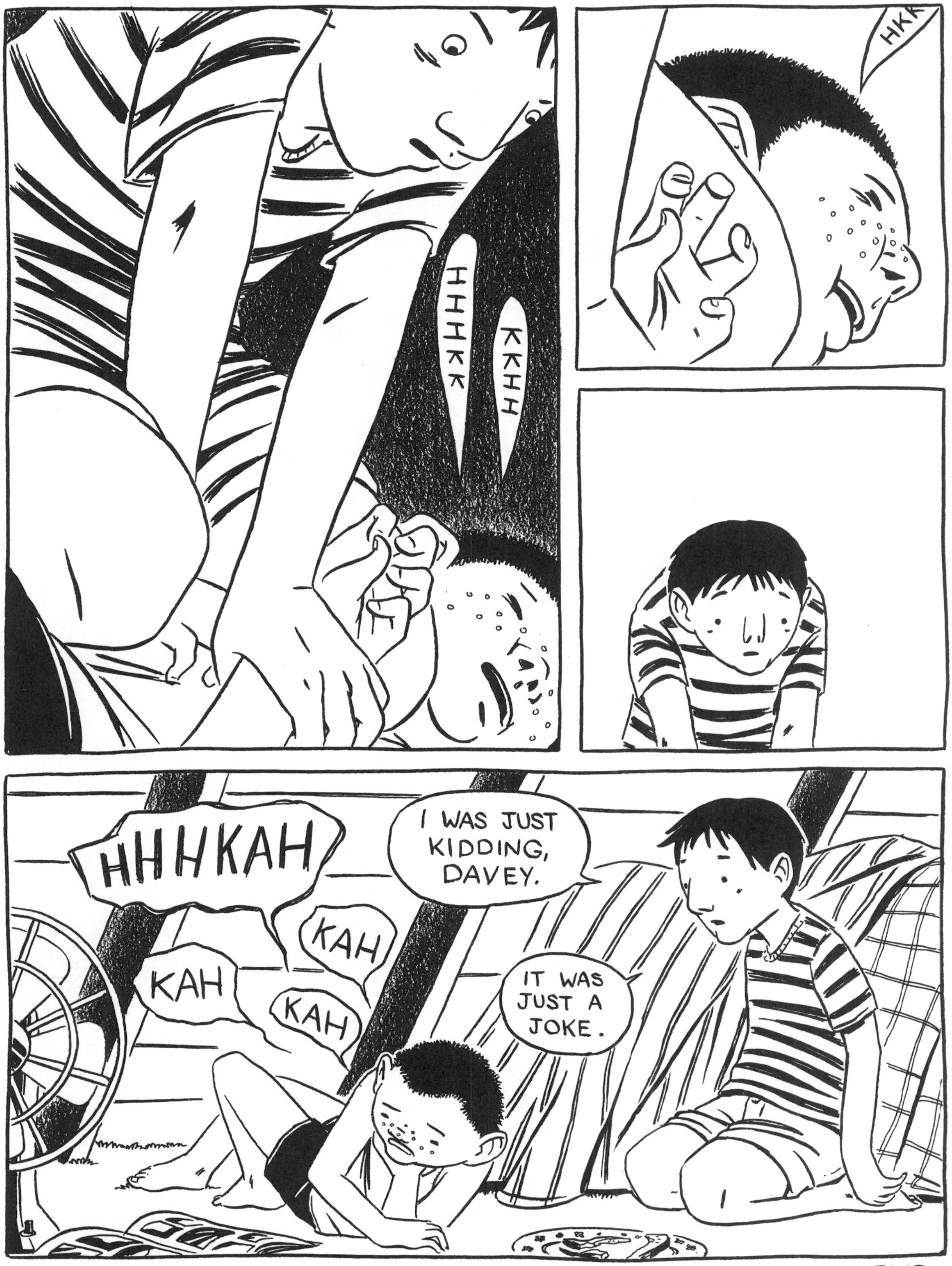
HHHKK
KKHH
HKK
HHHKAH
I WAS JUST KIDDING, DAVEY.
KAH
KAH
KAH
IT WAS JUST A JOKE.

END

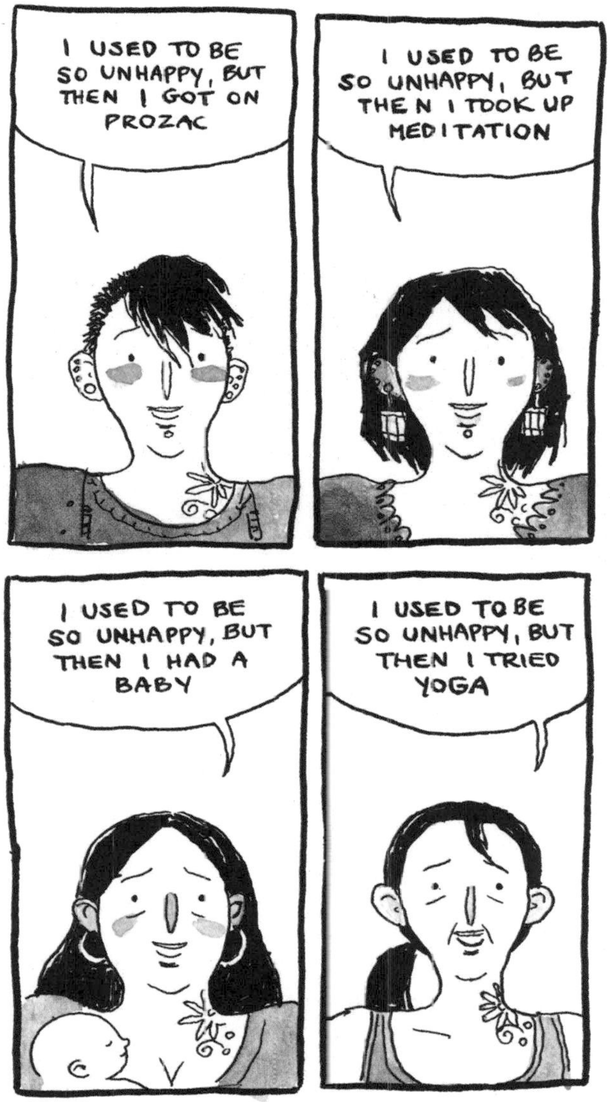
I USED TO BE SO UNHAPPY, BUT THEN I GOT ON PROZAC
I USED TO BE SO UNHAPPY, BUT THEN I TOOK UP MEDITATION
I USED TO BE SO UNHAPPY, BUT THEN I HAD A BABY
I USED TO BE SO UNHAPPY, BUT THEN I TRIED YOGA

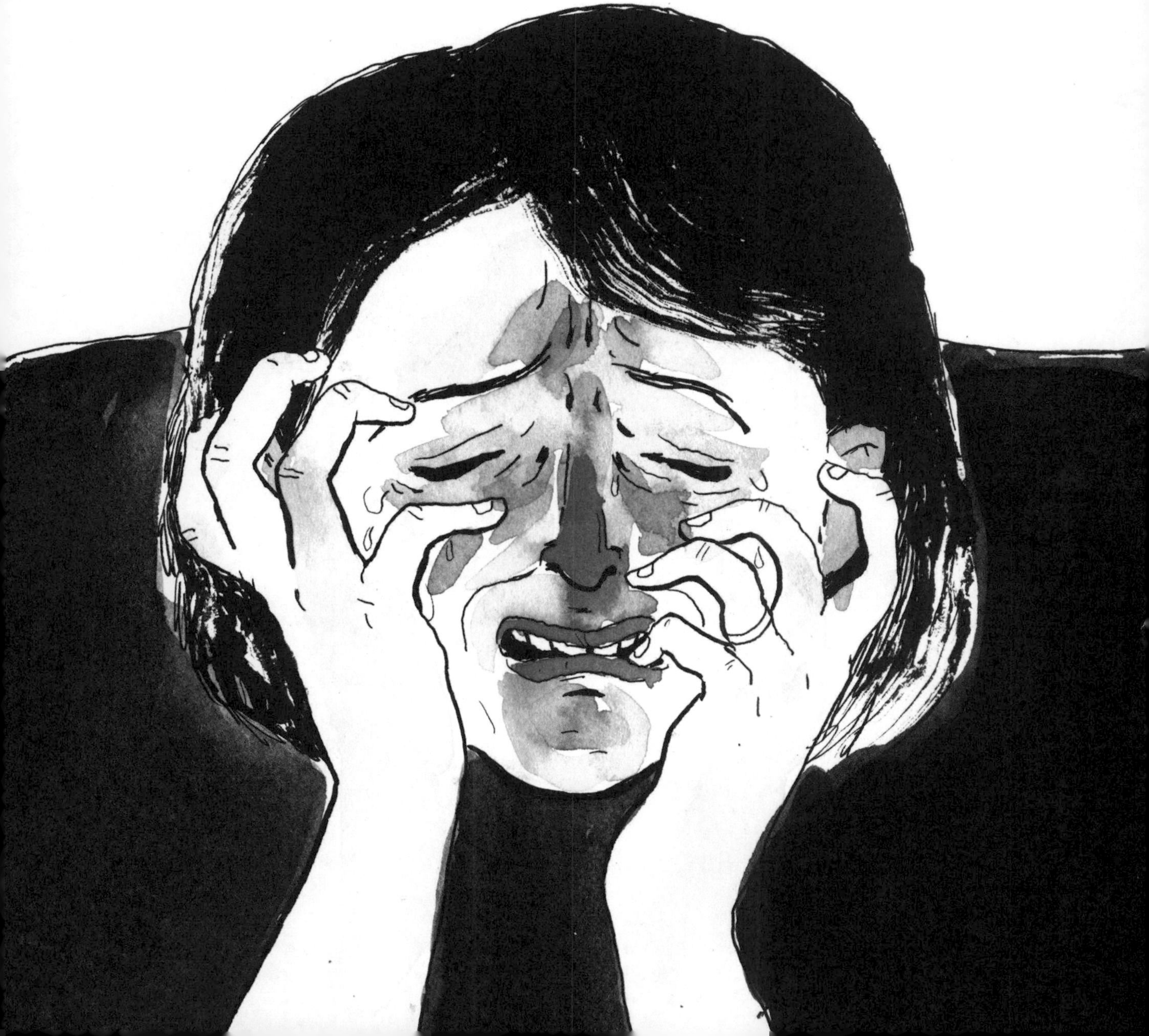

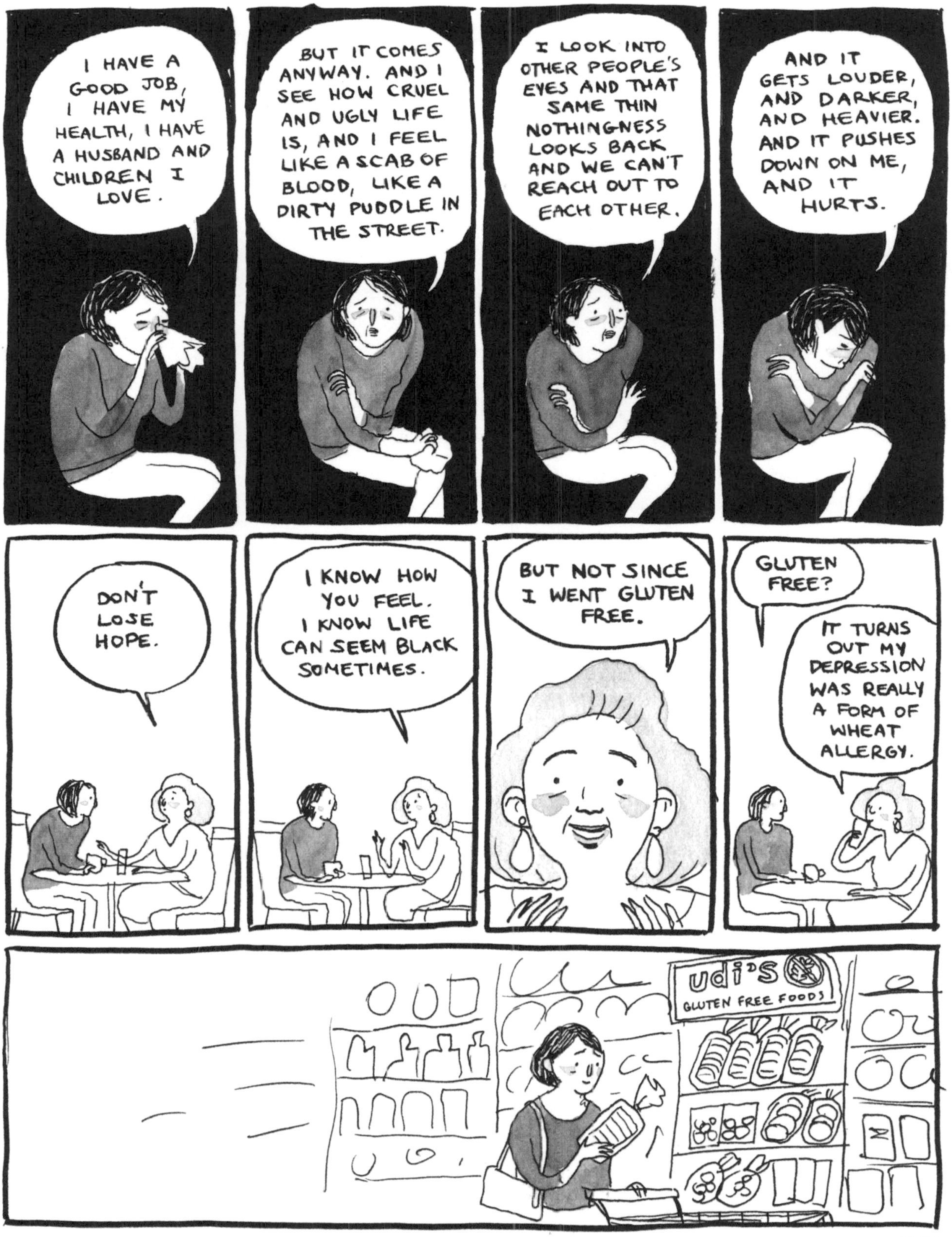
I HAVE A GOOD JOB, I HAVE MY HEALTH, I HAVE A HUSBAND AND CHILDREN I LOVE.
BUT IT COMES ANYWAY. AND I SEE HOW CRUEL AND UGLY LIFE IS, AND I FEEL LIKE A SCAB OF BLOOD, LIKE A DIRTY PUDDLE IN THE STREET.
I LOOK INTO OTHER PEOPLE'S EYES AND THAT SAME THIN NOTHINGNESS LOOKS BACK AND WE CAN'T REACH OUT TO EACH OTHER.
AND IT GETS LOUDER, AND DARKER, AND HEAVIER. AND IT PUSHES DOWN ON ME, AND IT HURTS.
DON'T LOSE HOPE.
I KNOW HOW YOU FEEL. I KNOW LIFE CAN SEEM BLACK SOMETIMES.
BUT NOT SINCE I WENT GLUTEN FREE.
GLUTEN FREE?
IT TURNS OUT MY DEPRESSION WAS REALLY A FORM OF WHEAT ALLERGY.
udi's
GLUTEN FREE FOODS

END

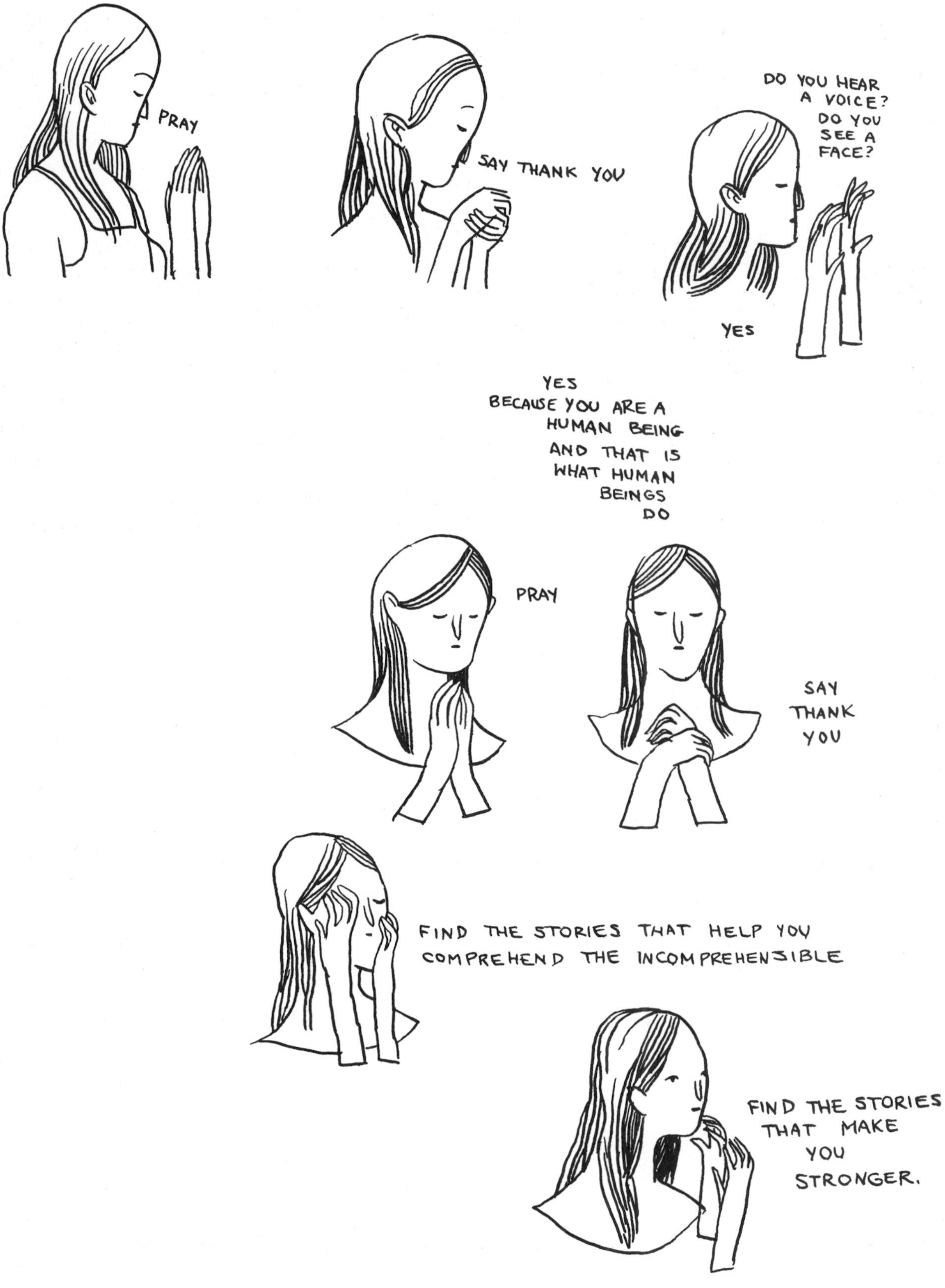
PRAY
SAY THANK YOU
DO YOU HEAR A VOICE? DO YOU SEE A FACE?
YES
YES BECAUSE YOU ARE A HUMAN BEING AND THAT IS WHAT HUMAN BEINGS DO
PRAY
SAY THANK YOU
FIND THE STORIES THAT HELP YOU COMPREHEND THE INCOMPREHENSIBLE
FIND THE STORIES THAT MAKE YOU STRONGER.

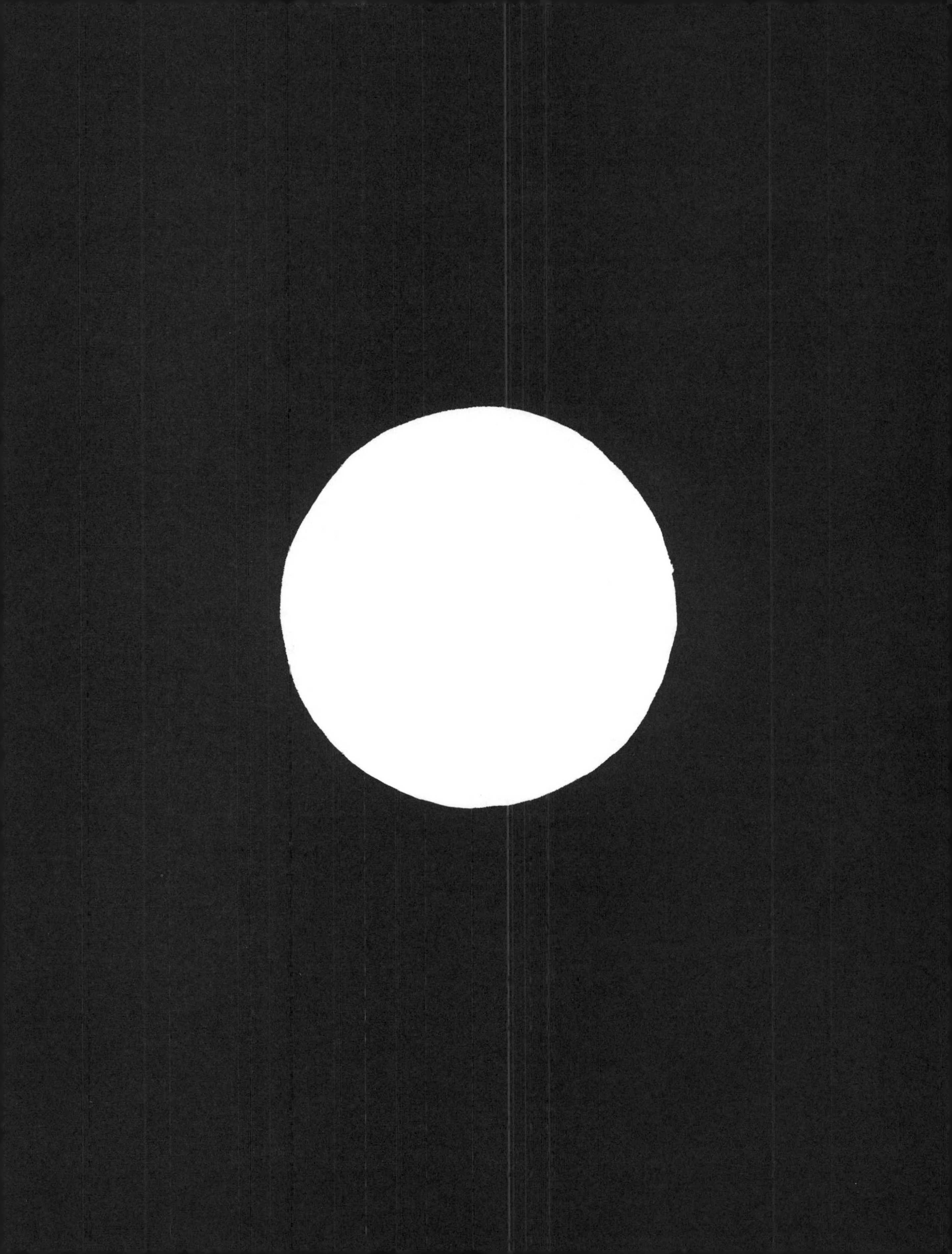

IN 2006 I TOOK A GREYHOUND FROM GEORGIA TO LOS ANGELES

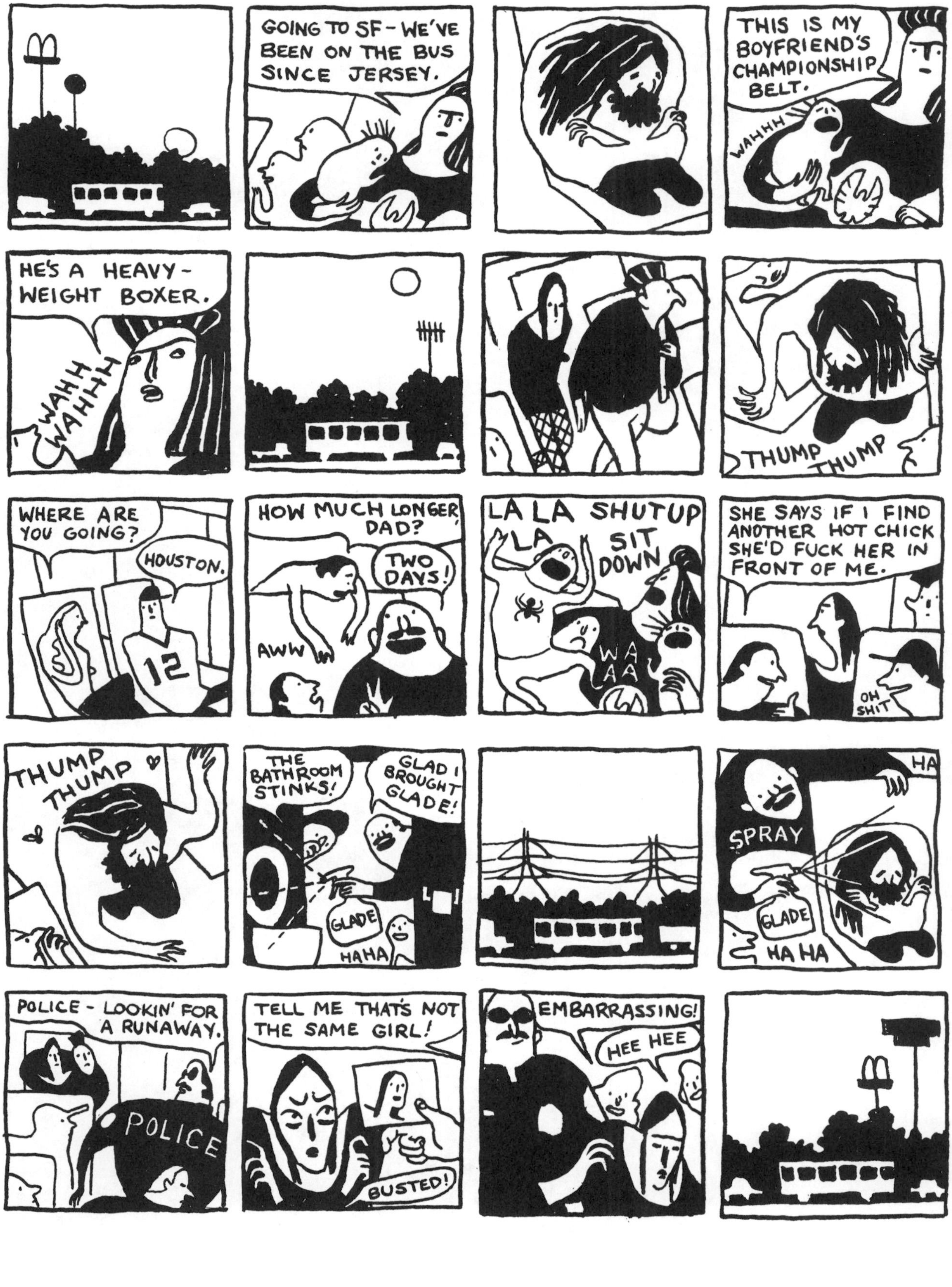
GOING TO SF - WE'VE BEEN ON THE BUS SINCE JERSEY.
THIS IS MY BOYFRIEND'S CHAMPIONSHIP BELT.
WAHHH
HE'S A HEAVY-WEIGHT BOXER.
WAHH WAHHH
THUMP THUMP
WHERE ARE YOU GOING?
HOUSTON.
12
HOW MUCH LONGER DAD?
TWO DAYS!
AWW
LA LA LA
SHUTUP SIT DOWN
WA AA
SHE SAYS IF I FIND ANOTHER HOT CHICK SHE'D FUCK HER IN FRONT OF ME.
OH SHIT
THUMP THUMP
THE BATHROOM STINKS!
GLAD I BROUGHT GLADE!
GLADE
HAHA
HA
SPRAY
GLADE
HA HA
POLICE - LOOKIN' FOR A RUNAWAY.
POLICE
TELL ME THAT'S NOT THE SAME GIRL!
BUSTED!
EMBARRASSING!
HEE HEE

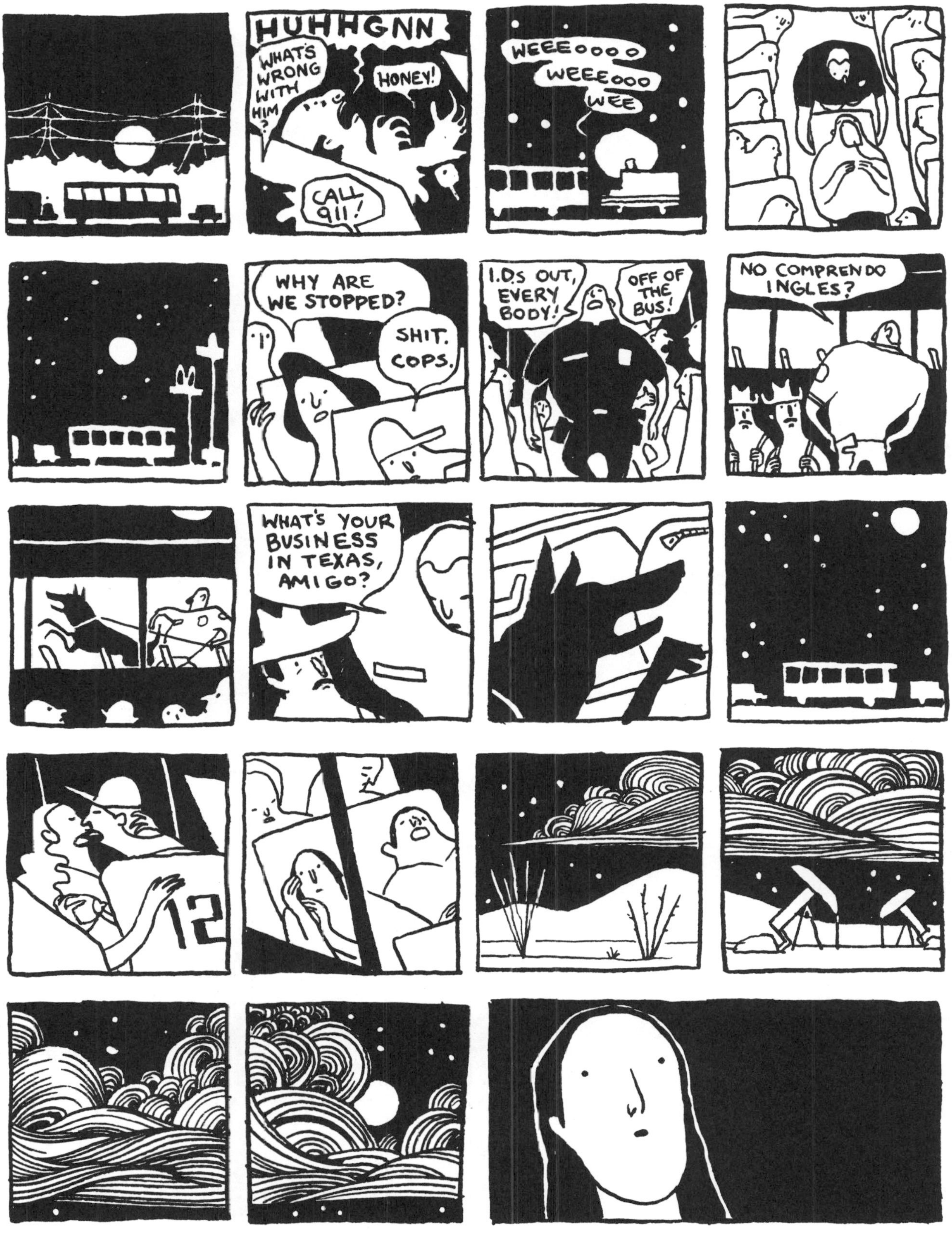
HUHHGNN
WHAT'S WRONG WITH HIM?
HONEY!
CALL 911!
WEEEoooo
WEEEooo
WEE
WHY ARE WE STOPPED?
SHIT. COPS.
I.D.s OUT, EVERY BODY!
OFF OF THE BUS!
NO COMPRENDO INGLES?
WHAT'S YOUR BUSINESS IN TEXAS, AMIGO?
12

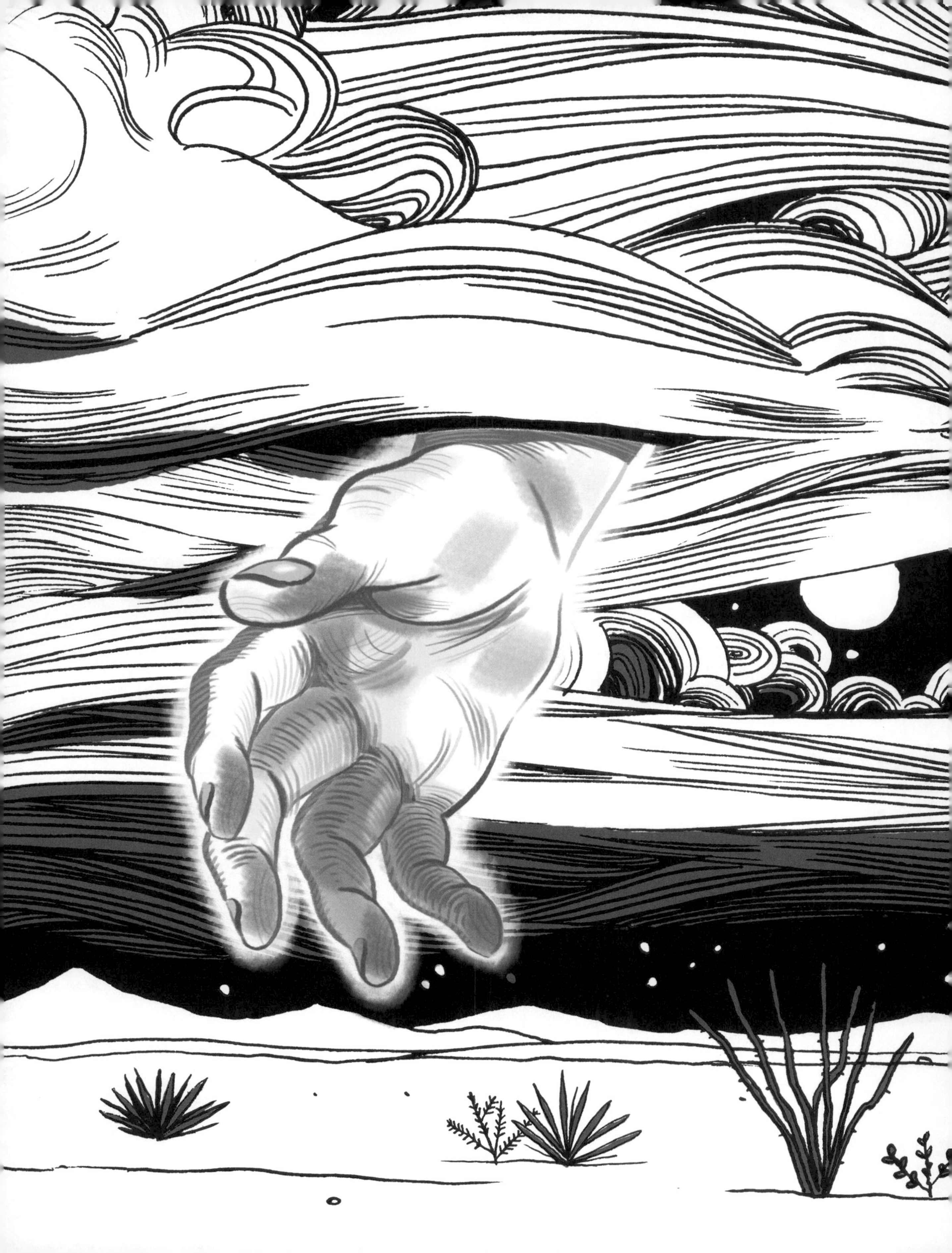

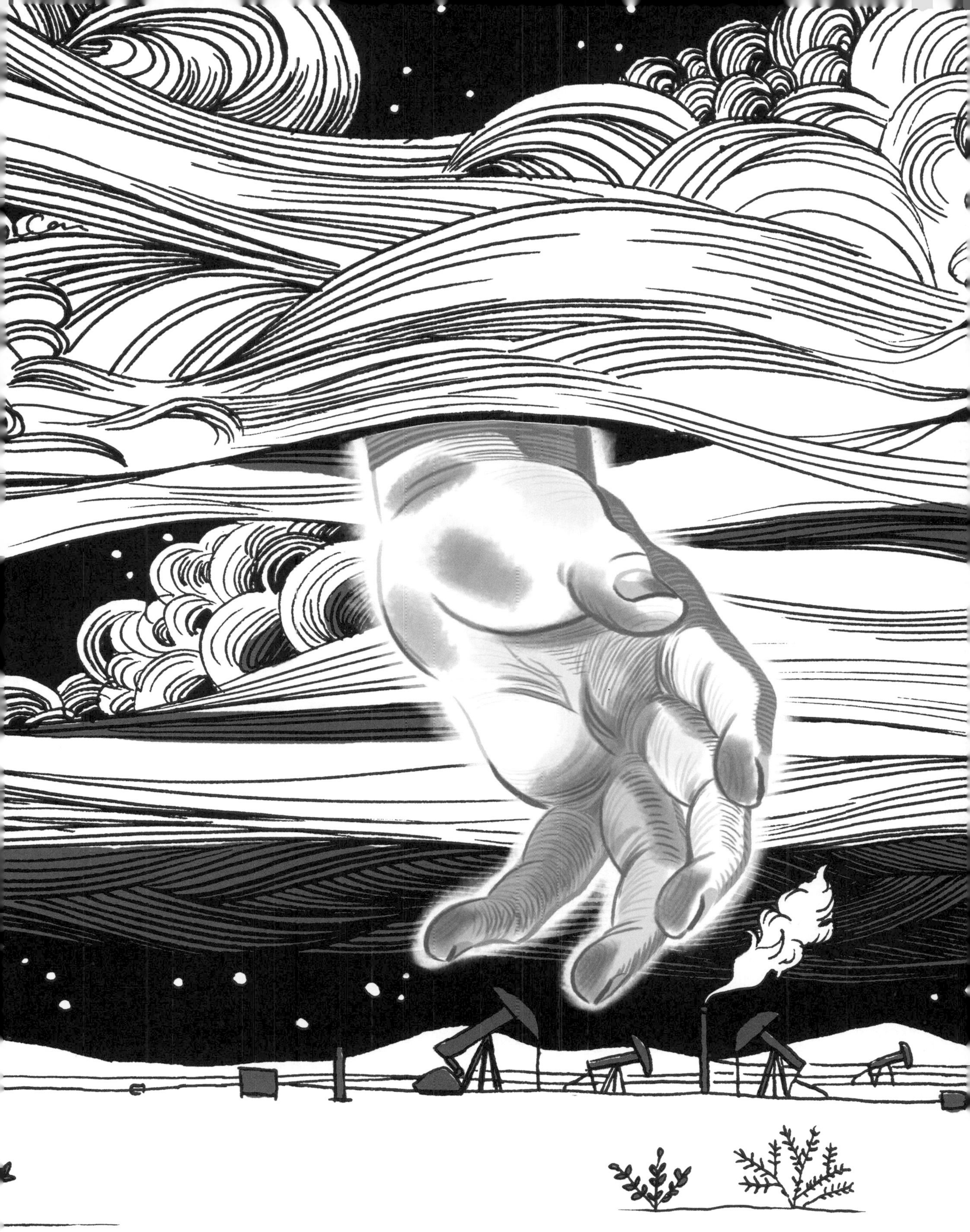

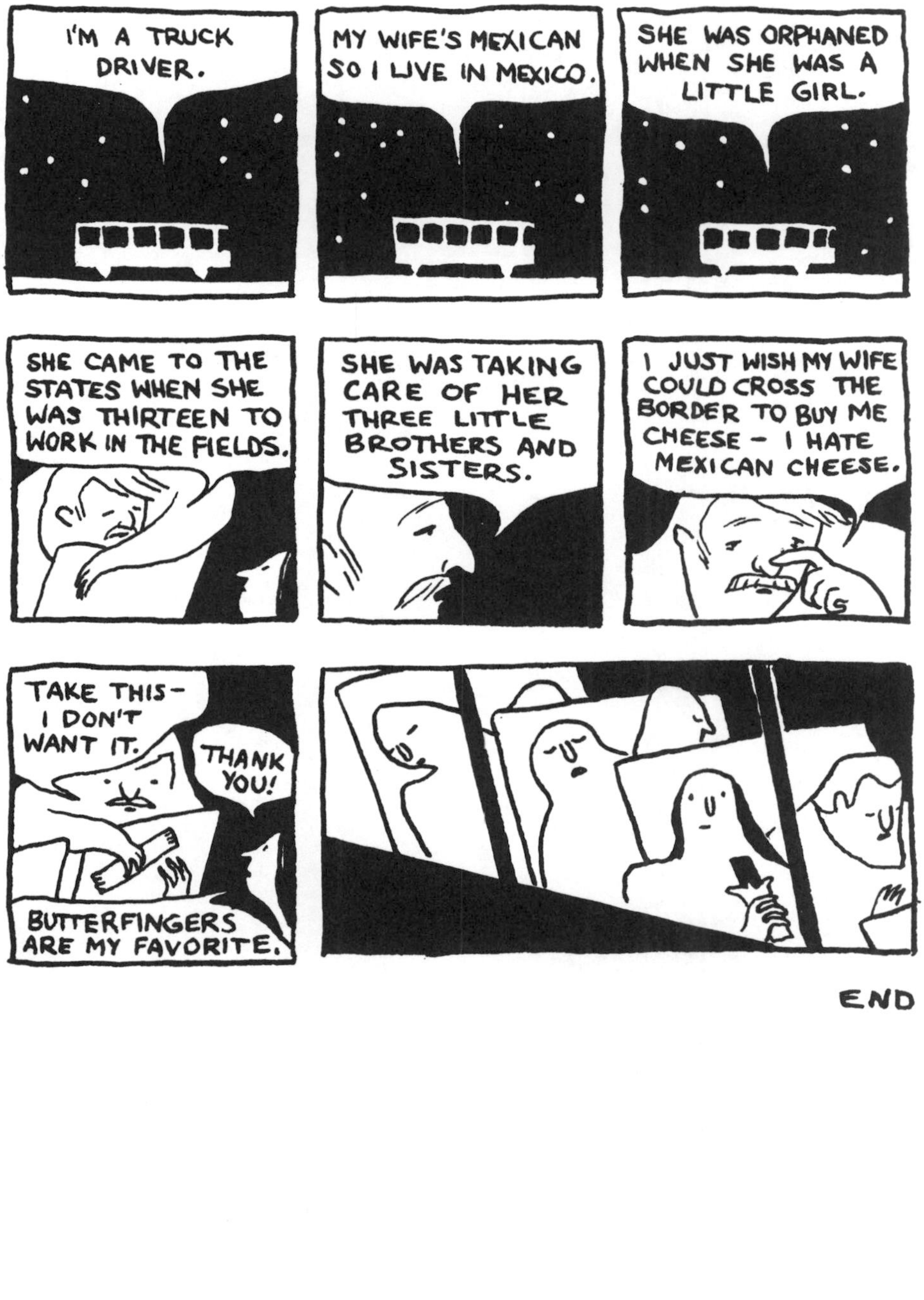
I'M A TRUCK DRIVER.
MY WIFE'S MEXICAN SO I LIVE IN MEXICO.
SHE WAS ORPHANED WHEN SHE WAS A LITTLE GIRL.
SHE CAME TO THE STATES WHEN SHE WAS THIRTEEN TO WORK IN THE FIELDS.
SHE WAS TAKING CARE OF HER THREE LITTLE BROTHERS AND SISTERS.
I JUST WISH MY WIFE COULD CROSS THE BORDER TO BUY ME CHEESE - I HATE MEXICAN CHEESE.
TAKE THIS- I DON'T WANT IT.
THANK YOU!
BUTTERFINGERS ARE MY FAVORITE.
END

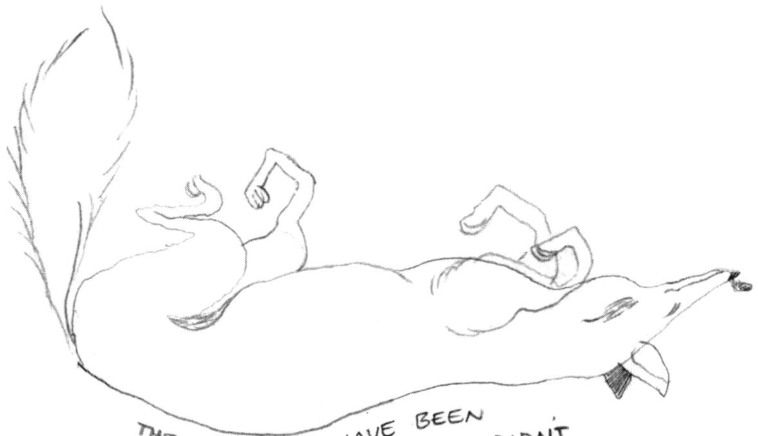

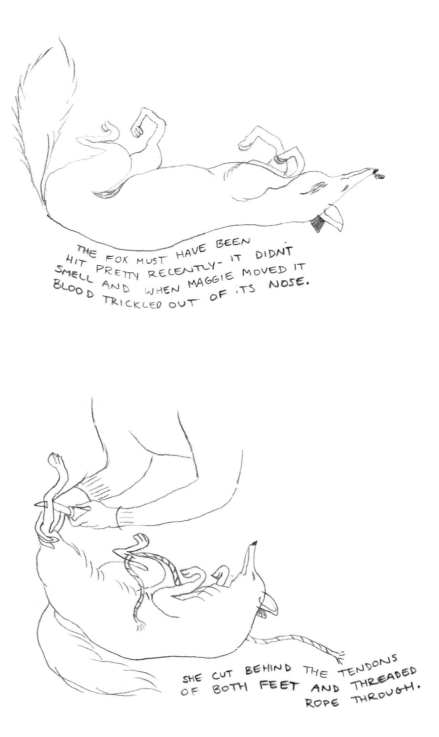

THE FOX MUST HAVE BEEN
HIT PRETTY RECENTLY- IT DIDN'T
SMELL AND WHEN MAGGIE MOVED IT
BLOOD TRICKLED OUT OF ITS NOSE.

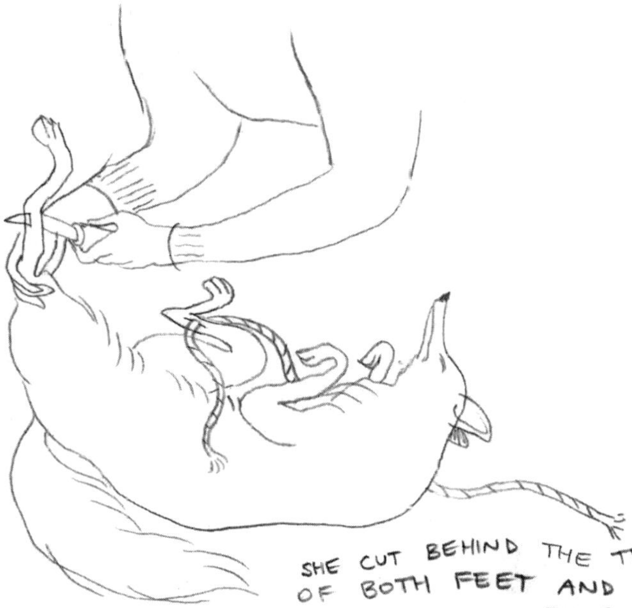

SHE CUT BEHIND THE TENDONS
OF BOTH FEET AND THREADED
ROPE THROUGH.

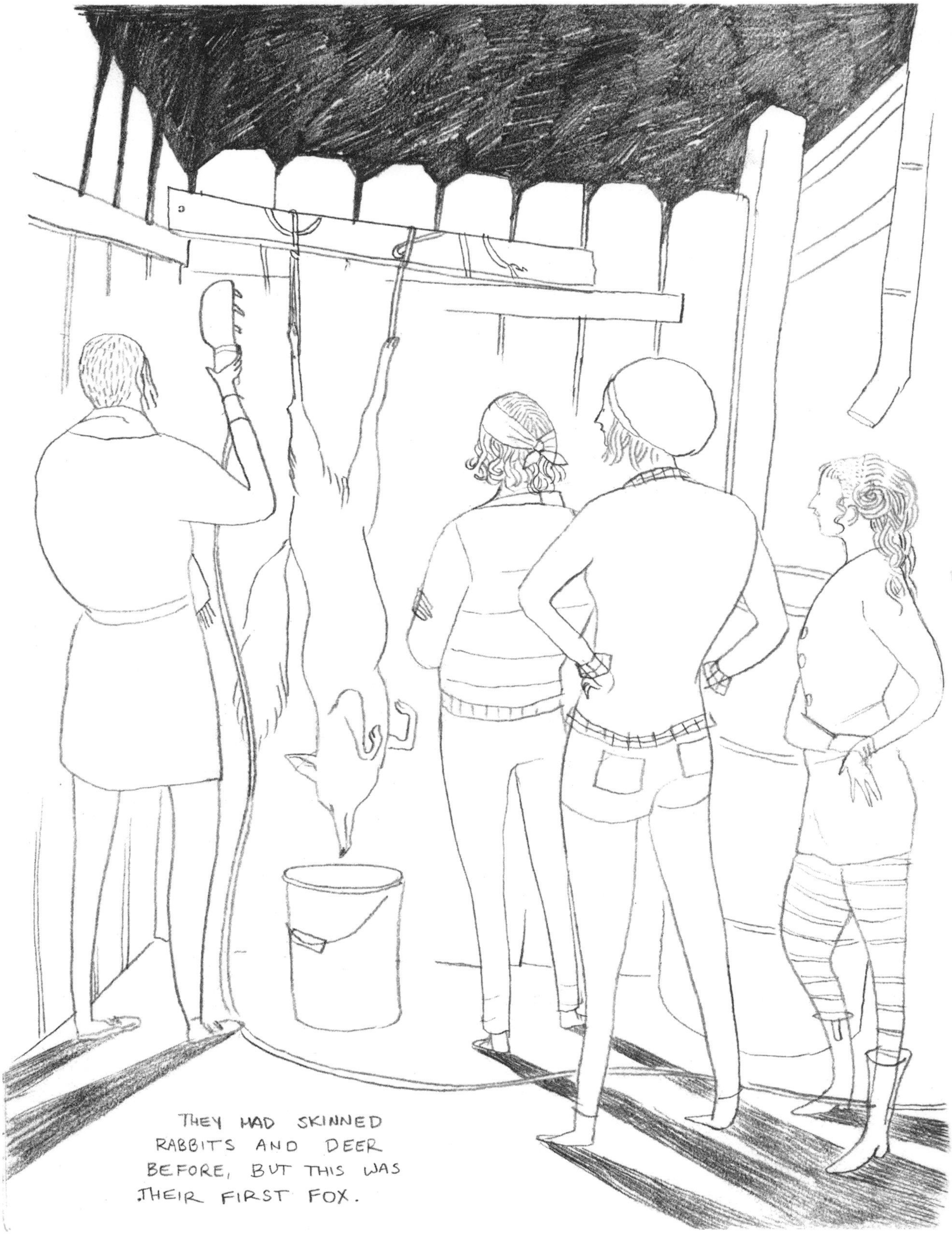
THEY HAD SKINNED RABBITS AND DEER BEFORE, BUT THIS WAS THEIR FIRST FOX.

FIRST MAGGIE
CUT RINGS
AROUND EACH
FOOT, DOWN
THE BACKS
OF THE LEGS,
AND AROUND
THE VENT.

HE SMELLED
STRONG NOW,
UP CLOSE,
BUT IT WAS
THE STINK
OF HIS
GLANDS,
NOT ROT
OR BOWELS.

THEY
PEELED
AWAY THE
SKIN ON
THE LEGS,
SHOWING
DARK RED,
GLISTENING
MUSCLE.

THERE WAS AN UGLY
HUGE GASH ON HIS
CROTCH THAT WAS
HARD TO LOOK AT.

BUT THE CLEAN FAT LEG MUSCLES WEREN'T HARD TO LOOK AT AT ALL.

YOU CAN TELL THEY'D BE GOOD TO EAT

LAURA SKINNED AS FAR UP THE TAIL AS SHE COULD & THEN CUT IT BETWEEN TWO BONES.

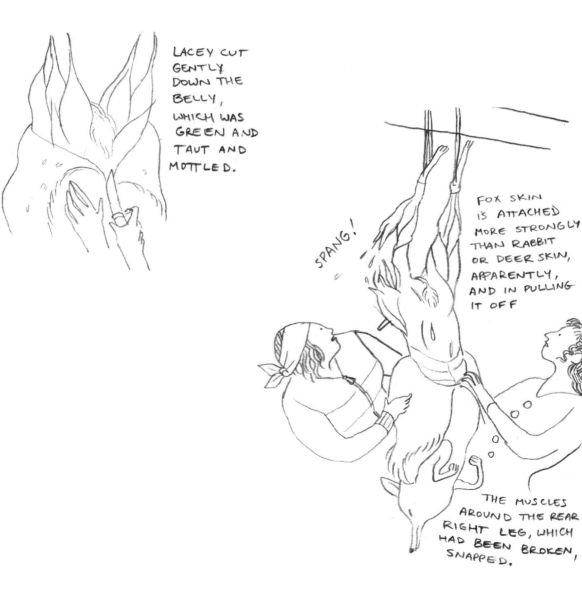

LACEY CUT
GENTLY
DOWN THE
BELLY,
WHICH WAS
GREEN AND
TAUT AND
MOTTLED.

SPANG!

FOX SKIN
IS ATTACHED
MORE STRONGLY
THAN RABBIT
OR DEER SKIN,
APPARENTLY,
AND IN PULLING
IT OFF

THE MUSCLES
AROUND THE REAR
RIGHT LEG, WHICH
HAD BEEN BROKEN,
SNAPPED.

WITHOUT HIS FUR THE FOX'S MUSCLES AND BODY LOOKED LIKE A MONKEY OR A LITTLE MAN.

NOW THEY WERE TO THE HEAD. THE NECK WAS VERY LONG AND THE SKIN WAS VERY THICK.

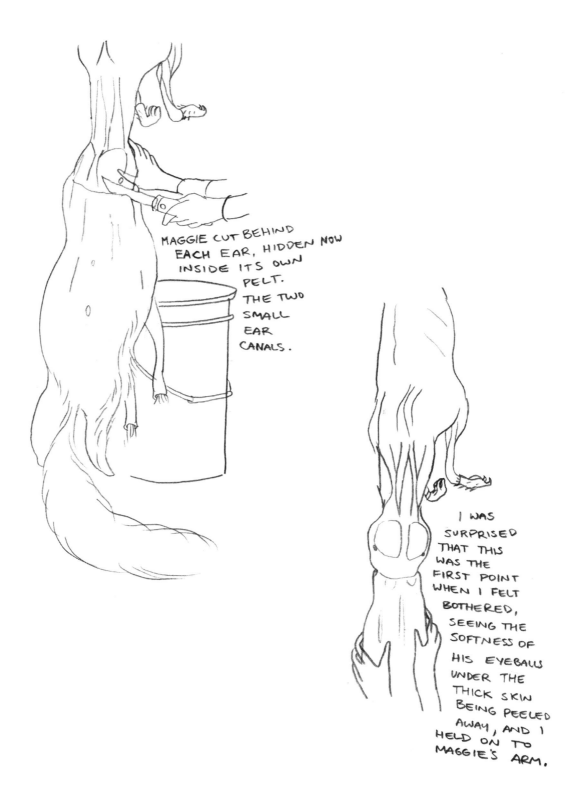

MAGGIE CUT BEHIND
EACH EAR, HIDDEN NOW
INSIDE ITS OWN
PELT.
THE TWO
SMALL
EAR
CANALS.

I WAS
SURPRISED
THAT THIS
WAS THE
FIRST POINT
WHEN I FELT
BOTHERED,
SEEING THE
SOFTNESS OF
HIS EYEBALLS
UNDER THE
THICK SKIN
BEING PEELED
AWAY, AND I
HELD ON TO
MAGGIE'S ARM.

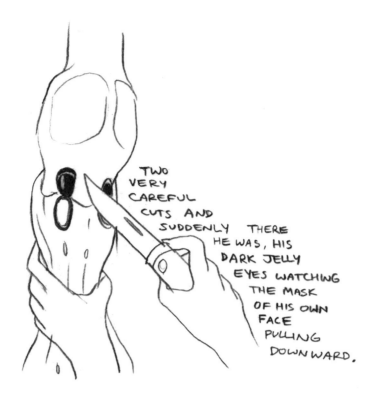

TWO VERY CAREFUL CUTS AND SUDDENLY THERE HE WAS, HIS DARK JELLY EYES WATCHING THE MASK OF HIS OWN FACE PULLING DOWNWARD.

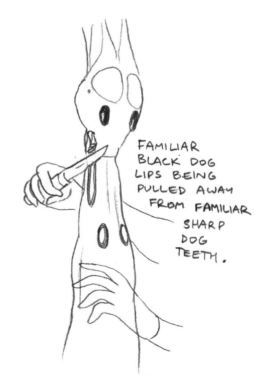

FAMILIAR BLACK DOG LIPS BEING PULLED AWAY FROM FAMILIAR SHARP DOG TEETH.

AND FOR
A MOMENT
THERE WERE
TWO FOXES,
KISSING

UNTIL
LACEY
CUT THROUGH
THE NOSE
CARTILAGE AND
THEY WERE
SEPARATED.

THE WOMAN FEELS
SADNESS

THE WOMAN FEELS
JOY

THE WOMAN FEELS
ANGER

THE WOMAN FEELS
FEAR

THE WOMAN FEELS

THE WOMAN FEELS
NOTHING

THE WOMAN

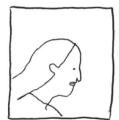

128

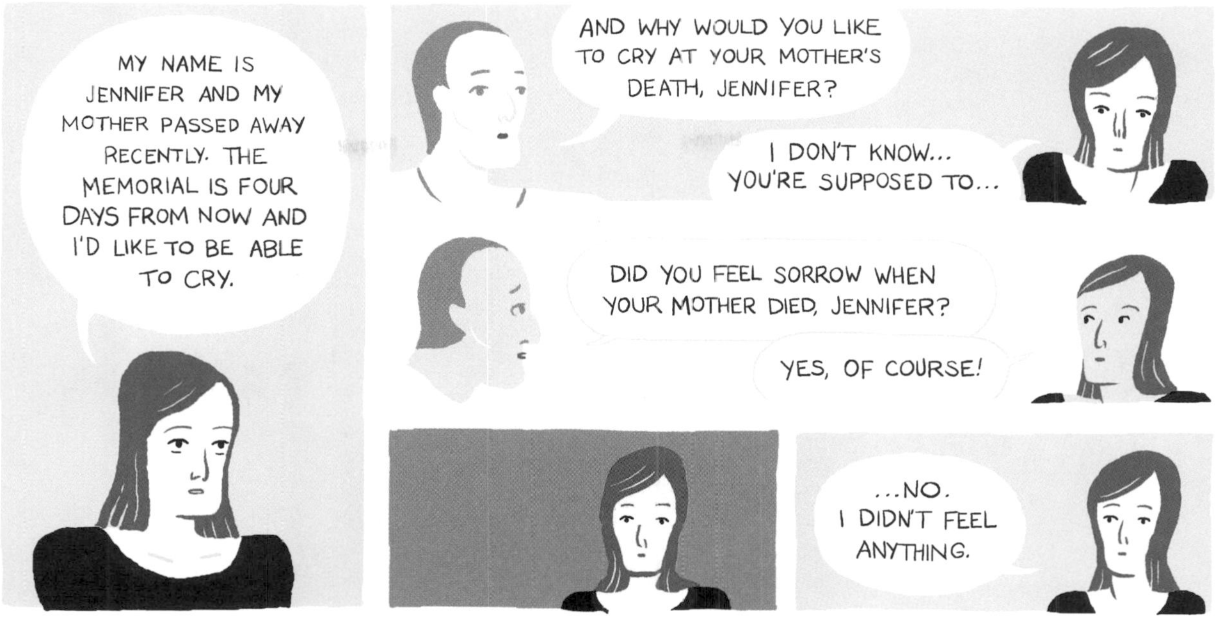
MY NAME IS JENNIFER AND MY MOTHER PASSED AWAY RECENTLY. THE MEMORIAL IS FOUR DAYS FROM NOW AND I'D LIKE TO BE ABLE TO CRY.
AND WHY WOULD YOU LIKE TO CRY AT YOUR MOTHER'S DEATH, JENNIFER?
I DON'T KNOW... YOU'RE SUPPOSED TO...
DID YOU FEEL SORROW WHEN YOUR MOTHER DIED, JENNIFER?
YES, OF COURSE!
...NO. I DIDN'T FEEL ANYTHING.

NO TEARS, NO SORROW

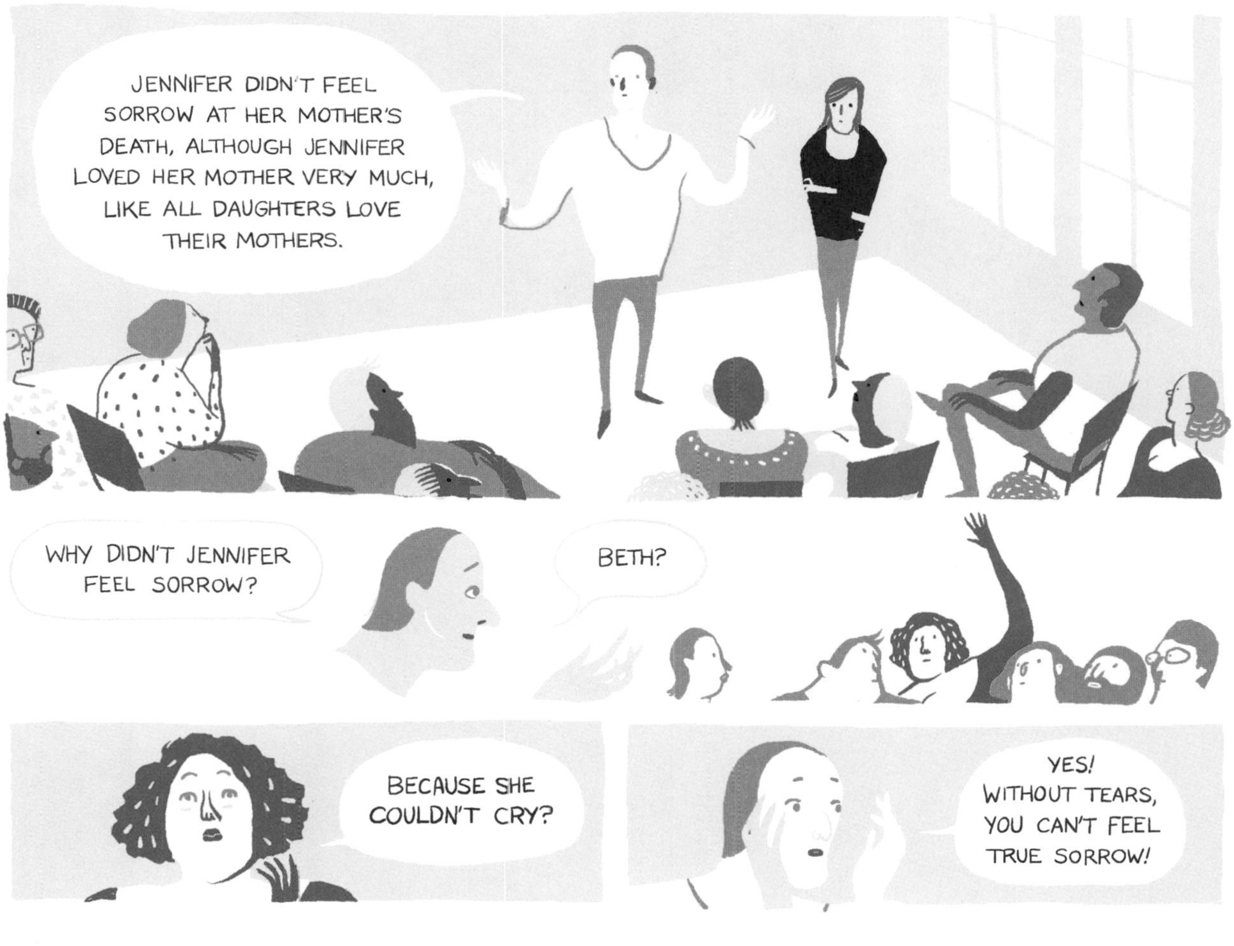
JENNIFER DIDN'T FEEL SORROW AT HER MOTHER'S DEATH, ALTHOUGH JENNIFER LOVED HER MOTHER VERY MUCH, LIKE ALL DAUGHTERS LOVE THEIR MOTHERS.
WHY DIDN'T JENNIFER FEEL SORROW?
BETH?
BECAUSE SHE COULDN'T CRY?
YES! WITHOUT TEARS, YOU CAN'T FEEL TRUE SORROW!

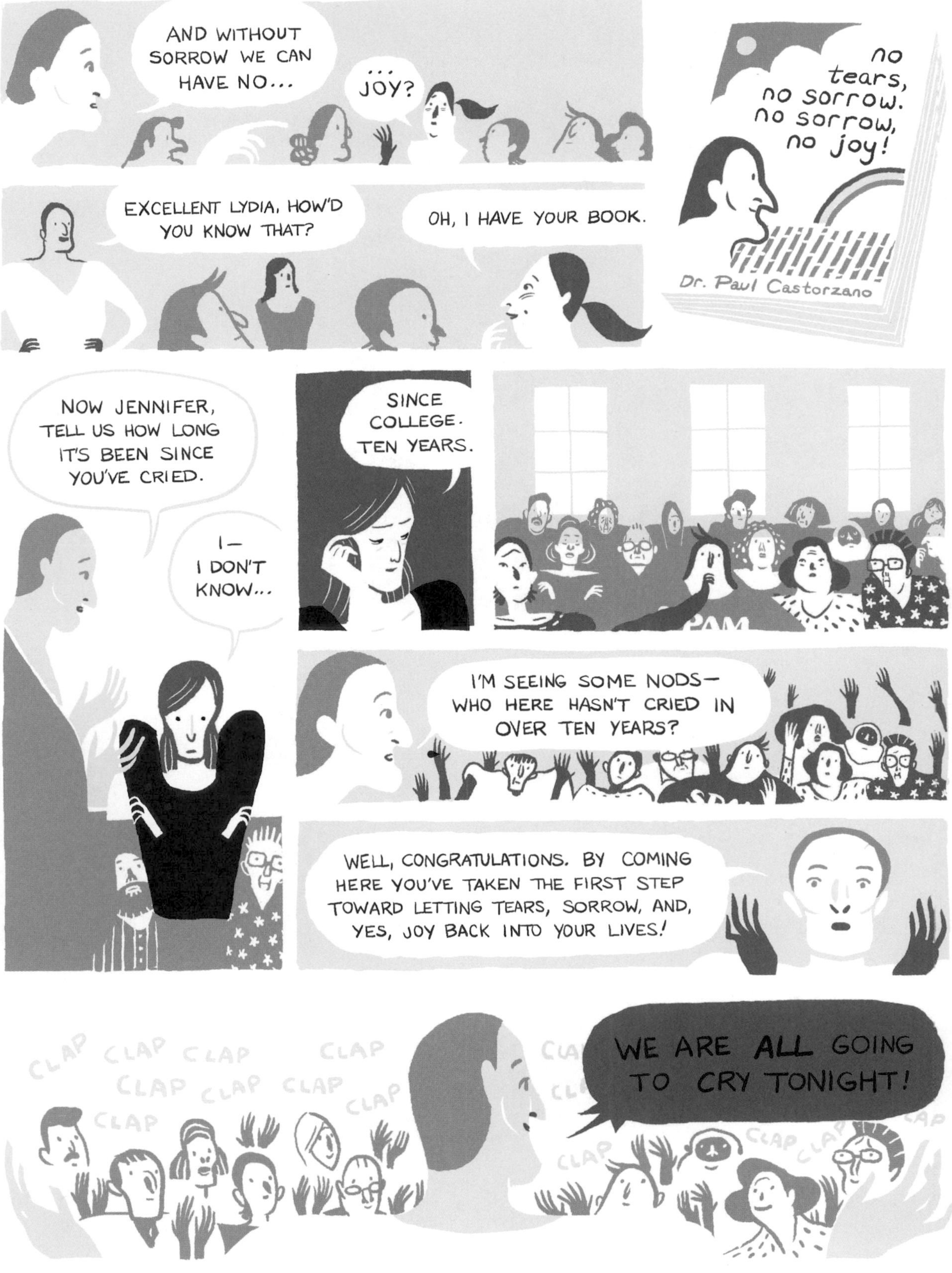
AND WITHOUT SORROW WE CAN HAVE NO...
... JOY?
no tears, no sorrow. no sorrow, no joy!
Dr. Paul Castorzano
EXCELLENT LYDIA, HOW'D YOU KNOW THAT?
OH, I HAVE YOUR BOOK.
NOW JENNIFER, TELL US HOW LONG IT'S BEEN SINCE YOU'VE CRIED.
I— I DON'T KNOW...
SINCE COLLEGE. TEN YEARS.
I'M SEEING SOME NODS— WHO HERE HASN'T CRIED IN OVER TEN YEARS?
WELL, CONGRATULATIONS. BY COMING HERE YOU'VE TAKEN THE FIRST STEP TOWARD LETTING TEARS, SORROW, AND, YES, JOY BACK INTO YOUR LIVES!
CLAP CLAP CLAP CLAP CLAP CLAP CLAP CLAP CLAP
WE ARE **ALL** GOING TO CRY TONIGHT!

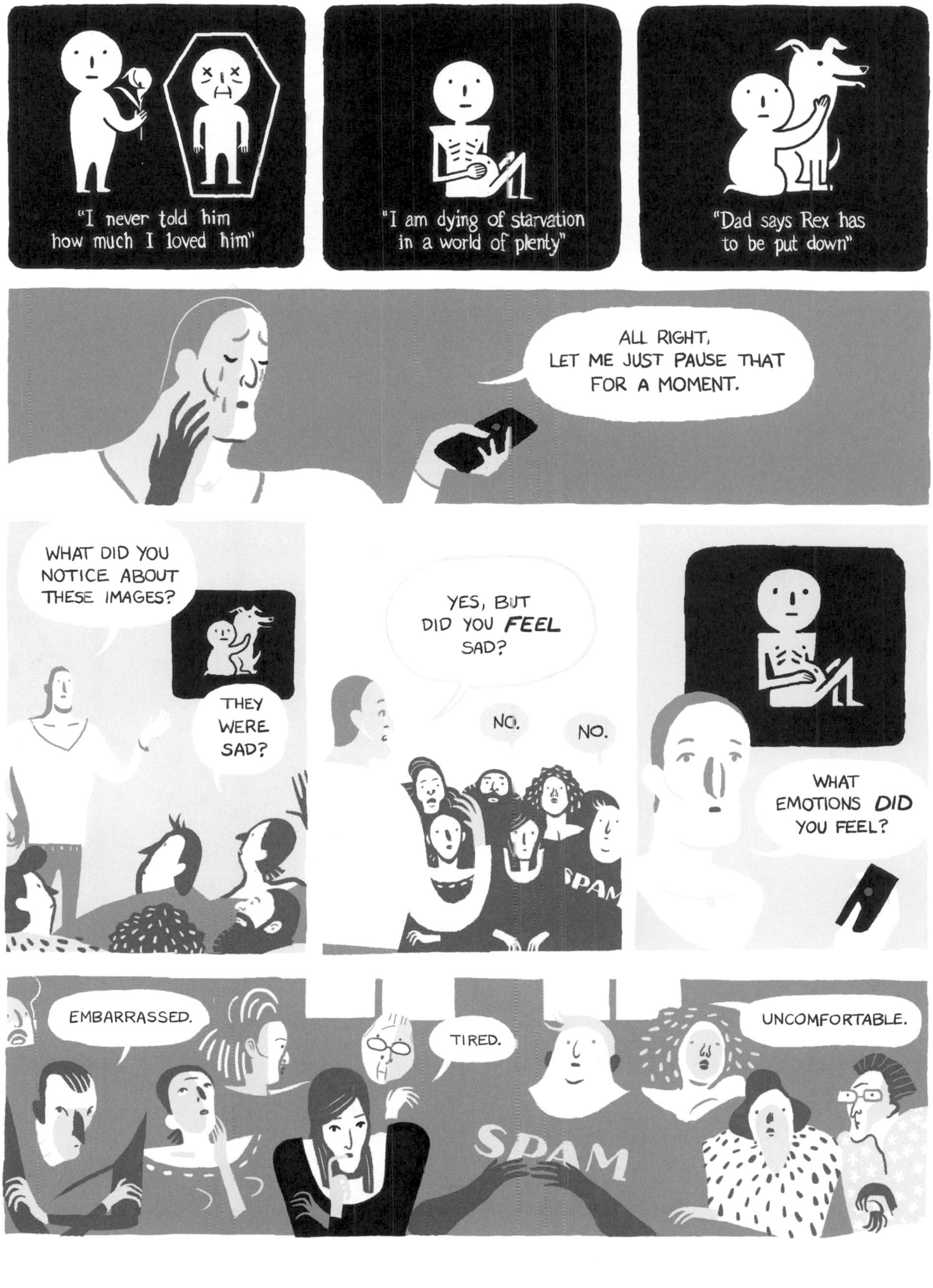
"I never told him how much I loved him"
"I am dying of starvation in a world of plenty"
"Dad says Rex has to be put down"
ALL RIGHT, LET ME JUST PAUSE THAT FOR A MOMENT.
WHAT DID YOU NOTICE ABOUT THESE IMAGES?
THEY WERE SAD?
YES, BUT DID YOU FEEL SAD?
NO.
NO.
SPAM
WHAT EMOTIONS DID YOU FEEL?
EMBARRASSED.
TIRED.
UNCOMFORTABLE.
SPAM

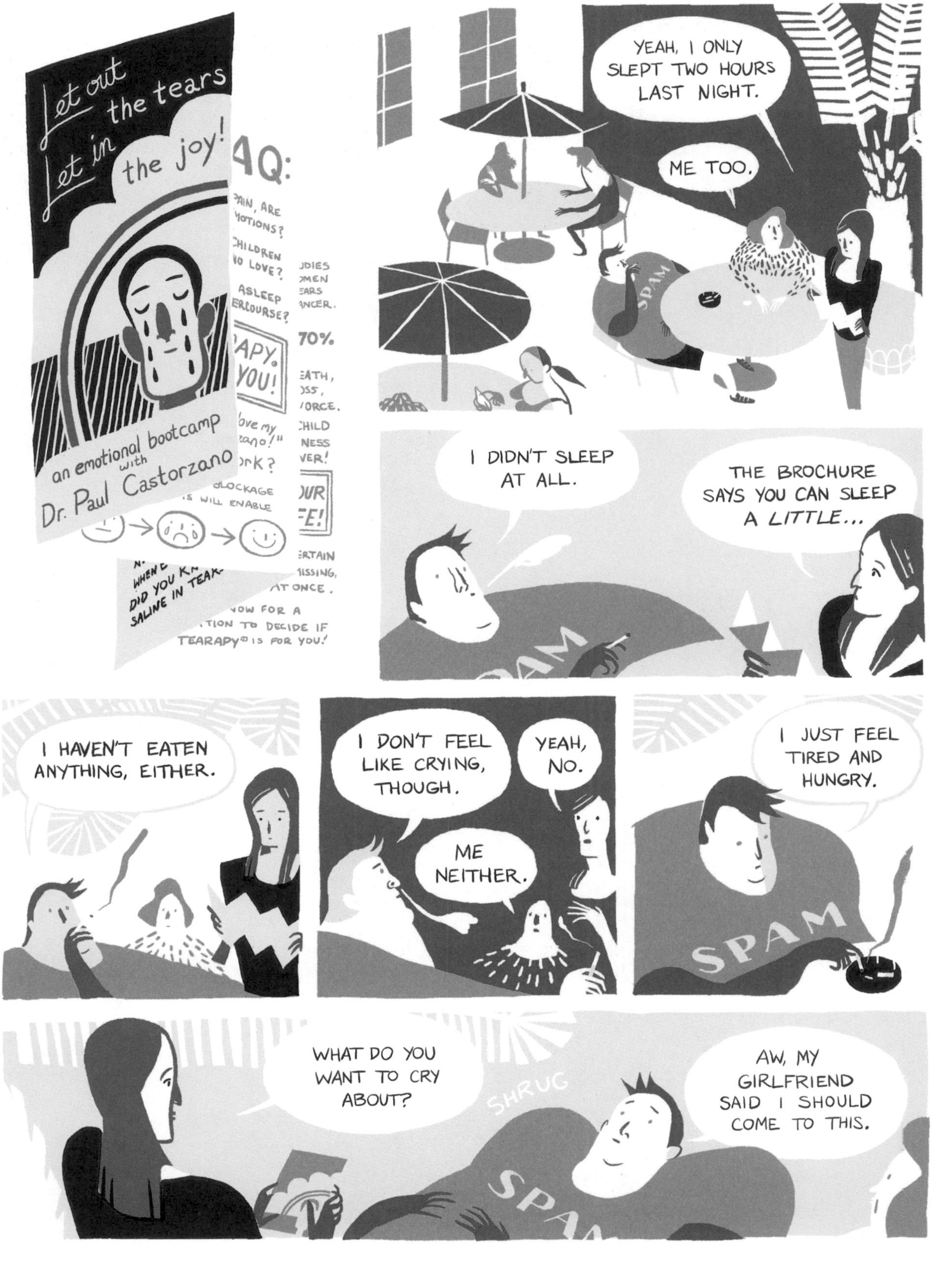
Let out the tears
Let in the joy!
an emotional bootcamp with
Dr. Paul Castorzano
YEAH, I ONLY SLEPT TWO HOURS LAST NIGHT.
ME TOO.
SPAM
I DIDN'T SLEEP AT ALL.
THE BROCHURE SAYS YOU CAN SLEEP A *LITTLE*...
I HAVEN'T EATEN ANYTHING, EITHER.
I DON'T FEEL LIKE CRYING, THOUGH.
YEAH, NO.
ME NEITHER.
I JUST FEEL TIRED AND HUNGRY.
SPAM
WHAT DO YOU WANT TO CRY ABOUT?
SHRUG
AW, MY GIRLFRIEND SAID I SHOULD COME TO THIS.

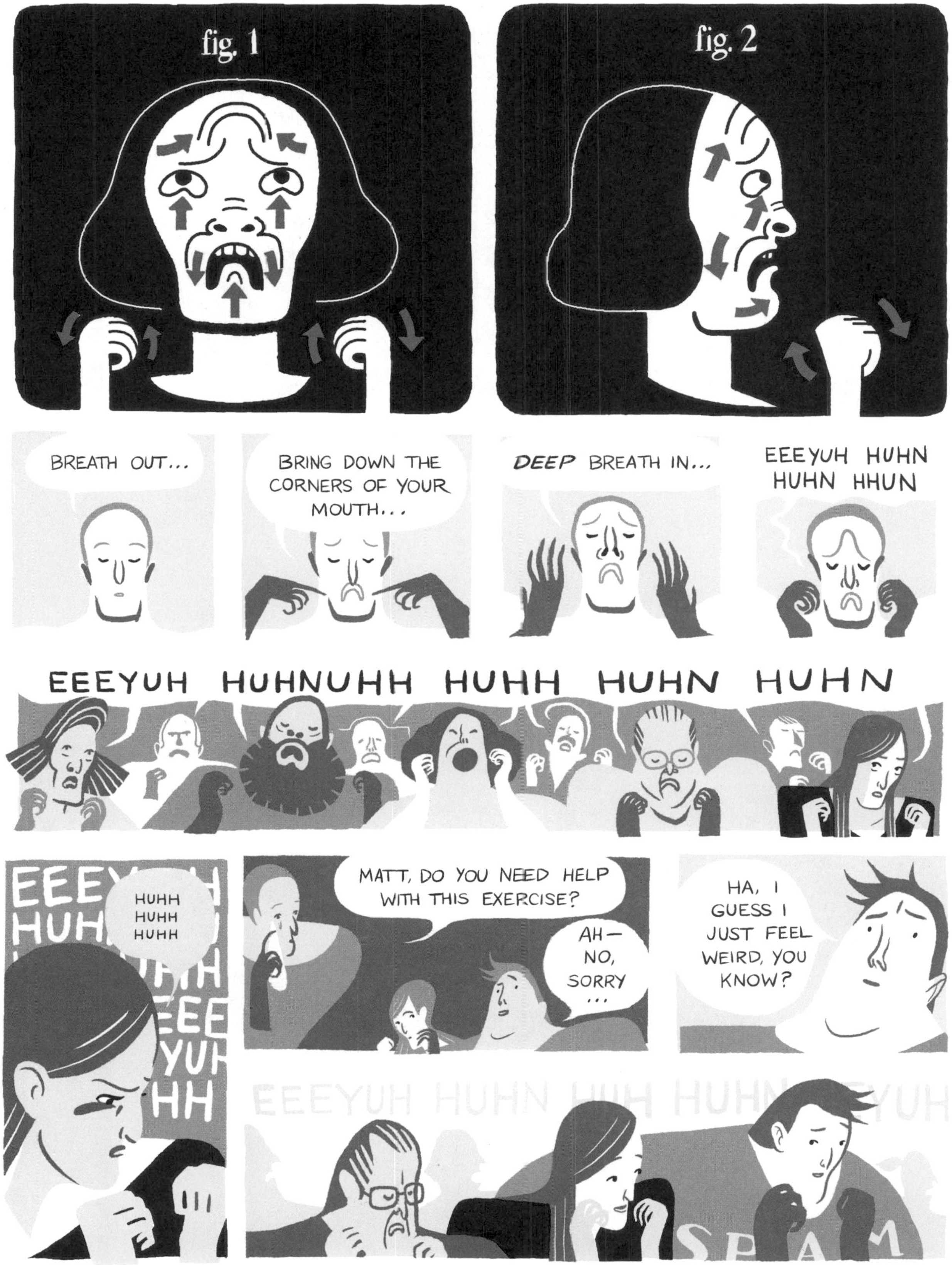
fig. 1
fig. 2
BREATH OUT...
BRING DOWN THE CORNERS OF YOUR MOUTH...
DEEP BREATH IN...
EEEYUH HUHN HUHN HHUN
EEEYUH HUHNUHH HUHH HUHN HUHN
HUHH HUHH HUHH
MATT, DO YOU NEED HELP WITH THIS EXERCISE?
AH— NO, SORRY ...
HA, I GUESS I JUST FEEL WEIRD, YOU KNOW?

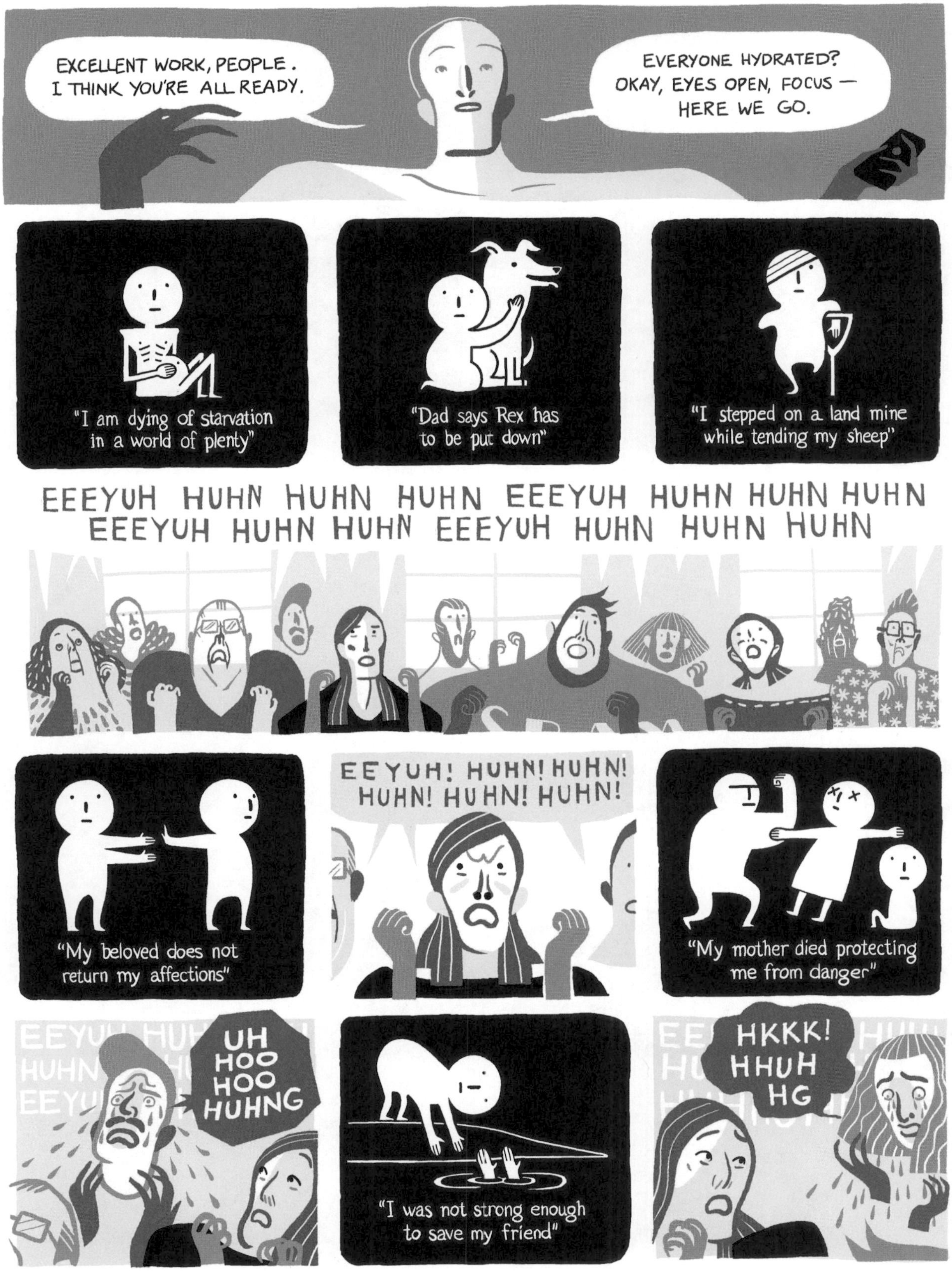

EXCELLENT WORK, PEOPLE. I THINK YOU'RE ALL READY.
EVERYONE HYDRATED? OKAY, EYES OPEN, FOCUS — HERE WE GO.
"I am dying of starvation in a world of plenty"
"Dad says Rex has to be put down"
"I stepped on a land mine while tending my sheep"
EEEYUH HUHN HUHN HUHN EEEYUH HUHN HUHN HUHN
EEEYUH HUHN HUHN EEEYUH HUHN HUHN HUHN
"My beloved does not return my affections"
EEYUH! HUHN! HUHN! HUHN! HUHN! HUHN!
"My mother died protecting me from danger"
UH HOO HOO HUHNG
"I was not strong enough to save my friend"
HKKK! HHUH HG

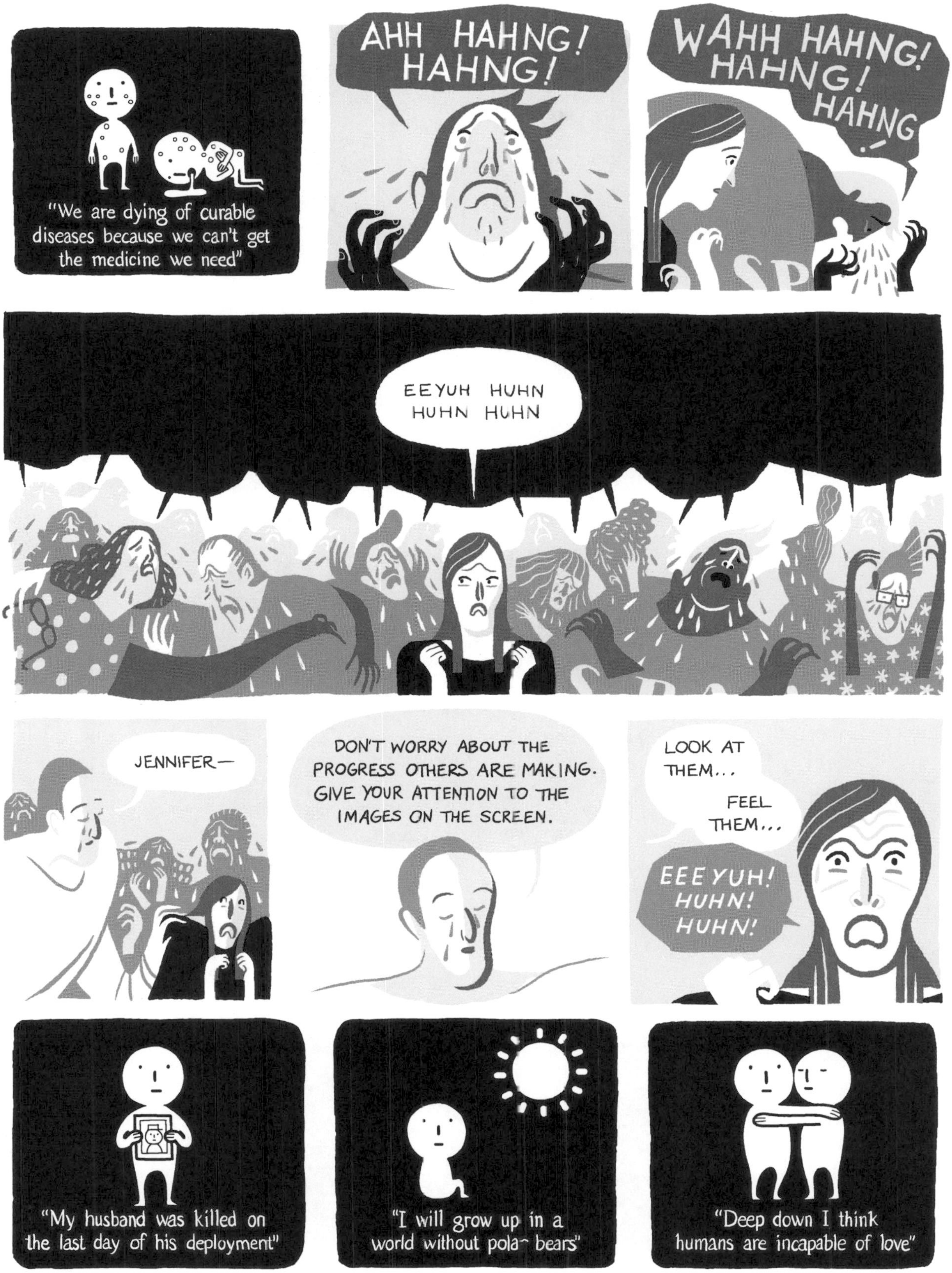
"We are dying of curable diseases because we can't get the medicine we need"
AHH HAHNG! HAHNG!
WAHH HAHNG! HAHNG! HAHNG!
EEYUH HUHN HUHN HUHN
JENNIFER—
DON'T WORRY ABOUT THE PROGRESS OTHERS ARE MAKING. GIVE YOUR ATTENTION TO THE IMAGES ON THE SCREEN.
LOOK AT THEM...
FEEL THEM...
EEEYUH! HUHN! HUHN!
"My husband was killed on the last day of his deployment"
"I will grow up in a world without pola~ bears"
"Deep down I think humans are incapable of love"

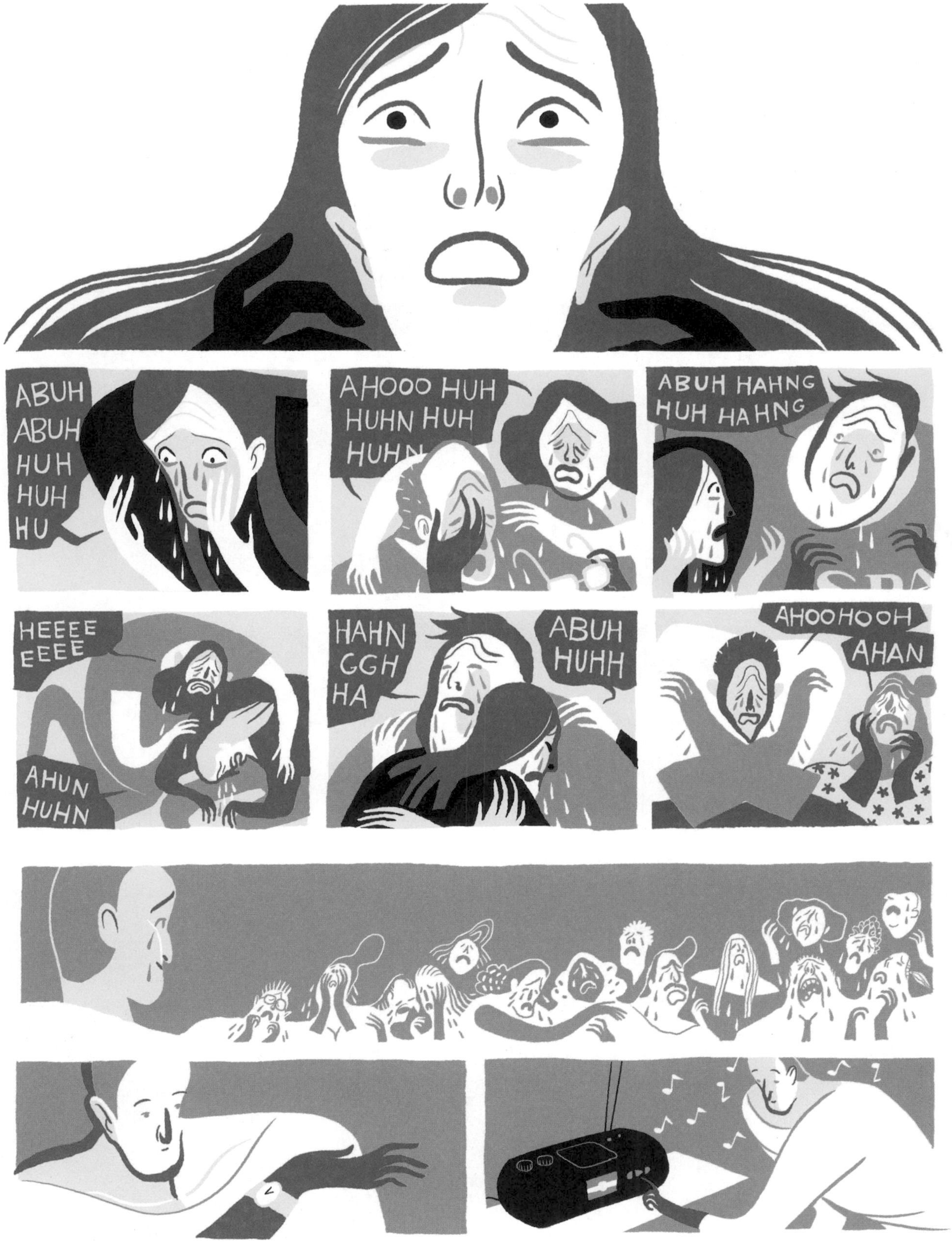
ABUH ABUH HUH HUH HU
AHOOO HUH HUHN HUH HUHN
ABUH HAHNG HUH HAHNG
HEEEE EEEE
AHUN HUHN
HAHN GGH HA
ABUH HUHH
AHOOHOOH
AHAN

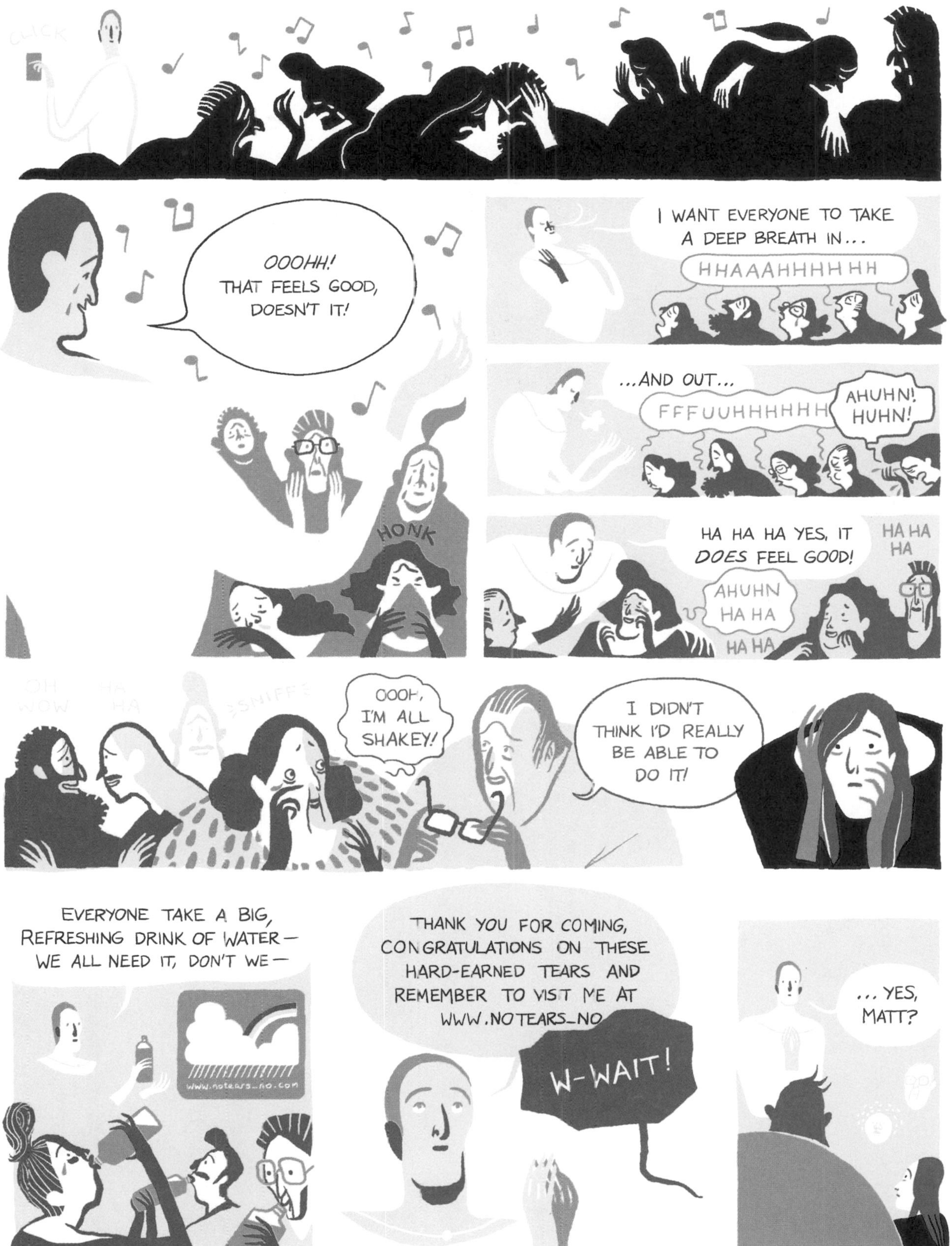
CLICK
OOOHH! THAT FEELS GOOD, DOESN'T IT!
HONK
I WANT EVERYONE TO TAKE A DEEP BREATH IN...
HHAAAHHHHHH
...AND OUT...
FFFUUHHHHHH
AHUHN! HUHN!
HA HA HA YES, IT DOES FEEL GOOD!
HA HA HA
AHUHN HA HA
HA HA
OH WOW
HA HA
SNIFF
OOOH, I'M ALL SHAKEY!
I DIDN'T THINK I'D REALLY BE ABLE TO DO IT!
EVERYONE TAKE A BIG, REFRESHING DRINK OF WATER— WE ALL NEED IT, DON'T WE—
www.notears_no.com
THANK YOU FOR COMING, CONGRATULATIONS ON THESE HARD-EARNED TEARS AND REMEMBER TO VISIT ME AT WWW.NOTEARS_NO
W-WAIT!
... YES, MATT?

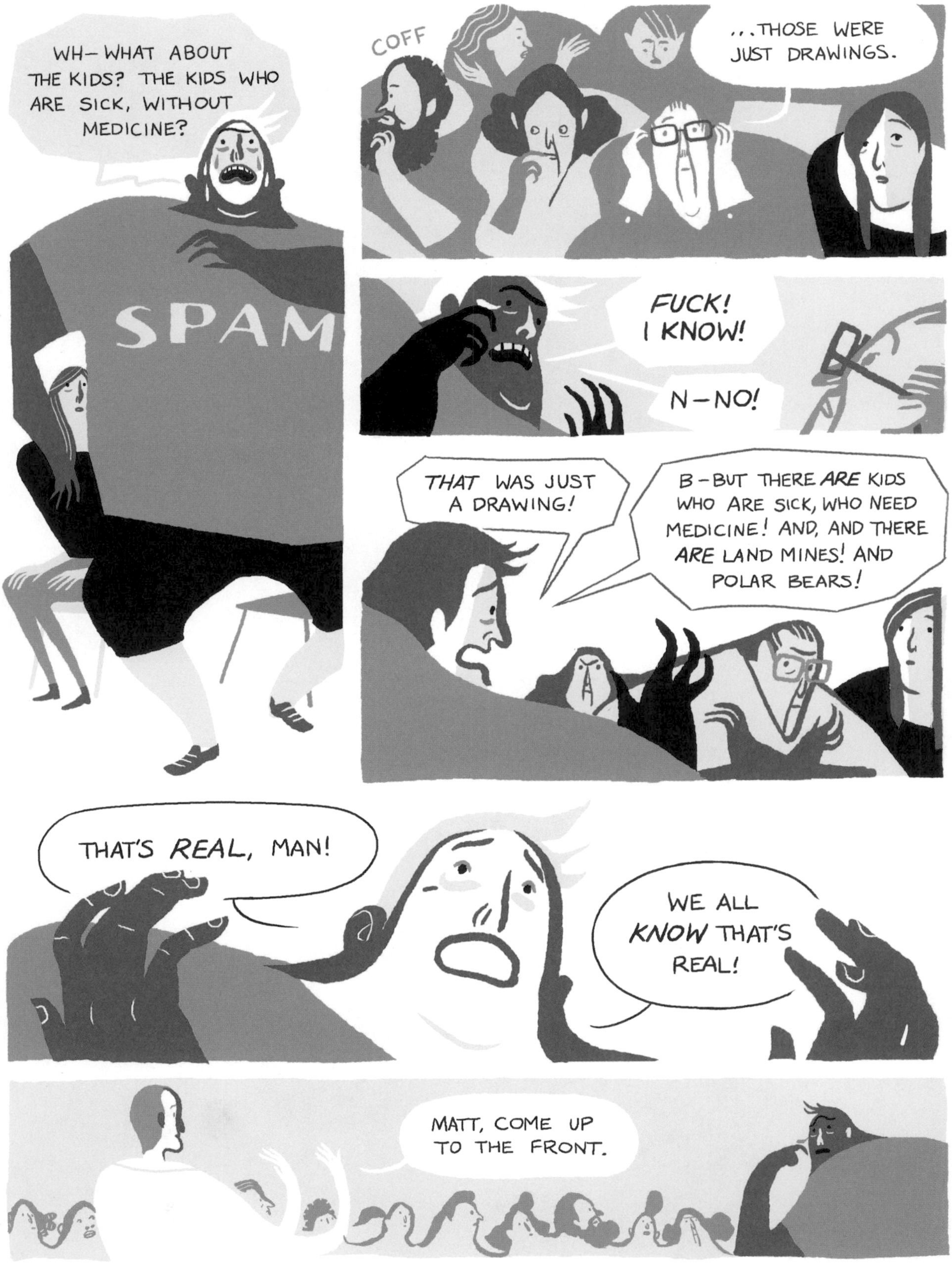
WH-WHAT ABOUT THE KIDS? THE KIDS WHO ARE SICK, WITHOUT MEDICINE?
SPAM
COFF
...THOSE WERE JUST DRAWINGS.
FUCK! I KNOW!
N-NO!
THAT WAS JUST A DRAWING!
B-BUT THERE ARE KIDS WHO ARE SICK, WHO NEED MEDICINE! AND, AND THERE ARE LAND MINES! AND POLAR BEARS!
THAT'S REAL, MAN!
WE ALL KNOW THAT'S REAL!
MATT, COME UP TO THE FRONT.

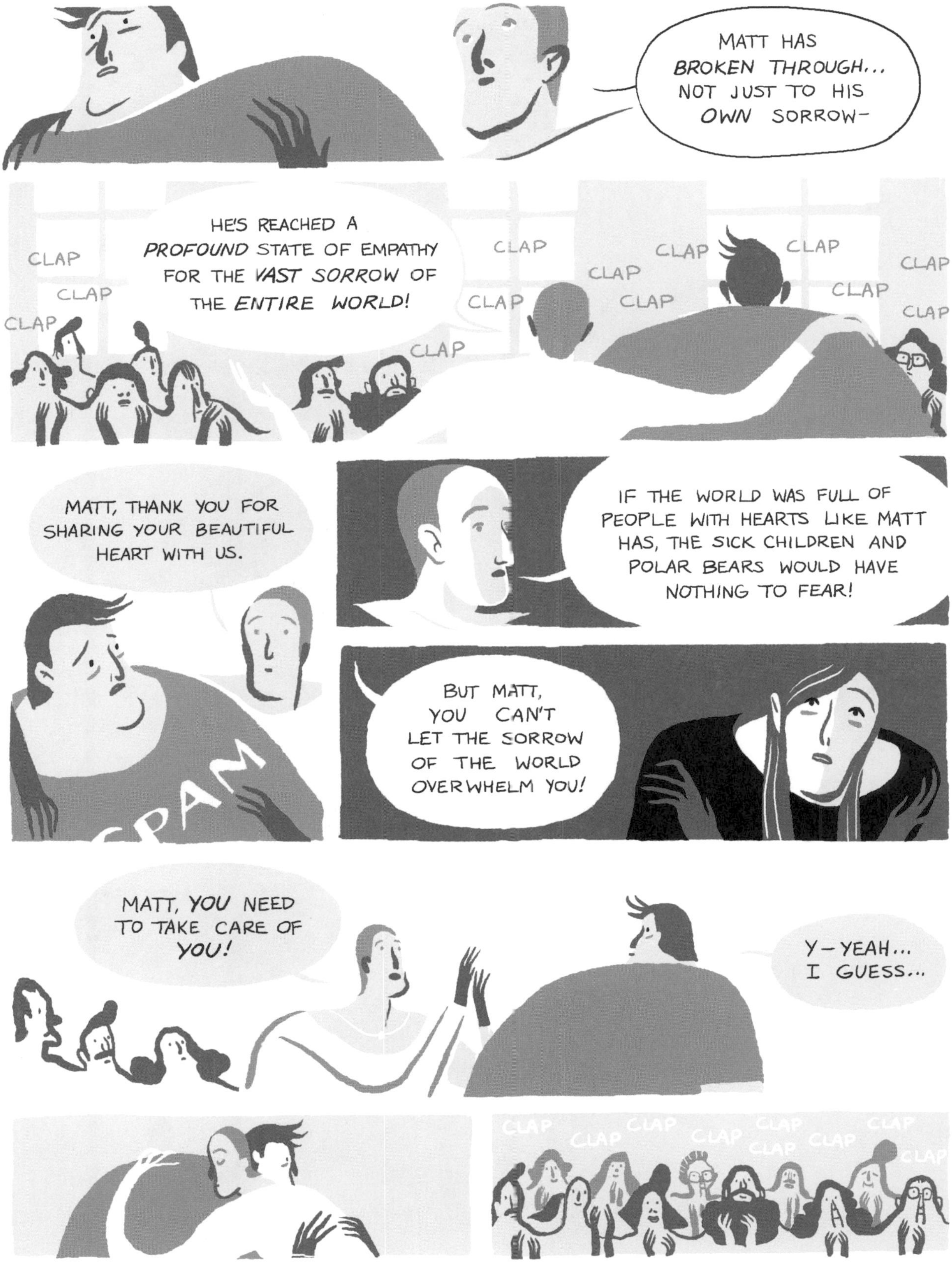
MATT HAS BROKEN THROUGH... NOT JUST TO HIS OWN SORROW-
HE'S REACHED A PROFOUND STATE OF EMPATHY FOR THE VAST SORROW OF THE ENTIRE WORLD!
CLAP CLAP CLAP CLAP CLAP CLAP CLAP CLAP CLAP CLAP CLAP CLAP
MATT, THANK YOU FOR SHARING YOUR BEAUTIFUL HEART WITH US.
IF THE WORLD WAS FULL OF PEOPLE WITH HEARTS LIKE MATT HAS, THE SICK CHILDREN AND POLAR BEARS WOULD HAVE NOTHING TO FEAR!
SPAM
BUT MATT, YOU CAN'T LET THE SORROW OF THE WORLD OVERWHELM YOU!
MATT, YOU NEED TO TAKE CARE OF YOU!
Y-YEAH... I GUESS...
CLAP CLAP CLAP CLAP CLAP CLAP CLAP CLAP CLAP

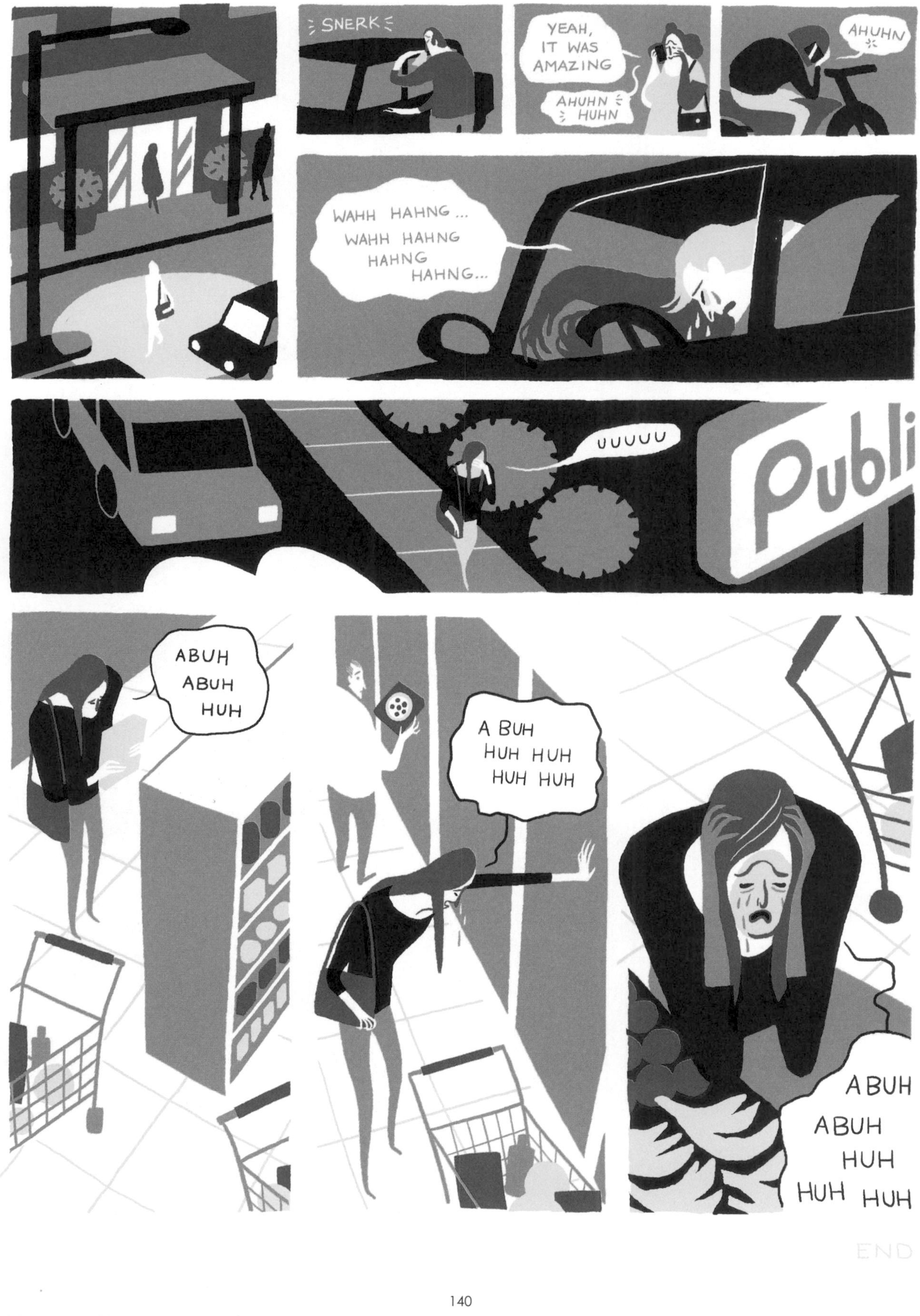
SNERK
YEAH, IT WAS AMAZING
AHUHN HUHN
AHUHN
WAHH HAHNG... WAHH HAHNG HAHNG HAHNG...
UUUUU
Publi
ABUH ABUH HUH
A BUH HUH HUH HUH HUH
ABUH ABUH HUH HUH HUH
END

9/26

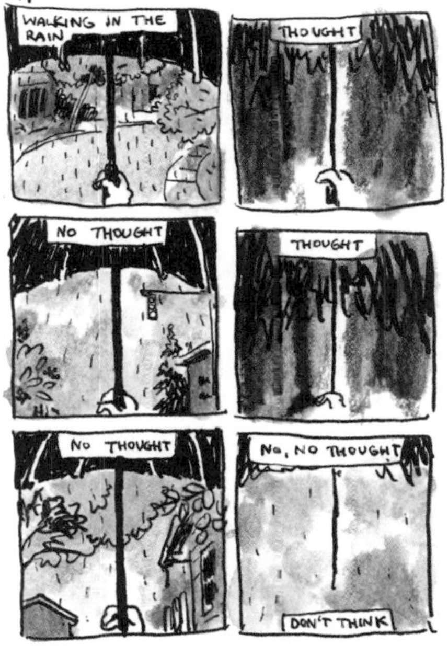
WALKING IN THE RAIN
THOUGHT
NO THOUGHT
THOUGHT
NO THOUGHT
NO, NO THOUGHT
DON'T THINK

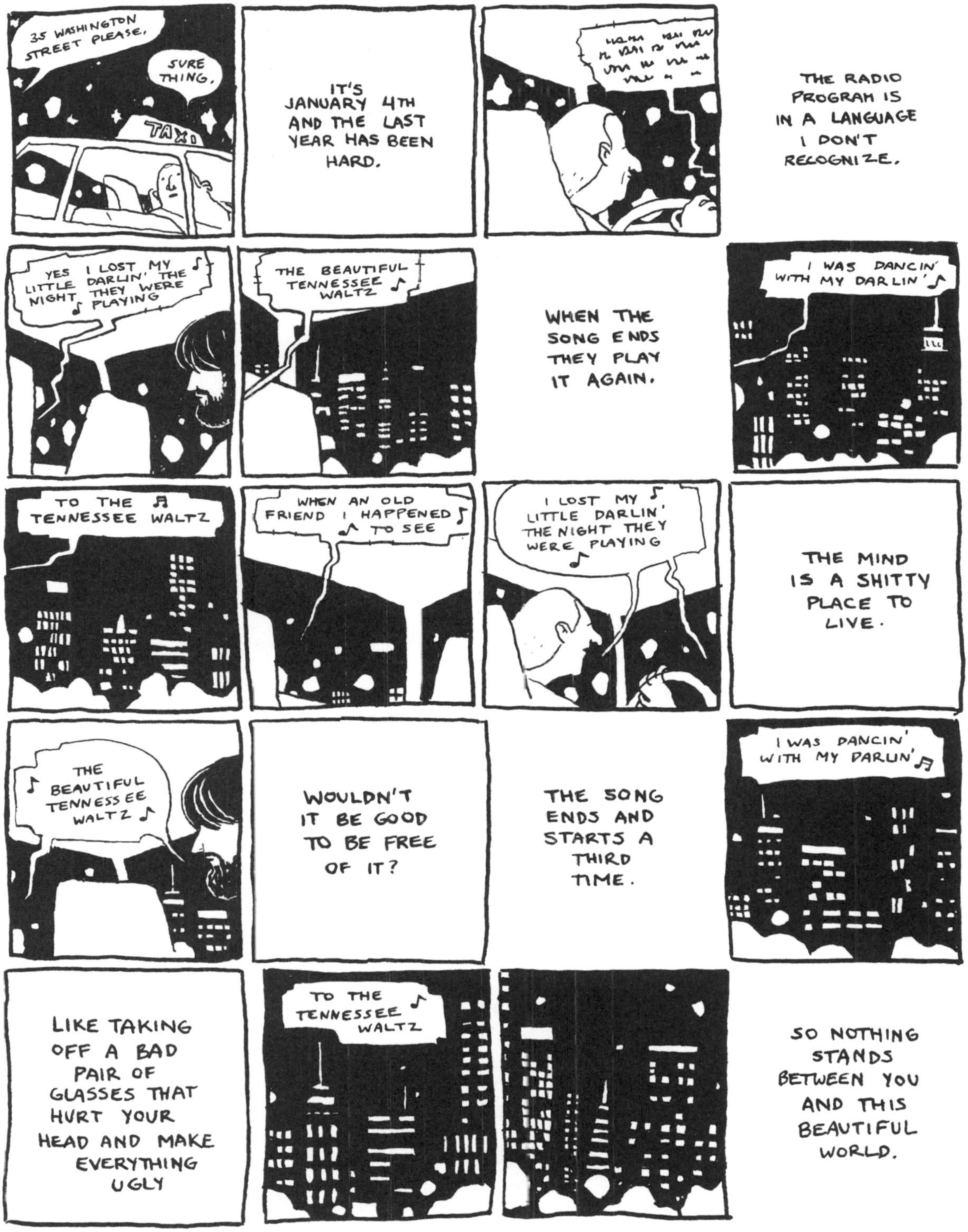

35 WASHINGTON STREET PLEASE.
SURE THING.
TAXI
IT'S JANUARY 4TH AND THE LAST YEAR HAS BEEN HARD.
THE RADIO PROGRAM IS IN A LANGUAGE I DON'T RECOGNIZE.
YES I LOST MY LITTLE DARLIN' THE NIGHT THEY WERE PLAYING
THE BEAUTIFUL TENNESSEE WALTZ
WHEN THE SONG ENDS THEY PLAY IT AGAIN.
I WAS DANCIN' WITH MY DARLIN'
TO THE TENNESSEE WALTZ
WHEN AN OLD FRIEND I HAPPENED TO SEE
I LOST MY LITTLE DARLIN' THE NIGHT THEY WERE PLAYING
THE MIND IS A SHITTY PLACE TO LIVE.
THE BEAUTIFUL TENNESSEE WALTZ
WOULDN'T IT BE GOOD TO BE FREE OF IT?
THE SONG ENDS AND STARTS A THIRD TIME.
I WAS DANCIN' WITH MY DARLIN'
LIKE TAKING OFF A BAD PAIR OF GLASSES THAT HURT YOUR HEAD AND MAKE EVERYTHING UGLY
TO THE TENNESSEE WALTZ
SO NOTHING STANDS BETWEEN YOU AND THIS BEAUTIFUL WORLD.

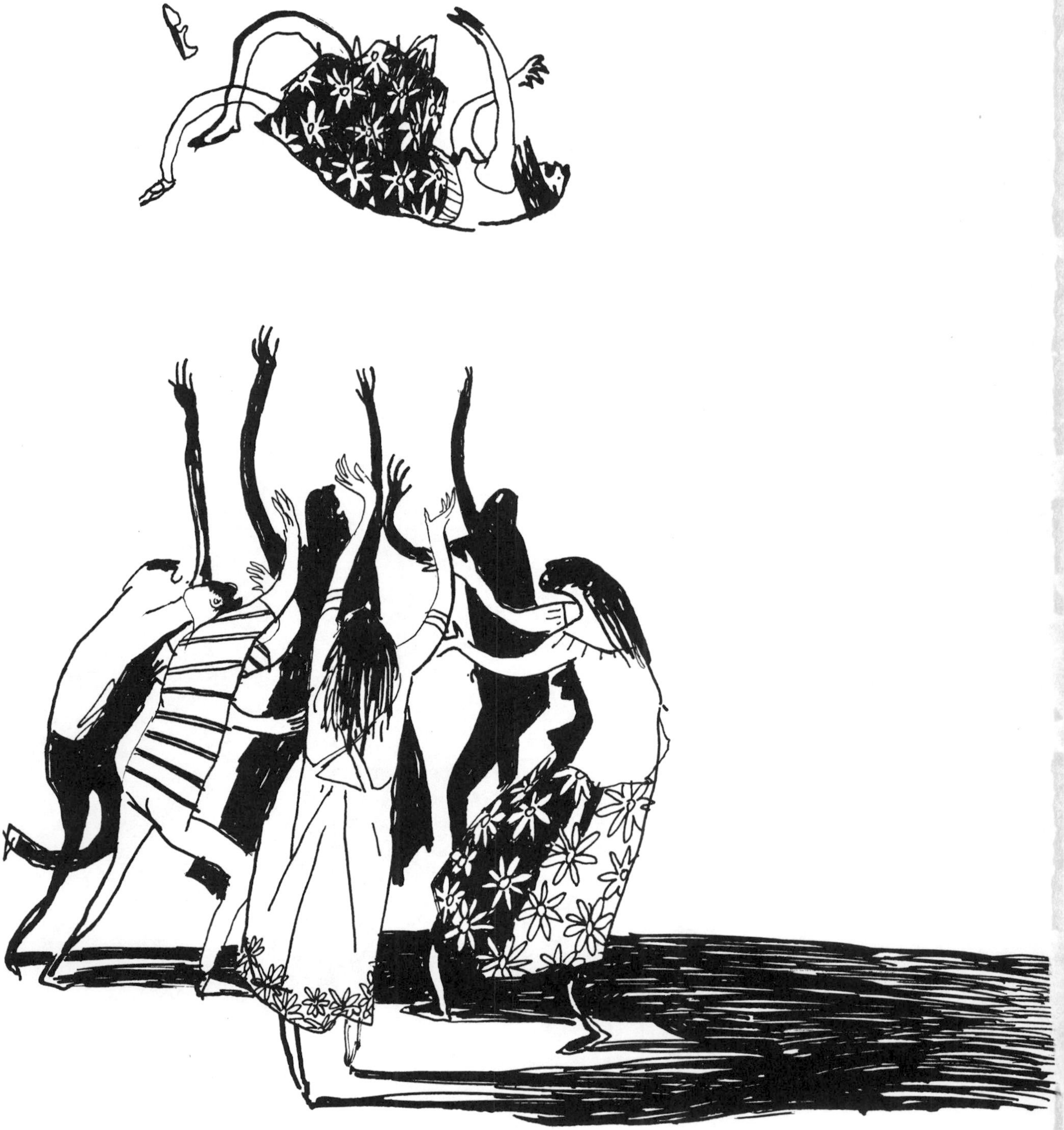